The
Ultimate Martial Arts
Q&A Book

750 Expert Answers *to* Your Essential Questions

JOHN CORCORAN and JOHN GRADEN

Contemporary Books

Chicago New York San Francisco Lisbon London Madrid Mexico City
Milan New Delhi San Juan Seoul Singapore Sydney Toronto

Library of Congress Cataloging-in-Publication Data

Corcoran, John, 1948-
    The ultimate martial arts Q&A book : 750 expert answers to your essential
questions / John Corcoran and John Graden.
        p.   cm.
    Includes index.
    ISBN 0-8092-9444-3
    1. Martial arts—Miscellanea.   I. Title: Ultimate martial arts question-and-
answer book.   II. Graden, John.   III. Title.

GV1101.C69   2001
796.8—dc21   00-65744

Contemporary Books

A Division of The McGraw·Hill Companies

1 2 3 4 5 6 7 8 9 0 VLP/VLP 0 9 8 7 6 5 4 3 2 1

ISBN 0-8092-9444-3

This book was set in Weidemann by Hespenheide Design
Printed and bound by Vicks Litho

Cover design by Monica Baziuk

McGraw-Hill books are available at special quantity discounts to use as premiums and
sales promotions, or for use in corporate training programs. For more information, please
write to the Director of Special Sales, Professional Publishing, McGraw-Hill, Two Penn
Plaza, New York, NY 10121-2298. Or contact your local bookstore.

This book is printed on acid-free paper.

To my wonderful cousin Kathleen "Cooky" Corcoran Schmidt, the sister I never had and within whose orbit I have been blessed with so much love and laughter.

—John Corcoran

To my parents, John and Susan Graden, and most of all to my best friend in the world, my treasured wife, Lynette, and our son Alexander.

—John Graden

CONTENTS

ACKNOWLEDGMENTS

The authors wish to thank the following writers, masters, instructors, publishing personnel, and family members for their invaluable input and/or contributions to this book.

First and foremost, we wish to acknowledge the superior efforts of Rob Colasanti, vice president of the National Association of Professional Martial Artists (NAPMA), whose meticulous organization of the photos saved an imminent deadline crisis—and potential receding hairlines. Another expert who saved our necks is Randall Hall, creative director of *Martial Arts Professional* magazine, who printed out the final manuscript and selflessly numbered the pages by hand when the computer's paginating function refused to work.

Next, but of equal importance, were the efforts of my cousin and cohort Maynard Schmidt, who shouldered the tedious task of sending out masses of permission release forms pertinent to this book. And last, John Schmidt, for sketching a template of the illustration in Chapter 5.

Content is one thing, but publishing is a major art and science of its own—and that's where the Contemporary Books staff excels. This book would not be a reality were it not for their martial arts acquisitions editor, Betsy Lancefield, whose belief in the project found a home for it in her fine house. Betsy's judgment as a businesswoman and editor is enhanced by the fact that she's also one of us—a practicing martial artist.

All of the other wonderful contributors to this work are acknowledged on the following pages in alphabetical order by last name under the specific chapter in which their material was used.

Chapter 1: John Bishop, Chino, California; Michael DeMarco, Erie, Pennsylvania; Buzz Durkin, Atkinson, New Hampshire; Andre Lima, Culver City, California; Carl Stone, Largo, Florida; Mike Swain, Campbell, California; Master Tat Man Wong, San Francisco, California.

Chapter 2: Kathy Fox, New York, New York; Jose Paman, North Highland, California; Warner Bros. Studios, Burbank, California.

Chapter 3: Dave Lowry, St. Louis, Missouri.

Chapter 4: Dr. Jerry Beasley, Christiansburg, Virginia; Master Sid Campbell, Oakland, California; Wayne Carman, Branson, Missouri; Ernie Reyes, Sr., San Jose, California; Grandmaster Jhoon Rhee, Washington D.C.; Master Kang Rhee, Memphis, Tennessee; Lee Wedlake, Fort Myers, Florida; Keith Yates, Garland, Texas.

Chapter 5: Karen Eden, Denver, Colorado; Grandmaster Joo Bang Lee, Downey, California; Master Bong Soo Han, Santa Monica, California; Grandmaster Jhoon Rhee, Washington D.C.; Master Scott Shaw, Redondo Beach, California; Rod Speidel, Bettendorf, Iowa; Charles Stepan, Youngstown, Ohio;

World Taekwondo Federation, Seoul, Korea; Keith D. Yates, Garland, Texas.

Chapter 6: Richard Baptista, Boston, Massachusetts; David Dorian-Ross; Nick Gracenin, Sharon, Pennsylvania; Willie Johnson, Laurel, Maryland; Rebecca Lee, Kissimmee, Florida; Brian Leung, Madison, Wisconsin; Allan Ondash, Courtdale, Pennsylvania; Scott Sheeley, Bellefontaine, Ohio.

Chapter 7: Carol Klenfner, SEG Sports, New York, New York; Andre Lima, Culver City, California; John Machado, Rio de Janeiro, Brazil.

Chapter 8: New Line Cinema, Los Angeles, California; Scott Rhodes, North Hollywood, California; United Artists Corporation, Los Angeles, California; Benny "The Jet" Urquidez, North Hollywood, California; Warner Bros. Studios, Burbank, California.

Chapter 9: Karen Eden, Denver, Colorado; Mike Swain, Campbell, California; Dr. Terrance Webster-Doyle, DeLand, Florida.

Chapter 10: Camille Bristow, St. Petersburg, Florida; Sarah Cunningham, St. Petersburg, Florida; Karen Eden, Denver, Colorado; Master

Jim Harrison, Missoula, Montana; Steve Shear, Lawrence, New York.

Chapter 11: Mitch Bobrow, Los Angeles, California; Al Garza, League City, Texas; Carol Klenfner, New York, New York; Tom Masterson, St. Petersburg, Florida; Rich Pelletier, Lewiston, Maine; Stephen Quadros, Burbank, California; Adrian Serrano, Milwaukee, Wisconsin; Shoto World Cup Karate Championships, Philadelphia, Pennsylvania; Mike Swain, Campbell, California; Master Toddy, Las Vegas, Nevada.

Chapter 12: Byron J. Cohen, Los Angeles, California; Columbia Pictures Corporation, Los Angeles, California; Bob Gilroy, Los Angeles, California; PM Entertainment, Sun Valley, California; Scott Rhodes, North Hollywood, California; T. J. Roberts, Los Angeles, California; Warner Bros. Studios, Burbank, California.

Chapter 13: Andrew Breen, Medford, Massachusetts; Master Sid Campbell, Oakland, California; Cannon Films, Los Angeles, California; Fred Degerberg, Chicago, Illinois; Dan Inosanto, Los Angeles, California; Diana Lee Inosanto, Los Angeles, California; Master Eric Lee, Los Angeles, California.

Chapter 14: Jeff Chinn, San Francisco, California.

INTRODUCTION

You're in for a treat. This is one of the rare books about martial arts that truly has something of interest for everyone. It has what I call universal appeal, and I've intentionally invested this quality in all my martial arts reference books over the years.

By universal appeal I mean that the contents are broad enough to appeal to everyone from beginners to black belts, no matter what art or style of martial art you practice. Further, the contents are written and presented in simple language that nonpractitioners—the so-called armchair enthusiasts—can also find educational and entertaining. And the simple question-and-answer format makes the information reader-friendly for children.

This book is divided into fifteen chapters that were very carefully selected for their wide, topical appeal in the martial arts field. Whether you seek information on traditional martial arts, eclectic arts, martial sports, exotic weapons, history, or movies and movie stars, you will find something of interest within these pages. In addition, included are some unique chapters on topics covering the higher values of the martial arts, fear and the fight-or-flight reflex, and how to choose a martial arts school.

We have scoured the United States to locate exceptional photographs to enhance the text. We hope that you will have found our search worthwhile and the images as visually stimulating as we do.

The martial arts have played a major role in my life, arming me with life skills and the strength to overcome everyday obstacles both large and small. This book is my way of sharing the many wonderful qualities of the martial arts with you, the reader.

—*John Corcoran*

What are the martial arts? If I were to ask ten black belts, all experts, I'd probably get ten different answers. If I were then to ask ten adult nonpractitioners, I'd get ten more. If I were to ask ten kids, I'd get ten more, and so on.

The martial arts mean different things to different people. Much of their perspectives, of course, are based upon their experiences and exposure to these arts. This book is designed to help make your experience with the martial arts a more positive one. Mine certainly has been.

On my first night of karate classes, February 12, 1974, I picked up the second issue of *Professional Karate* magazine. *Professional Karate*, I was to discover, was the standard by which all newsstand martial arts magazines were to be measured. It was also edited by my esteemed coauthor and friend, John Corcoran.

In those pages, I uncovered a world that instantly enraptured me. I was fascinated by the different styles and the bigger-than-life black belts who dominated the tournaments at that time. Many of those guys are legends today. Nearly three decades later, Chuck Norris, Joe Lewis, and Bill "Superfoot" Wallace are still three of the biggest names in martial arts circles throughout the world.

From that first night in class, I knew I was going to be a martial artist for life. I had found my career at the tender age of fourteen. I considered the karate school my institution of higher learning, and its degrees of black belt my degrees in education. It's been a wonderful ride.

My parents were certainly concerned about my choice of career. However, I've been very fortunate in that by all measures of success in our society, the martial arts have been completely rewarding for me. I have enjoyed every minute and would never consider doing anything else.

It's my hope that this book can have a similar effect on its readers. The martial arts are a wonderful, positive activity for participants of all ages. Through the pages of this book, I hope at least a small portion of the enthusiasm and passion John Corcoran and I share for the arts is transferred to you.

—*John Graden*

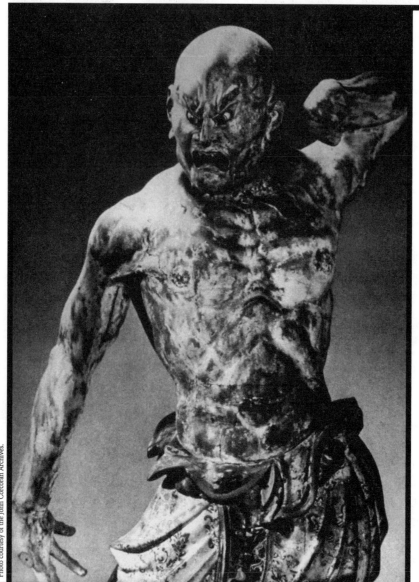

This formidable Japanese Nio Bodhisattva guardian deity glares fiercely and threatens evil trespassers with a karate-type fist. These kinds of giant sculptures are typically found guarding the gate entrances of Buddhist temples and are often composed in martial arts–like postures.

BASIC MARTIAL ARTS

*D*eadly, *mysterious, spectacular, amazing, bizarre, mystical, astonishing, incredible*—these and many other such terms have been used by Westerners to describe the martial arts. Ever since the first Western explorers set foot in Asia, their tales of the fighting skills of the Chinese boxers and the Japanese samurai have fascinated all who've heard them.

Millions of Westerners from all walks of life have practiced some form of the Eastern martial arts ever since *judo* was first introduced to Americans in 1902 and to Europeans in 1906. America's connection with the martial arts goes back even farther. In what is now the state of Hawaii, a martial art called *lua* ("dislocation of joints") has been practiced since A.D. 600. In 1849, during the California Gold Rush, Chinese laborers practiced *kung-fu* in secret. By

1868, again in Hawaii, Okinawan and Japanese immigrants were practicing *karate* and *jujutsu*.

The martial arts, however, are by no means Asian inventions. According to the article "The Importance of Martial Arts Research and Practice," in the summer 2000 edition of the *Journal of Asian Martial Arts*, publisher Michael DeMarco writes, ". . . artwork depicting detailed techniques of hand-to-hand combat have been found at a temple complex at Beni Hassan in Egypt and the Mesolithic cave paintings found at Morela la Vella, Spain, both dating over 22,000 years ago."

Furthermore, the Greek art of *pankration* thrived as a sport in the ancient pre-Christian Olympic Games from its inception in 648 B.C. to the end of the B.C. era, and has been abundantly documented in writings, paintings, vases, and sculptures from that period. Astonishingly, pankration embraced techniques found centuries later in both judo and karate and even kung-fu, although historians can find no indisputably direct link for its transmission between Europe and Asia.

Today, the martial arts have spread through Western society in surprising ways, chiefly because they truly offer something of

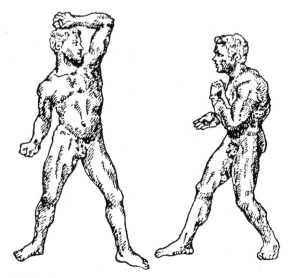

The Greek art and sport of pankration is the world's most well-documented form of ancient martial arts and Europe's first total form of fighting. In one of the most notorious ancient pankration bouts, Demoxenus (right) and Creugas fought to a standstill in a prolonged contest and agreed to allow each other one last unimpeded blow to decide the winner. After Demoxenus weathered a blow to the head, he ordered Creugas to lift his arm, as depicted in this drawing. Demoxenus then delivered an open-hand, spearlike strike with his fingertips that reputedly penetrated Creugas's side, instantly killing him. Drawing courtesy of the John Corcoran Archives.

value for everyone, from the handicapped to white-collar professionals to the rich and famous. How famous? As early as 1902, in fact, an American president, Theodore Roosevelt, was receiving private instruction in judo. Decades later, another famous American, perhaps the most popular singer in history, Elvis Presley, was a karate black belt who trained in the martial arts for almost half of his life.

In spite of all the enormous media and person-to-person exposure that Westerners have had to the martial arts over the years, a considerable degree of mystery and mystique still surrounds this popular activity. This chapter will answer many of the most frequently asked questions about the martial arts by both novice devotees and nonpractitioners.

IN THE BEGINNING

What is a martial art?

Although most people consider martial arts to be fighting systems from Asia, the term can be used to describe any fighting system from any country. This includes both weapons systems such as various types of sword and knife fighting, and unarmed systems like karate, jujutsu, kung-fu, and wrestling.

The trademark of a martial art is that it was created for self-defense, and not for sporting purposes.

Where did the martial arts come from?

Many historians believe that the first martial arts came from India. Though recorded history is sketchy, there are ancient writings, legends, and statues indicating that as early as 1000 B.C., India's warrior caste, the Kshatriya, practiced a fighting system whose primary weapon was the closed fist. It was called *Vajramushti*. This system, or parts of it, was transmitted to different parts of Asia.

However, a twentieth-century archaeological dig at the Beni Hassan tomb in Egypt unearthed a spectacular series of color wall murals depicting wrestling and stick-fighting techniques. These murals predate any other pre-Christian evidence of systemized fighting arts.

Probably the most important contribution to the Asian fighting arts was made by the Indian prince Bodhidharma, who brought both Zen Buddhism and an Indian fighting system to China in the fifth century A.D. Many of the kung-fu systems from China, Southeast Asia, and the karate systems of Okinawa and Japan descended from Bodhidharma's teachings at China's Shaolin Monastery.

What is karate?

Originally, *karate* (meaning "empty hand" in Japanese) was a term used to describe the martial arts of Okinawa. These arts were a

Chinese kung-fu, as demonstrated here by San Francisco, California's Master Tat Man Wong, is the forerunner of all Eastern martial arts. Because the many styles of kung-fu were practiced in secrecy for centuries, they still retain the most mystique of all the martial arts.
Photo courtesy of Master Tat Man Wong.

blend of Chinese kung-fu and indigenous Okinawan fighting arts such as *Okinawa Te.* These sixth-century striking arts emphasized hand strikes, foot strikes, blocks, evasive movements, and a limited number of grappling techniques. These karate systems differed somewhat from region to region. In the early 1900s, they spread to Japan.

Today, the word *karate* has become a generic term used to describe just about any striking system that emphasizes hand and foot strikes. We now see *taekwondo* and *tang soo do* sometimes referred to as "Korean karate," Chinese *kenpo* referred to as "Chinese karate" or "Hawaiian karate," and even some eclectic systems referred to as "American karate."

What is kung-fu?

Kung-fu, the popular generic term for hundreds of the Chinese martial arts, simply means "skill" or "ability." Kung-fu, which is the forerunner of all the Asian martial arts, encompasses systems that can be classified into three main types: for combat, for show, and for health. There have been over four hundred types of kung-fu throughout China's history.

What is a grappling system?

Grappling systems are self-defense styles that primarily use techniques such as joint-locks, throws, takedowns, strangulation techniques, and control holds. Various strikes and kicks are also used sparingly.

The most well-known and widely practiced grappling system is Japan's jujutsu (art of

Judo was the first Asian martial art taught publicly in the United States. It was taught in New York in 1902 by Yoshiaki Yamashita. Yamashita was also the personal instructor of President Theodore Roosevelt. Here World Champion Mike Swain of Campbell, California, performs one of judo's vast selections of throwing techniques. Photo courtesy of Mike Swain.

gentleness). Many people consider jujutsu to be a complete system since it uses joint-locks, throws, control holds, hand strikes, and kicks. Of course, the amount of emphasis on particular techniques depends on the style of jujutsu.

The martial art known as *aikido* is a descendant of jujutsu. Aikido emphasizes the joint-locking techniques and stepping patterns of jujutsu.

The martial sport of judo is also a descendant of jujutsu. Judo emphasizes the throws and control holds of jujutsu that were deemed safe for sporting contests.

Were early martial artists really able to kill an adversary with a single blow?

Many martial artists used various methods to train their hands to break hard objects such as wood and bricks. Most notable were the Okinawans, who allegedly were able to kill a foe with one blow.

The Okinawan karate practitioners used a training device called the *makiwara*. This was a 4″ × 4″ board that was tapered from bottom to top. The wide part was sunk into the ground and the narrower top (approximately 1″ × 4″) was left at shoulder level. The top 12″ or so were then wrapped with straw rope.

The practitioner would then strike this board several times a day to toughen all the striking surfaces of the body such as the knuckles, balls of the feet, and sides of the hands. Because the board was tapered it would bend, giving just enough resistance to toughen the striking surface and improve strength.

Since most early martial arts employed weapons, why was the ability to kill with one blow necessary?

In the case of the Okinawans, the need came out of self-defense necessity. In 1477, the Japanese occupied Okinawa. As part of this occupation all Okinawans were disarmed, leaving them with just karate as a means of self-defense.

When involved in a fight with an adversary armed with a sword or spear, a person would be lucky to get in just one blow. By toughening the striking surfaces of their hands and feet, the Okinawans were able to render blows that were powerful enough to break through the bamboo armor the Japanese soldiers wore and kill or maim them.

Why didn't the Okinawans create some type of improvised weapons?

They did. But since they were prohibited from carrying weapons of any kind, they learned to fight with farm tools that they normally had in their possession at any time. The five main Okinawan weapons were the *sai*, *bo*, *kama*, *nunchaku*, and *tonfa*.

How were these implements used as both farm tools and weapons?

The sai was a tool used to make furrows in the ground for seed planting. It was a pronged truncheon with a main stem about fifteen to twenty inches long and tapered to a sharp point. On both sides of the main stem are shorter prongs that are about three inches long and two inches apart from the main prong. The sai could be used to strike or stab. The shorter prongs could also be used to catch a sword blade or spear shaft. At times, the sai was also thrown like a knife.

The bo was a six-foot staff used as a walking stick or balanced across the shoulders to carry a bucket or basket at both ends. As a weapon it was used to strike, block, poke, and trip an attacker.

The kama was a sickle-type bladed tool used to cut rice or other grains. As a weapon it was used to block, slash, and stab.

The nunchaku consisted of two sticks that were approximately twelve inches long and connected by a cord of three to six inches. As a farm tool it was used to flail rice. As a weapon it was used to strike, block, seize, and strangle.

The tonfa was the handle of a millstone. It was approximately twenty-four inches long and had a handle set in the side about six inches from the end. It was used to block, strike, poke, and catch. The modern-day side-handle batons used by police officers descend from the early tonfa.

TRADITIONS

Why do students bow so often in martial arts schools?

Bowing is an Asian custom used as a greeting or to show respect. When entering and leaving a martial arts school, a student will bow to show respect for the place of learning. Once inside the school, students will bow to the instructors and other students both to show respect and as a greeting.

If there are pictures of the system's founders or masters on the wall, they are normally bowed to at the beginning and the end of class.

Does this bowing and meditation bear any religious overtones?

In most systems, no. As explained in the previous answer, bowing is an Asian custom that is basically equivalent to the Western custom of shaking hands.

Meditation before class is used to clear the mind of outside thoughts and worries so the student can concentrate on the training. Meditation after class should clear the mind of the workout's stresses so the student can return to the normal routine outside of class.

A few systems have strong religious content, but instructors will make the prospective student aware of this before the student decides to join the class.

What is a Professor?

High-ranking judo and jujutsu practitioners were first to use the formal title Professor. It became popular among practitioners of Hawaiian systems such as *kenpo* and *kajukenbo* because in their developmental years they were affiliated with Professor Henry Okazaki's American Jujutsu Institute.

In terms of rank, the title may represent a practitioner holding a rank of sixth-degree black belt or higher, depending on the system.

What is a grandmaster?

In the early days of the martial arts, the term *grandmaster* was used to describe the head or founder of a particular system. Because of that there were very few grandmasters.

Today, the term is commonly used to denote an instructor of advanced rank, no matter what age or experience level. Some Korean systems have applied the term to instructors as low as sixth-degree black belt.

In response to the many modern grandmasters, some individuals have embellished the title by prefacing it with words such as *great*, *supreme*, or *senior*.

What are the formal titles used in Chinese systems?

In many Chinese systems, only the titles Master and Student are used. Other Chinese kung-fu systems use the following titles. Sihing denotes a senior student, normally of brown-belt rank. Sibak is used to describe an assistant instructor of black-belt rank. Sifu (male) or Simo (female) is used by the chief instructor of the school. Sigung denotes a teacher's teacher, or high-ranking instructor. Sijo denotes the founder of the system.

What are the formal titles used in Japanese systems?

The most commonly used titles are Sempai, which is used by senior students of brown-belt rank or above; Sensei (Teacher), which denotes a black-belt instructor; Shihan (Master), which is normally used by high-ranking instructors of seventh-degree or higher; and Soke (grandmaster), which is the title given to the founder of the system.

Martial arts students wear a wide variety of colored belts. What do the colors of the belts mean?

Originally, no colored belts were used in the martial arts. Tradition tells us that students usually wore light-colored belts to hold their uniforms together. These belts were never washed, so as time went on they darkened and became more soiled. Thus, it was evident how long a student had been training.

The modern use of colored belts probably comes from the judo system, which was founded by Jigoro Kano in 1882. Judo practitioners were awarded belts of varying colors as symbols of rank advancement.

The belt colors used today vary from system to system, but those most commonly used are in the following order: white, yellow, orange, purple, blue, green, brown, and black. In Korean systems, the red belt is used at a level equivalent to the brown belt. In other systems, the red belt is used to denote a high-ranking black belt.

Traditional karate practitioners typically wear a pure white uniform with a minimal amount of style or school embroidery on the left side of the jacket, as worn by Uechi-ryu instructor Buzz Durkin of Atkinson, New Hampshire. Schools are commonly wooden-floored, uncluttered, and well-lighted.
Photo courtesy of Buzz Durkin.

Chinese stylists will sometimes use silk sashes of varying colors.

Is there a pure traditional martial arts system?

Many traditional martial artists claim to practice a pure system, but closer examination of their styles usually reveals information to the contrary. It may be possible to locate a pure system, but it may not be beneficial.

System founders adopted techniques from other systems because they believed the new techniques would enhance the overall effectiveness of their existing systems. No single system can contain all the techniques necessary to defend against every possible attack situation. It would be foolish to ignore a technique from a different system if it filled a void in your own system.

MARTIAL ARTS IN AMERICA

When and where were the Asian martial arts first practiced in America?

Even though it did not become a state until 1959, Hawaii should be acknowledged as the first place in America where the martial arts were practiced.

The Polynesians who settled the Hawaiian islands in A.D. 600 brought with them a fighting art called *lua* (dislocation of joints). This system is similar to jujutsu in that it favors joint-locks and dislocations. It also contains many spear and knife techniques.

Probably the first martial arts practitioners in mainland America were the Chinese laborers who were imported to work in the gold rush camps in 1849. Although many qualified kung-fu instructors were probably among these immigrants, they practiced their arts in secret and kept their knowledge exclusively to themselves.

The Korean art and sport of taekwondo is the most widely practiced martial art in the Western world. Renowned for its vast repertoire of flamboyant kicking techniques, like the flying kick demonstrated here by Culver City, California's Andre Lima, taekwondo became an official Olympic sport in the 2000 Games in Sydney, Australia.

Photo courtesy of Andre Lima.

When were martial arts first taught to the general public in America?

Judo was the first Asian martial art taught publicly in America. Yoshiaki Yamashita introduced it in New York in 1902. Yamashita was also the personal instructor of President Theodore Roosevelt.

Karate was first publicly taught in Hawaii at the Hawaii Young People's Karate Club in 1933. These classes were taught by Thomas Miyashiro, an Okinawan Shorin-ryu stylist. Shorei-ryu stylist Robert Trias established the first karate school on the mainland United States in Phoenix, Arizona, in 1946.

Kung-fu was first taught to the American public in the late 1950s. Three Chinese instructors opened their doors to all races. The first was, most likely, Jimmy H. Woo, who opened a kung-fu school in El Monte, California, in 1959. Around that same time, Bruce Lee started teaching a small group of students in Seattle, Washington. Ark Y. Wong opened his Five Animals kung-fu school in Los Angeles, California, in 1964.

Taekwondo was first taught in San Antonio, Texas, in 1955 by Atlee Chittim. At the time, Chittim was only a brown belt. The first black belt to teach in America was Jhoon Rhee, whom Chittim brought to Texas from Korea in 1956.

By the mid-1970s, some form of martial arts was being taught in every major city in America.

Are there any American forms of martial arts?

America is a world leader because its people have always been innovative and hardworking. So it was inevitable that Americans would look for ways to improve or alter the Asian fighting arts to better fit their indigenous needs. Of course, there are only so many ways to execute a hand strike or kick, so American innovation has focused on combining techniques from various systems to avoid the weaknesses certain systems may have had.

Other American innovations are usually philosophical and/or address self-defense or sporting needs in American society versus in Asian societies.

Two of the major American systems are kajukenbo and American kenpo. There are also many minor systems, with far fewer practitioners, that fall under the heading of American karate or American martial arts.

What was the first American martial art?

Kajukenbo, America's first martial arts system, was founded in Hawaii in 1949. Kajukenbo's inception came about in 1947 when five Hawaiian martial arts masters, calling themselves the Black Belt Society, cooperated on a project to develop a complete self-defense system.

Using Chinese kenpo as a base, kajukenbo incorporates techniques from various martial arts into a complete system: tang soo do kicks, jujutsu joint-locks, judo throws and ground fighting, and the circular techniques of *sil-lum pai* kung-fu. The name *kajukenbo* derives from the combination of the names of the arts that merged to form it: *ka* for karate, *ju* for judo and jujutsu, *ken* for kenpo, and *bo* for Chinese boxing (kung-fu).

Like most karate systems, kajukenbo has kata or forms. These fourteen kata are known as the Palama Sets 1 through 14.

Kajukenbo's self-defense techniques are arranged and categorized into fifteen grab-arts, twenty-one punch counters, fifteen knife counters, thirteen club counters, nine two- and three-man attack counters, and twenty-six advanced alphabet techniques.

Today, over 100,000 people practice kajukenbo in fourteen countries.

Who were the five Hawaiian masters who called themselves the Black Belt Society, and how did they develop kajukenbo?

These five men were Peter Choo, the Hawaii welterweight boxing champion and a tang soo do black belt; Frank Ordonez, a *sekeino* jujutsu black belt; Joe Holck, a Kodokan judo black belt; Clarence Chang, a master of sil-lum pai kung-fu; and Adriano D. Emperado, a Chinese kenpo black belt and *escrima* expert.

Together these men trained for several hours each day, taking advantage of each system's strengths and weaknesses to develop their new art. When Joe Holck and Peter Choo would spar, Holck could see his weaknesses in striking techniques, and Choo would realize his vulnerability once he was on the ground. Emperado was able to show Choo how a kenpo man could work inside a kicker with quickly executed hand strikes. Chang showed the others how the circular, flowing techniques of sil-lum pai were used to evade and strike. And Frank Ordonez showed everyone how to flow with an attacker's force and then redirect it back on the attacker with painful locks and throws.

What is the advantage of creating an American system like kajukenbo?

A created system like kajukenbo allows for more effective self-defense. By combining techniques from the five arts, a kajukenbo stylist can defend him- or herself in many ways. The stylist can use soft, circular kung-fu techniques to evade and strike. Or the stylist can use judo or jujutsu to control an attacker or throw the attacker to the ground.

In most kajukenbo counterattacks these techniques are combined. If the attacker punches, for example, the kajukenbo stylist may step into the attack at a 45-degree angle while blocking with a soft palm block. The stylist would then counterattack with several rapid-fire kenpo hand strikes followed by a judo foot sweep. Once on the ground, the attacker could be struck again or controlled with a jujutsu lock.

Combination techniques flow naturally because each technique sets up the next by following the reaction of the attacker's body. Although some traditional martial artists describe this as "overkill," the theory behind this American system is that it is better to counter with multiple techniques that can be ended when the threat no longer exists, than to rely on one technique and find that it is not enough.

Which state has had the most influence on American martial arts?

Long known as the melting pot of the Pacific, the Hawaiian culture represents all the major Asian countries. No other place in the Union has made as many major martial arts contributions to America as has Hawaii. Many of America's first schools, systems, and champions came from this state.

Since they first settled on the islands in A.D. 600, Hawaiians have practiced a fighting system that they brought with them, the most common name for which is lua.

The first Asians to arrive in Hawaii were the Chinese, who brought several styles of kung-fu with them. The next group of immigrants, the Japanese, brought judo and jujutsu. The Okinawans brought karate with them.

In the early 1900s, Henry S. Okazaki broke with tradition and opened a judo and jujutsu school to all races on the islands. This school was known as the Kodenkan and was the origin of the Danzan-ryu jujutsu system.

The first kung-fu school outside of China, the Chinese Physical Culture Association of Hawaii, was also opened in Hawaii, in 1922. And America's first karate demonstration was given by Okinawan Shorin-ryu master Kentsu Yabu, at Honolulu's Nuuanu YMCA in 1927.

WOMEN AND THE MARTIAL ARTS

Can women become proficient at the martial arts despite their small statures?

Many of Asia's martial arts masters are as small or smaller than the average American woman. Some of the strengths of a martial artist are the use of balance, use of leverage, and the ability to use as many muscle groups as possible when executing a technique. This allows a person of small stature to generate more power than some larger and stronger people.

One characteristic of martial arts such as karate and kung-fu is their highly systemized methods of "dirty" fighting. Self-defense techniques like groin kicks, knee breaks, eye pokes, and strikes to the throat require very little strength to make them highly effective.

If a smaller person concentrates on attacking the eyes, throat, and groin, that person can successfully defeat a larger attacker.

What is the number of women taking martial arts in the United States?

Just as the number of young students has increased, more and more women are involved in training as well. The violent nature of our crime-ridden modern society has created a perceived need for some kind of self-protection, and the martial arts are, of course, one of the best means of self-defense.

Still, many more men than women are enrolled in the typical American karate class.

Are there fewer women involved in karate because it's too hard for them to learn?

Not at all. In fact, women often have more natural flexibility, better coordination, and a higher level of determination than men do. However, the martial arts still carry a popular image of machismo, and some factions in our culture still think learning to fight is unlady-like. Until this changes, there will probably always be more men than women practicing the martial arts in the United States.

What techniques should a woman use in defending herself?

The techniques mentioned previously are highly effective when used by women. Women should also use their common sense to try to avoid a dangerous situation or to talk their way out of one.

A loud scream can sometimes summon help or make an attacker flee rather than risk detection and apprehension. In fact, everyone should attempt to escape a dangerous situation, if the possibility presents itself.

Why do some instructors consider women to be better students than men?

Most women will admit that they know nothing about self-defense and trust their instructor to teach them what they need to know to defend themselves. Since women are more likely to be violently attacked and less physically able to defend themselves than men, they are very serious about their training.

Men are not any less serious about their training, but the fact that many attacks against women are life-and-death situations cause women to work hard at learning self-defense techniques. Further, men and women grow up differently: men learn to fight from an early age while women learn to avoid physical confrontations. In general, men are also more often involved in competitive sports than women.

Men take up the martial arts for various reasons. They are interested in self-defense, want to be skilled street fighters, want the exercise, or are interested in the competitive sport aspect. In general, women are primarily interested in the self-defense aspects of the martial arts.

When it comes to receiving instruction, some men who have been involved in contact sports or have received military training will have preconceived notions about self-defense. They will always want to be shown that a technique works. They will also question why one specific technique is used in a situation instead of another.

Why are women more flexible than men?

All considerations being the same, women are not more flexible than men. What makes them appear to be more flexible is the way they approach physical activity while they are growing up.

Many men grow up doing activities such as weight lifting and running, which tend to strengthen and tighten their muscles. So when they decide to take up the martial arts, they suddenly have to start stretching the muscles they have spent so many years tightening.

Conversely, many women grow up participating in activities like dance and aerobics, where stretching and flexibility play an important role. Thus when they start martial arts training, they may already be more flexible than anyone in their class.

Were any martial arts systems founded by women?

In early China it was not uncommon for Buddhist nuns to be proficient at kung-fu, just as Buddhist monks were. The popular Wing Chun style of kung-fu was founded in China in the late 1700s by a Buddhist nun named Yim Wing Chun. She had received her instruction from another Buddhist nun named Ng Mui, who trained at the famed Shaolin Temple in the Henan province of China.

A popular Indonesian legend credits the founding of *pentjak silat* to a Sumatran peasant woman. According to this legend, while at a stream fetching water this woman observed a tiger and a large bird fight for several hours. As the woman was preparing to return home, her angry husband arrived at the stream and scolded her for taking so long. When he tried to punish her, she evaded his strike with a technique she had seen the animals use. Later on, she taught the techniques to her husband, and thus pentjak silat was born.

GENERAL INFORMATION

Where should I concentrate my gaze when I fight?

This is a topic of endless debate among instructors. Some teachers, from more traditional backgrounds, instruct their students to stare into their opponent's eyes to intimidate them and erode their confidence. A more current school of thought dictates focusing on the opponent's feet. A person cannot commence an attack without transporting the weaponry to the battle. By watching an opponent's feet, a fighter can tell how fast, and from which side, the attack will come.

The third and most practical approach comes from Joe Lewis—the great karate and kickboxing champion and technical genius.

He advocates keeping your gaze focused around chest level—as if to read the lettering on your adversary's T-shirt. Not everyone has the confidence and steadiness of nerves to successfully engage in a staring contest with an opponent. By focusing your field of vision slightly lower, it may appear to an opponent that you are, in fact, locking gazes with him or her and are totally unfazed. Additionally, any movement an opponent might undertake with either hands or feet would fall well within range of your field of vision.

What mental quality is most critical for a warrior's survival in real combat situations?

Acuity—keenness of thought and vision—is most critical for a warrior in combat. A warrior needs to be able to size up situations instantly, and make accurate assessments of their immediate surroundings.

Are sprays and gases effective for street defense?

Yes and no. While these types of weapons are currently fashionable, they have some very real disadvantages. First, in an enclosed area, such as a car, it is unavoidable that the user will also be in contact with the noxious fumes. Second, in an open area if the wind direction is not favorable the same situation may occur. Last, a sprayer of any kind requires the user to properly position the nozzle and ensure it is pointed away from the user and toward the assailant.

Some sprayers have safety tabs that must be released before using. In times of violent stress, these seemingly simple adjustments and extra steps can erode the user's margin for survival.

What is the single most important physical attribute a warrior requires in order to prevail in a street encounter?

The protracted duels that moviegoers watch are strictly products of an industry dedicated to providing visual stimulation. What really happens when angry people go after each other is neither stimulating nor terribly visual. Most genuine violent conflicts last anywhere from four to fourteen seconds. If you blink, you miss it. The outcome usually is determined almost instantly. For this reason, the most critical quality could best be described as sustained explosiveness.

If one were to compare fighters to automobiles, the car that can accelerate from 0 to 120 miles per hour the fastest, and stay at that level the longest, has the greatest chance for success (all other factors being equal). Traditionally, professional warriors have always trained for endurance—to last however many rounds the particular contest required. In the real world, the advantage is less with the aerobically fit individual and more with the anaerobically prepared participant.

A common staple of modern movies is the ruthless, unscrupulous martial arts instructor who sends his students into competition and into the streets as hordes of bullies. Do such people really exist?

The common misperception created by these films is that martial arts institutions conduct recruitment and corruption of the innocent. This kind of unscrupulous attitude is very rare in the martial arts school business; 99.9 percent of the schools teach ethical conduct and high ideals to accompany the self-defense instruction.

Those looking to learn biker-barroom techniques or win-at-all-costs, mercenary-type training would have to search hard for the 0.1 percent of schools that might provide this kind of service.

Can a person learn the martial arts from books or videos?

While external aids like these are excellent ways to help you remember sequences and even learn some new moves, nothing can substitute for actual hands-on instruction from a knowledgeable teacher. A book can't correct your balance, and a video can't insist that you perform just one more technique.

Bad habits, such as leaning over when kicking, are easy to develop and hard to get rid of. You need to have regular instruction from a black-belt instructor.

How much can a person learn from an instructional videotape?

Instructional videotapes are an extremely valuable supplement to dojo training. Seasoned martial artists use them to round out their arsenals and add further sophistication and refinement to their existing systems. Videos enable novices to sample a wide variety of disciplines outside of their own without committing to memberships in twenty different schools. This visual exposure may prompt students to change areas of specialization, if they find they gravitate more readily to another art.

Is it possible that video–CD-ROM instruction will ultimately replace the martial arts school in the future?

No. There have always been closet practitioners in the martial arts. These people, either due to social discomfort, physical disabilities, or time or money constraints, practiced in the privacy of their homes. Often, their parents never knew they were behind closed doors imitating the postures they saw in the pictures and drawings in books.

The new teaching technology offered in CD-ROM and videos is the next evolutionary step in a food chain that began in America with the Bruce Tegner how-to books. In learning any kind of physical motor skills, nothing can ever substitute for person-to-person coaching. In much the same way that people cannot learn to drive without someone sitting beside them to coach and correct as they learn to operate the car, people cannot develop a true proficiency in the martial arts without the direction, correction, and immediate feedback of an instructor.

In most cases, expert closet practitioners know just enough to get themselves hurt.

Is there a martial art designed especially for police officers?

Yes, the Koga Method, later renamed Koga Jutsu, contains techniques from aikido, jujutsu, judo, and wrestling, but all have been modified for police use. Police recruits are taught approximately thirty to forty hours of this system.

Instructors are taught in 120-hour blocks covering instruction in thirty-six areas such as interviewing positions, footwork, rolls, searching techniques, handcuffing techniques, takedowns, control holds, and twist locks.

Robert Koga, who many consider America's foremost trainer of police officers, founded this system. Born in San Francisco, California, in 1930, Koga first got involved in the martial arts when he was twelve years old. He ultimately earned black belts in judo, jujutsu, and aikido. In 1955, Koga became a police officer with the Los Angeles Police Department, where he worked until his retirement in 1979.

No man in this country has had a greater influence on the training of more police officers than has Koga. Since 1961, over a hundred thousand police officers, federal agents, and military personnel have been trained by Koga or by one of his disciples.

Is there an ultimate martial art?

Over the years, especially in recent times, many systems have claimed to be the ultimate martial art. Some of these claims come from a true belief shared by the system's practitioners; other claims have been made for strictly personal or commercial reasons.

The fact of the matter is there is no ultimate martial art. If there were, nobody would want to practice the other "inferior" martial arts—leaving just one martial art to study.

There are hundreds of martial arts. And because everybody has their own individual reasons for studying martial arts, no single martial art can meet every person's individual needs. So the ultimate martial art is the one that ultimately meets all, or most, of your personal requirements.

What is an eclectic martial art?

Eclectic is a term used to describe the more modern martial arts that in their evolution have deviated from strict tradition. These types of martial arts may hold to some traditional philosophy and beliefs, but they tend to take a practical view of physical techniques.

As an example, a system that has become involved more and more in sport would probably have its techniques altered for competition. It would adopt techniques from other systems if they were useful for competition. The same is true of a primarily self-defense system: it would embrace and adopt techniques that add to its effectiveness.

Kajukenbo, American kenpo, and Bruce Lee's jeet kune do are good examples of eclectic systems.

What is the difference between a hard style and a soft style?

Hard styles, or external systems, use hard, powerful techniques primarily executed in linear patterns. Although *hard style* is used in reference to Chinese systems, Japanese systems like Shotokan karate and Korean systems like taekwondo are also considered hard styles.

Soft styles, or internal systems, stress circular techniques that flow with soft fluidity. They are referred to as internal because they stress the use of *chi* (internal energy).

What is chi?

Although some scientists believe there is no such thing as chi, others believe it is a biophysical energy generated through breathing techniques, such as those practiced in the martial arts.

Many martial artists believe that the development of chi is much more important than the development of physical technique. They believe chi greatly enhances both the power of physical techniques and the ability to withstand physical punishment.

What famous celebrities are genuine martial artists?

There are far too many to list. They range from presidents and politicians to professional athletes and actors. Even members of European royal families—including King Juan Carlos of Spain, who's a legitimate karate black belt—have practiced the martial arts. The martial arts have found favor with people from all walks of life, famous or not.

What is the world record for breaking bricks and ice?

There are no legitimate world records for breaking. This is because there is no standard for the structural strength of the items that are broken.

Although many breaks are true examples of the power that can be achieved with dedicated training, others are no more than carnival tricks done to impress the uninformed. One way to make breaking easy is to bake boards in an oven to dry them out, making them more brittle and thus easier to break. Another way is to purchase inferior bricks that cannot be used for construction because they contain too much sand and are thus susceptible to easy breakage.

If you have the opportunity to observe a breaking demonstration, do so with a critical eye. If someone breaks a stack of bricks and a lot of dust fills the air, the bricks contain a high measure of sand content. If someone is stacking the blocks of ice or cinder blocks separated with "spacers," such as two-by-four

This spectacular head break of flaming cinder tiles by Largo, Florida's Carl Stone demonstrates the inherent danger in such stunts, even for the experts.

Photos courtesy of Carl Stone.

pieces of wood or other materials, that person is making the break easier. The weight of the top block, when broken, will break the blocks below it in a domino fashion.

Was there really a Shaolin Temple?

Yes. The Shaolin Temple (Young Forest Temple) located in the Henan province of China is considered the birthplace of today's martial arts. Emperor Hsiao Wen built this temple during the Northern Wei dynasty (A.D. 386–534). Martial arts have been practiced there, starting with their introduction by the Indian monk Bodhidharma in about A.D. 502, up to the present time.

In its early days, the Shaolin monks made up a formidable army that was used by the emperor for both training purposes and warfare. This army of monks was said to number five thousand at one time.

Although the Shaolin Temple has been destroyed and rebuilt on a number of occasions over the centuries, it is still in exis-

tence today and is now a popular tourist attraction. Monks are still trained in martial arts there.

The "martial artist as Superman" myth was largely dispelled in this stunt gone awry for the 1981 nationally televised season-opener of the controversial reality TV show *That's Incredible*. Californian Steve Pyle galloped toward two sports cars speeding bumper-to-bumper toward him at 120 mph (192 km/hr). He intended to leap over both cars as they raced beneath him. The lead car, however, caught his trailing left foot, somersaulting him to the ground. It was never discovered whether or not he lost his left foot in the mishap, but it was certainly severely damaged at the time. Doctors predicted he would be crippled for life.

MARTIAL ARTS MYTHS

2

One fascinating aspect of the martial arts is its rich folklore and mythology. Many trades, occupations, vocations, and persuasions have their own colorful folklore. But the martial arts surpass most of them both in sheer number and, quite understandably, uniqueness of stories.

First, martial arts myths extend back some two thousand years to ancient times. Second, they depict flamboyant tales of physical prowess, heroism, combative skill, and even psychic powers. Handed down largely through word of mouth (and fairly recently through books, magazines, and videos), these myths have the distinct power to make blind believers out of otherwise reasonable folk.

These myths commonly serve to place the martial arts practitioner at a supposedly higher level than the average mortal. The stories perpetuate fantastic claims that even if only half-true would still prove to be far beyond credible human capabilities. But a fantastic claim is like a miracle, which has been most colorfully described by one sage as "an event described by those to whom it was told by men who did not see it!"

Such claims include the master who could thrust his bare hand into a person's chest and pull the heart out; the timed "death touch" wherein the exponent lightly taps his subject at a prescribed point, thereby causing that person's death up to two years afterward; and the tenacious practitioner who defeated a ferocious tiger in unarmed combat! These and many more are all standard fare in the field of martial arts mythology.

It is curious that over time seemingly nonsensical practices have likewise surfaced, and have been criticized within the martial arts community itself: the training "attacker" who steps in neatly and freezes in the lunge-punch position so the opponent can masterfully dismantle him; the arts that advocate using only high kicks; and the weapons practitioners who oppose each other with sticks of equal size and design. These and other practice procedures have been passed on unquestioned for years. While amusing in nature, these training methods continue to this day and perhaps will be perpetuated for as long as there are followers to adhere to them. Whether they are practical and have utility in the real world is largely up to the individual's belief and confidence in them. In the martial arts, after all, a practitioner is able to get out of such methods what he or she is willing, or able, to put into them.

Here is a lighthearted look at some of the more widely circulated martial arts myths. The strange practices that have puzzled both outsider and exponent for years will also be examined.

Martial artists often claim they have extraordinary control of their bodies. Is this so?

Martial artists are able to perform physical feats quite beyond the reach of nonpractitioners. Any discipline that fosters an innate awareness of movement, balance, and breathing will generally develop outstanding physical control.

Besides martial artists, other people with notable control of their bodies are yogi, gymnasts, and ballet dancers.

Are there really closed-door, bare-knuckle fights similar to the popular televised bouts?

Everybody these days, from martial arts instructors to film stars to enterprising young men selling instructional books and videotapes, claims to be some sort of bare-knuckle fighting champion. The frequency with which such claims circulate would imply that each major city, as well as some small towns, has its own underground champion.

There is no way to verify the existence of these bouts, however, short of actually attending such a meet. In fact, we know only one person whom we believe participated in these kinds of contests: New York's Paul Vizzio, who later became a recognized kickboxing world champion.

Was the televised Ultimate Fighting Championship (UFC) the first bare-knuckle bout in the United States?

No. There are many accounts of public bare-knuckle fights during the early days of the Union. These fights were said to have been a mixture of boxing and wrestling in which headlocks, throws, butting, and kicking, as well as punching, were fair game.

Martial arts–based bouts of this nature took place as early as the 1970s. One, the infamous Taunton Death Matches (in which no one actually died or got maimed) in Massachusetts, featured eye pokes and groin grabs. Similar contests also occurred in New York and New Jersey during that period of time. Some of the known participants were Tayari Casel, Errol Bennett, and Happy Crump.

The UFC, however, was the first bare-knuckle, no-holds-barred tournament presented to a wide audience, and it has since been imitated by others.

Is ikken hisatsu, the "one punch" (or "one fist") kill of karate, really possible?

Yes and no. This is one of the most common myths attached to karate. No one knows where it originated. Perhaps it started with primarily Okinawan *karateka*, who intensely "conditioned" their hands by striking progressively harder and coarser objects until they developed a grotesque mass of calluses and calcium deposits that grossly enlarged their knuckles. Tales of Okinawan karate masters killing an attacker with a single blow from these ironlike fists were widely circulated for decades.

Such hand conditioning was still a normal part of serious Okinawan karate training from the 1950s to the 1970s, when the art was taught to U.S. servicemen, who perpetuated the practice upon their return from Asia by teaching what they had learned. Today, the practice of conditioning the hands is considered "prehistoric" and entirely unnecessary in the process of becoming adept at karate. Furthermore, it has been known to cause premature acute arthritis of the hands.

A kenpo master claims to have knowledge of a one-punch killing technique that can destroy a person's skeletal and nervous system. Is this possible?

This sounds like a variation of Shotokan karate's *ikken hisatsu*. A good question to ask of people claiming to know such a technique is whether they have ever applied it in combat. Because unless they have, they don't know whether the technique will work.

Is it possible for a martial artist to use a spear hand to plunge into someone's chest and pull the heart out?

This is a complete fabrication. If you're not convinced, try thrusting your fingers into a slab of raw meat. It won't take much to figure out that this is just a silly myth.

Another purported martial arts power involves killing someone from a distance, without physical contact. Can a person achieve this extraordinary feat?

You can, in fact, kill someone from a distance, but it's not necessarily a martial arts technique: you use an implement such as a gun, rocket launcher, or bow and arrow.

So the belief, generated by certain internal-power practitioners, that a person can gain long-distance destructive ability by repeating certain movements is not all true?

To illustrate, consider a story that happened a few years ago. An old man claiming to teach gung-fu had his eager student stand in a shallow horse stance, hold his right vertical fist forward with his index finger sticking out, and instructed him to alternately bend and straighten the finger.

After a few months, the master declared the student's training was over. The student protested, saying he had learned nothing about protecting himself, upon which the master handed him a .38 Special revolver. As it turned out, he wasn't mispronouncing "gun-fu" after all.

Is the "death touch," and its related mystical beliefs in secret vital points, internal destructive power, and delayed killing properties, for real?

The age-old myth about the delayed death touch, where the practitioner could supposedly touch the opponent lightly and thus cause his or her demise up to two years later, is allegedly based on the same principal points, called meridians, used in acupuncture.

Acupuncture does work. The death touch technique, however, has largely circulated on the strength of superstition and word-of-mouth tradition. There are no known documented incidents showing definite effects of the technique.

One explanation that has been offered to support this phenomenon has to do with the reportedly inferior diet in ancient China. Diet directly affects general fitness and health, and there were not as many people knowledgeable in the martial arts in ancient China as there are now. Therefore, according to this theory, it may have been easy to have attributed someone's death to a soft tap administered by a kung-fu practitioner some time prior, even though the recipient already had an existing fatal condition.

But even if the delayed death touch really worked, there remains the problem of dealing with the opponent in the present:

attackers don't typically wait around to suffer the effects of such a delayed touch. In other words, if you're confronted by a 250-pound raging bully, you better drop both the "delayed" and the "touch" concepts. Instead, deliver your technique with the speed and power of a jet-propelled pile driver. Otherwise, the "death" you cause just might be your own!

What about the enduring tale surrounding the so-called "poison hand"? Is it true?

The poison hand reputedly gave one the capacity to inflict damage on an opponent in a manner similar to the death touch. Again, however, there is no evidence to show it actually worked. One practical manifestation would have been for one to wear a cyanide-laced metal glove. A substantial cut from such a weapon would produce lethal results.

What do practices like running in the snow and showering under a freezing waterfall have to do with the martial arts?

They mainly illustrate how mental discipline can translate to the achievement of unusual feats. This activity has little significance as far as translating into combat, unless you count getting caught in a violent encounter in a colder climate.

Can martial artists really defeat armed attackers?

Martial arts movies, demonstrations, and books are replete with images of practitioners handily defeating attackers armed with knives, machetes, *katana*, and even firearms. Don't buy it: disarming a foe with a bladed weapon is hazardous at best.

Opposing a blade-wielding opponent, even under controlled conditions, often leads to injuries. Imagine a crazed attacker intent on disemboweling or decapitating you and you'll get the idea. For obvious reasons, firearms pose an even worse proposition.

There is a popular demo technique where the barehanded defender catches the attacker's downward sword swing by slapping his palms together upon the sword. Is this really possible?

It is only possible if the swordsman purposely stops the stroke in mid-air. In a real encounter, though, the joined-palms position would be a good one to use for praying that the opponent doesn't chop your limb or head off.

Can a person use the martial arts as protection against wild or rabid animals?

Through the years, various martial artists have been credited with using their techniques to defeat animals. A Chinese iron-palm master supposedly killed a horse with a single slap. In Indonesia, two men once were found dead beside a tiger. Observers concluded that the two, who were reputed to be silat experts, engaged the tiger in a life-and-death struggle, killing it but sustaining mortal injuries themselves in the process.

One Japanese karateka was rumored to have killed a tiger, a rumor he himself is said to have denied. Once a magazine ad featured another karateka who purportedly defeated a wild boar.

Legendary karate strongman Masutatsu Oyama is said to have fought over fifty bulls in his prime. The conditions, however, were somewhat contrived: the bouts were preset, and the bulls were not really intent on combat.

Are there any documented accounts of martial artists defeating an attacking animal?

A documented account of not a martial artist but a possibly untrained woman surfaced in early 1992, when a 120-pound Navajo woman from Texas was attacked by her pet, a 130-pound wolf-malamute hybrid. When she received a leg wound from the wolf-dog's teeth, she first tried to conceal the cut to prevent the animal from getting more enraged. The wolf-dog was unrelenting, however, and the woman soon found herself fighting for her life. With unusual presence of mind, she wrapped her legs around the wolf-dog's midsection, grabbed it by the throat, and started squeezing. It took over four tortuous minutes, but she succeeded in rendering the animal unconscious, whereupon she used its collar to gain control. She did kill it.

Martial artists will recognize this defensive action as the jujutsu and judo technique where the practitioner wraps his or her legs around the opponent and chokes the opponent out. The practitioner may simply retain the opponent in the scissorlike hold while applying the choke, or else use the legs to squeeze the subject's ribs in the technique known as *dojime* (trunk constriction). Dojime is forbidden in sport judo, but is part of the older, combat-oriented jujutsu tradition.

It is not clear whether the Navajo woman was a martial artist, but she clearly demonstrated ideals normally displayed by only advanced martial arts practitioners: fortitude, poise, determination, and above all, the ability to gain victory.

She also expressed deep concern for the wolf-dog, indicating that she did not engage the animal for publicity purposes as perhaps some of today's martial artists might do.

With martial arts training, can people develop the ability to sense an opponent's presence without looking?

Although some practitioners claim to have developed extrasensory powers from their martial arts training, many resort to tricks, such as strategically placed mirrors, see-behind glasses, and radio transmitters.

Some of the best people to learn aware-ness from, however, are peripherally involved in martial arts practice: law enforcement offi-cers, military combat personnel, and ex-convicts. As a general rule, these people pos-sess the uncanny ability to read body lan-guage and to sense imminent danger before the average person can perceive it.

Do black belts really have to register their hands?

This myth seems to have circulated widely among the uninformed. But here's how this one started and to what end it has evolved.

This misconception started in the 1960s with U.S. Marines stationed in Okinawa who trained in karate. According to retired world heavyweight karate champion Joe Lewis, a former U.S. Marine who trained there, marines training in karate in Okinawa were required by the Marine Corps to register as karate students.

This rule was due to the many fights that broke out involving off-duty marines on the island. The military police could then be informed whether any rowdies were trained in karate and thus might be more difficult to deal with on a physical level.

The myth further evolved with some unknown black belt warning his opponent, "My hands are licensed weapons," in an effort to scare him away.

There is no known law, as of this writing, that requires black belts to register their hands with any state or federal law enforce-ment agencies. Be aware, however, that most state laws cite that you can only defend your-self with a force equal to the attack. So if a bully was just calling you names and you crip-ple him for life, you could be held responsi-ble. Use common sense in all self-defense situations.

Is a person who has earned a black belt considered a "lethal weapon"?

A professional competitor or a professional instructor, by legal definition, is absolutely a lethal weapon. That's why such profession-als have to be especially careful to avoid physical confrontations. Lately, U.S. citizens live in a so-called litigious society, and any professional black belt who defends himself with more force than was leveled against him could be sued for a large amount of money.

Martial artists have been sued by their attackers in recent years and have lost an unspecified but growing number of these cases in court. In one memorable case, the instructor, a famous Korean master, lost a suit waged against him even though his attacker challenged him inside his school during a class, and in front of dozens of witnesses, initiated the confrontation by throwing—but not landing—the first blow!

Hard-core devotees of kata training insist a person can only be effective in a fight by having proper form. How true is this?

Anyone who has observed or been in an actual violent encounter will tell you this is not true. Bar fights, for example, are mostly sloppy exchanges or free-for-alls featuring none of the neat, clinical techniques seen in martial arts training. Often, factors other than technique—such as awareness, presence of mind, quick reaction to danger, you and your opponent's abilities to withstand pain, and just plain old dumb luck—figure prominently in the outcome of a fight.

In the final analysis, the opponent will not care if you use perfect form in hitting him or her. Your opponent will fall if hit properly in a vulnerable spot, whether or not you look aesthetically correct while doing it.

It's generally acknowledged that boards don't hit back when struck. What about bricks?

That may depend on the brick . . . and the breaker! At a demonstration in California, a kung-fu practitioner was on stage repeatedly trying to break a brick that just wouldn't seem to cooperate. He first hit it against his head, but it remained intact. He tried again with more force, but all it did was stagger him to the extent that he almost fell off the stage.

Next, he asked a volunteer to hold it up vertically so he could break it with a straight punch. But the volunteer didn't know how to lock his arms to stabilize the object, so the brick kept moving every time it was hit. In disgust, the kung-fu performer placed it on his palm and slammed it with a knife-hand blow, whereupon it plummeted, whole until it broke upon contact with the floor!

The obstinate brick delivered the coup de grâce when it splintered and a chip flew into a nearby spectator's eye. "That brick's alive!" someone yelled as the embarrassed demonstrator quickly made his exit.

Is there a trick to breaking ice?

Ice, being heavier than wood or bricks, tends to move slower and poses less of a threat to the breaker, save the danger of it falling on

Breaking bricks, concrete slabs, or ice blocks can actually be very easy when one knows the tricks of the trade. The use of wooden spacers, as in this triple-slab ice break by black-belt Kathy Fox, makes the feat far easier than it appears.
Photo courtesy of the John Corcoran Archives.

someone's feet. One interesting fact about ice-breakers, incidentally, is that they generally don't compete in free-sparring. Maybe they're concerned they'll break the other opponent's bones, as they do the ice. Or maybe they're afraid the opponent will counterattack, unlike the ice.

Professional wrestling is laughingly denounced by some as mere showmanship and theatrical foolishness, yet many of the moves in the sport resemble martial arts techniques. Is there a connection between the two disciplines?

Perhaps because of the participants' flamboyant and sometimes outrageous behavior, pro wrestling is usually seen as pure showmanship. Pro wrestling is, by law in the United States, considered an exhibition sport where the outcome must be predetermined.

But don't let that fool you. Many excellent martial artists over the years have been involved with or trained in wrestling in one capacity or another. These include boxers Joe Louis (the Brown Bomber), "Two Ton" Tony Galento, Primo Carnera, and Muhammad Ali himself, who fought a tune-up bout against one wrestler before squaring off against Brazilian Antonio Inoki in Japan.

From the karate ranks came Masutatsu Oyama and America's Everett Eddy, who also battled with Inoki. Judoka Kukichi Endo and Masahiko Kimura are two more. It is sometimes said that Kimura's involvement in pro wrestling may have been the reason why the greatest judoka of all time died in April of 1993 as a mere seventh Dan. America's "Judo" Gene LeBell, famous for his cinematic stuntwork and his mixed-match victory over boxer Milo Savage, also participated in the sport.

Kodenkan Danzan-ryu jujutsu founder Henry Seishiro Okazaki provided training for professional wrestlers at his dojo in Hawaii.

Sumotori Rikidozan, who was fatally stabbed in a nightclub, was Kimura's tag-team partner.

On the subjects of wrestling, boxing, and judo, some people observe that wrestlers, boxers, and judoka are sportsmen and not true martial artists. Are they inferior to those who practice the so-called deadly arts like kung-fu and karate?

Combat-sports participants are true martial artists. Their training places them through the same rigorous path shared by exponents of the other martial arts. In their given range, these fighters can be very effective in actual combat since they are accustomed to applying their techniques in a spontaneous and, except for pro wrestling, unrehearsed manner. In the area of fitness, furthermore, combat-sports participants tend to be superior since they have to remain in excellent shape to be competitive.

Most martial arts schools, particularly those that teach Japanese and Korean styles, require the wearing of the gi. Does this practice inhibit a student from fighting well in street clothes?

The *gi* worn in *dojo* and *dojang* serves a multifaceted purpose. First, it prepares the student for practice by placing him or her in the proper mind-set. Second, it allows the student to train without fear of ripping his or her clothing. Also, it promotes a uniform look in the particular group working out.

A gi shouldn't inhibit fighting ability in the street unless you happen to feel you have to change to the gi before doing battle—like Superman. On the other hand, some progressive schools shun the use of the gi because it's "unrealistic." Does wearing or not wearing the gi truly affect fighting ability?

It can be argued that Thai kickboxers and Western-style boxers don't wear the gi yet are effective in combat. As far as looking for proponents of the gi, look no farther than the Gracies of Brazil, who have proven their abilities in actual fighting—always while wearing a gi.

Is it true, as some practitioners of the weapons arts like kobudo, arnis, *and* kenjutsu *claim, that techniques using the stick, knife, sword, or staff are infinitely superior to empty-hand techniques?*

Using weapons techniques against a barehanded opponent does indeed give a fighter several marked advantages. There is the superior reach afforded by the weapons. Also, points, sharpened edges, and hard, unfeeling striking surfaces provided by these weapons increase the potential for damage to the opponent.

It would be a big mistake, however, to practice weapons techniques to the exclusion of everything else. Since the weapon is necessarily an extension, not a natural portion, of the human body, it will only work if the practitioner has time to reach for it, and then only if it is closely accessible to begin with.

Contrast this to the hands, which can be just as formidable: they're always by your side, you never have to reach for them, and they'll never let you down.

Does air travel have any effect on martial arts rank?

It seems to, considering that there are first-degree black belts who left the Orient (and sometimes even Hawaii) only to step off the plane on the mainland as seventh-, eighth-, and even ninth-degree black belts.

It seems there were only four color-belt ranks—white, green, brown, and black—in most styles at one time. Now there are a dozen or so. What are some of the varieties of these current color-belt ranks?

Before the four-color belt system there was only one kind with three variations: white, brown, and black, popularized by Kodokan judo. Today, some styles use white, yellow, orange, purple, blue, green, brown, and black, with various stripes in between.

Some styles don't follow the conventional color progression. Blue belt, for instance, is the equivalent of black belt in some tang soo do groups. The deep blue is said to represent profound knowledge and experience. Black, the "color of death," according to proponents of such groups, is not used in their grading systems.

Also, the red belt, highest in Japanese karate and judo, is the equivalent of the brown belt in many taekwondo schools. So don't panic if you see someone in his or her early twenties wearing a red belt; they are not necessarily young wannabes trying to pass themselves off as ninth or tenth Dans.

In his later years, judo founder Jigoro Kano returned to the white belt as the highest rank, signifying that he transcended the system he created and was starting anew.

Mail-order belt promotions sometimes appear in martial arts ads. Can I really get my belts through the mail?

Yes, and you don't even need to take any tests. Just send a check for the cost of the belt, plus shipping and handling. Or better yet, go to a local martial arts supply store and buy one so you can save on the shipping and handling charges.

Various dubious facts, often presented as truth by some "experts," seem to prevail in the Filipino martial arts. Is it true, for instance, that arnis was developed by half-naked jungle inhabitants?

No. Because of popular media depictions (accounts of World War II combat veterans who saw jungle fighting in the Philippines, and even modern "cultural" presentations), Filipinos are thought to have been, until recently, primitive jungle dwellers.

In fact, because of heavy foreign influence, first by the Spaniards and then the Americans, Filipinos have generally dressed in Western-style clothing since the 1500s. Just as there are Arabs who have never seen a camel nor been to the desert, there are many Filipinos who have never been to the jungle.

So who did develop arnis?

Much of arnis (or *escrima* or *kali*, the latter of which is not used or recognized in the Philippines itself), in its current form, was developed in relatively recent years by the Doce Pares and the Presas groups. Not a major factor in actual combat since the onset of fully automatic firearms and high explosives, arnis had nearly become extinct until it was reintroduced into the Filipino public and private high school institutions in 1973.

It's commonly stated that while arnis uses sticks instead of blades for safety reasons, the stick movements translate directly to bladed techniques. Is this true?

Stick and blade techniques represent two distinct yet complementary aspects of arnis combat. Although the movements with each weapon are essentially identical, training with the stick alone doesn't adequately acquaint a student with the proper edge-to-target orientation necessary to make an effective cut with the blade.

The same argument is sometimes leveled at sport kendo players by practitioners of kenjutsu and *iai*, who claim that only by practicing with an actual sword can one gain expertise in swordwork.

There are those who state, however, that arnis stick techniques can be effectively put into use with a rolled-up newspaper. Is this so?

Anyone trying this approach to weapons fighting will realize the futility of fighting with newspaper. Paper, even in a rolled-up condition, is extremely flimsy and offers little in the way of striking or locking an attacker—unless, of course, the attacker is a pesky fly or mosquito.

Do all Filipinos really practice arnis?

That's like saying all Brazilians know *capoeira* or all Japanese karate. This kind of stereotype is commonly perpetuated by foreigners and curiously even by some nonnative Filipinos who attempt to portray romanticized images of all Filipinos training in their native art.

Some Filipinos choose other systems such as kung-fu, karate, or taekwondo. Others prefer Western boxing or competitive judo. Many more, burdened by the need to make a living, do not practice any martial art at all.

It's sometimes stated that arnis was widely practiced by the national heroes of the Philippines. Is this so?

This account is often told by modern-day arnis practitioners and instructors to somehow boost the historical importance of their art. Older, scholarly studies and photographs of the national heroes depict the brothers Antonio and Juan Luna practicing European fencing. Andres Bonifacio wielded a bolo (machete) as a revolutionary.

Going back a little further, Lapu Lapu and his men reportedly used pointed, fire-hardened sticks in their battles against Spanish forces in general and Magellan's group in particular. None of this, however, points to any use of arnis, in name or in concept.

José Rizal, the Filipino national hero, was recorded as having been skilled in the use of the yo-yo. Now a child's toy, the yo-yo was originally a weapon in the nineteenth-century Philippines.

Japanese-style sword practitioners often cut fruits and vegetables in demonstrations of their sword arts. Does this improve their skill with the sword?

The trick with this type of demonstration is largely to challenge the possibility of cutting the person who is holding the fruit or vegetable against his or her body. While visually spectacular, this type of cutting does not necessarily indicate any outstanding skill with the sword.

One striking activity of the members of the Society for Creative Anachronism (SCA) is the practice of combat with armor and mock weapons. Would this be considered martial arts training?

Only by those with an eye toward realistic combat training. Followers of the SCA who engage in this activity commonly possess courage, strength, combative ability, and the capacity to continue doing battle after being struck with hard blows. Their mock combat could roughly be considered the Western equivalent of Japanese kendo.

Martial myths commonly serve to place the martial arts practitioner at a supposedly higher level than the "average mortal." They perpetuate fantastic claims that even if only half-true would still prove to be far beyond credible human capabilities. For example, the Shaolin monk character Master Po, from the original TV series *Kung Fu*, was blind but performed as if he were not.
Photo courtesy of Warner Bros. Television.

Chi-kung *practitioners sometimes roll around in broken glass on the ground. What does this feat signify?*

It means that the practitioner can keep fighting even after crashing through a glass window. Apparently, it also means the fighter has pretty tough skin.

Sometimes styles with unusual-sounding names surface. Do the strange names mean these styles are fake?

Just as beauty is in the eye of the beholder, the term *fake* lies in the mind of the observer.

The nonsensical blending of words from different Oriental languages often means that the "founder" didn't have the requisite linguistic skill to name his style. This is not to say these styles can't be effective, though. Some arts, despite their unusual titles, have some pretty tough instructors and practitioners.

Can martial artists levitate, as sometimes portrayed in the movies?

Only, it seems, if they're elevated by wires. Not a phenomenon peculiar to the martial arts, levitation is normally demonstrated only by magicians, who, with rare exceptions, are not martial artists.

Some practitioners of jujutsu, particularly the scholarly types, insist that jujutsu *is the proper and only valid spelling for the art and that those who spell it otherwise are not practicing the real thing. Is this true?*

Although *jujutsu* seems to be the form currently accepted as linguistically valid, this was not always the case. The rendering *jujutsu* was popular around the turn of the twentieth century, particularly in the older instructional manuals on the subject.

The version *jujutsu* became especially common during the World War II era in the 1940s, when elements of the Japanese martial art were taught as part of American military combatives' training.

The throws, locks, chokes, and strikes, however, hurt just as much and take equal effect whether you spell the art *jujutsu*, *jiu-jitsu*, or *jujitsu*. One would also do well not to get into arguments on its proper spelling with any Brazilians.

Are most jujutsu systems really centuries old as they claim to be?

Check their terminology and you'll find out. Jujutsu styles that use judo terms like *ogoshi*, *osoto-gari*, and *de ashi barai*, or aikido terms like *ikkyo*, *shiho-nage*, and *tenchi-nage*, were probably formed fairly recently. Judo and

aikido, after all, were founded around the turn of the twentieth century.

Is ground grappling, as claimed by certain experts, really the ultimate in self-defense?

Ground grappling does seem to stymie those unfamiliar with that category of technique. Certain surfaces, however, may be hazardous to a ground-grappler's health. Some of these are broken glass, lava, quicksand, and a bed of hot coals. Another would be the floor of a crowded cowboy bar, where the buddies of the man you're rolling around with might try to line dance on your head.

Is it a waste of time to learn grappling?

Absolutely not. Grappling is a vital element in the arena of all-out unarmed combat. Most real fights result in grappling within five seconds. However, some excuses are widely circulated by skeptics who think it is useless. Obviously, these few have never seen the televised bare-knuckle fights like the Ultimate Fighting Championship.

Some of these excuses include: it's not glamorous in appearance; it's a more complex skill to learn than striking; it requires greater energy; you need to admit defeat at times; you have an uncomfortable feeling working up close with members of your own sex; you have a fear of falling; and you have stylistic prejudice.

Some throws in aikido and jujutsu demonstrations look so effortless yet send the subjects flying in acrobatic flips. Are these throws real?

Many aikido and jujutsu throws are painfully real and are effected by applying pressure on a joint. The acrobatic manifestations often seen in demonstrations, however, are greatly enhanced by the falling and rolling skills of the persons being thrown.

In these instances, it's really the throwee, not the thrower, who creates the dramatic effect. In real life people don't just gracefully sail in the air and land solidly, only to rise unharmed.

People in the attacker's role at demonstrations seem to be afflicted by some ailment that stops them in the lunge punch position. What is this ailment?

This is the enigma of the Frozen Man wherein the attacker magically freezes upon reaching the lunge punch pose. Like the receiver who generally makes the jujutsu or aikido practitioner look good in demos, the Frozen Man makes the kung-fu or karate exponent really stand out by allowing him or her to deliver flawless-looking punching and kicking counters.

At least one aikido instructor advocates the practice of atemi-waza *on the makiwara. Isn't this antithetical to aikido philosophy?*

The practice of aikido's atemi-waza, like palm strikes and knife hands, on a makiwara facilitates their development for practical use. This wouldn't be considered contrary to aikido philosophy, since founder Morihei Uyeshiba was quoted as saying that aikido is, first and foremost, a martial art.

Some instructors try to sell their system based on the notion that a person doesn't need to be in good physical condition to apply their techniques in combat. Is this realistic?

Actually, chances are the people pushing this notion are themselves in great shape. Fitness is such a crucial factor in combat-effectiveness that it is sometimes said to represent one side of a triangle, the other two being practical techniques and proper mental attitude.

Are all martial artists with titles like Master really deadly fighters?

No. Some people dubbing themselves a grandmaster or a supreme ultimate grandmaster have reportedly lost real fights. On the other hand, there are masters who have never called themselves anything other than Bob, Harry, or John and can drop behemoths in a street fight.

Some observers claim that forms training in arnis crept in as a result of intermingling with karate and kung-fu. Are forms in arnis indeed a recent innovation?

Forms, alternately referred to as *sayaw* (dance), *anyo* (image), or *karenza* (apparently a corruption of the English word *cadence*), have existed in the many sects and subsects of the Filipino martial arts for a long time. They serve the same purpose as their Chinese or Japanese counterparts: the development of single and multiple striking and locking techniques.

The current head of
Hombu aikido,
Kisshomaru Uyeshiba,
performs a shiho
nage (four-directional throw)
at a 1976 demonstration
in Tokyo.

THE MARTIAL ARTS AND WAYS OF JAPAN AND OKINAWA

3

Perhaps more than any other nation, Japan is regarded as the central crucible in which the fighting arts of Asia were fired, melded, and brought to their purest and most potent form. Indeed, in considering those combative arts that have become, in the West, universally recognized entities—judo, karate-do, aikido, and others—Japan is the correctly credited source.

It is ironic that Japan should have established such an international reputation for belligerence. In its long history, up until its disastrous entrance into World War II, Japan's military incursions into other countries probably had been more limited than those of any other country in all of history. It was a nation, in fact, that for the bulk of modern history had been by its own choice virtually isolated from the rest of the world.

Sources of the original population of Japan remain a mystery. Historians know, however, that many influences on early Japanese civilization came from mainland Asia, including its methods of fighting. The earliest archaeological evidence of warfare in Japan is found in crude "swords" carved of stone, almost certain prototypes of weapons similarly shaped in China.

Japan, from the period circa A.D. 100, was not a *unified* nation in any modern sense of that word. It was a country comprised of small clans, largely isolated by geographic boundaries of rivers and mountains. The only central government, in the city of Nara, was regional, based upon a succession of emperors selected from a few families.

It was not until the rise of one of these families, the Fujiwara, in the ninth century, that the fighting man began to play a significant cultural role. The Fujiwara expanded their power through military force. At the same time, many of the smaller clans throughout Japan started to see the advantages in building their own armies. Thus was born the concept of the *bushi* (martial gentleman) who later came to be known by a borrowed Chinese term, the *samurai*.

The history of Japan from the tenth century forward to the middle of the ninth is marked heavily by the deeds of the bushi class. A succession of regional struggles for local power was waged. The Gempei War in the eleventh century was a clash between two great warrior families, the Taira and the Minamoto, in which the martial arts of archery, spearmanship, and fencing played prominent roles.

These and other fighting arts of the professional warrior evolved further during the Kamakura (circa 1200–1400) and Muromachi periods (circa 1336–1600) when internecine warfare split Japan into numerous militant factions. During these eras many distinct schools and traditions (*ryu*) of the classical martial arts were born.

In 1600, a warrior-general, Ieyasu Tokugawa, succeeded in allying some foes and crushing others, and his clan gained military and political control over the entire country. The Tokugawa regime enforced a ban on trade and any other official or social dealings with other nations. Japan entered a two-century epoch of almost complete isolation.

This Pax Tokugawa was a period where battlefield combat within the country was abandoned as well. That is not to say, however, that the fighting arts of the bushi withered. On the contrary, the samurai set about adapting these military disciplines on a more personal scale. Individual duels replaced large-scale encounters. At the same time, the spiritual and moral dimensions of these arts were more fully inculcated into the samurai's teaching and practice.

In 1853, the United States demanded that Japan, under threat of U.S. warships, open herself to commerce with the West. Japan entered a period in which Western ideas were quickly and enthusiastically imported. Among these were Western concepts of military strategy and armament: the gun replaced the sword.

At this time, the traditional fighting arts of Japan might have been extinguished for lack of use. They were retained, though, in two ways. First, many of the classical schools of swordsmanship and other combative arts were kept alive by those families and clans that had founded them centuries before. Some of these schools continue their instruction today on an extremely small and rare scale.

Second, some of these arts were transformed. Emphasis was shifted from their battlefield practicalities to their moral components.

For instance, jujutsu, the art of grappling in armor, evolved into judo, a method not meant primarily for combat, but for the personal cultivation of physical and moral fitness and for the beauty of its aesthetic form.

According to martial scholar Dave Lowry, "There are a number of Ways in Japan for various disciplines, but all of them have similar goals: a perfection of character, a pursuit of life's truths, and a polishing of the spirit."

These modern evolutions—judo, kendo, aikido—of more ancient fighting methods—jujutsu, kenjutsu, *aikijutsu*—have been imported and have become popular and well-known throughout the world.

A word must be inserted here about karate, a fighting art probably practiced by more adherents worldwide than any other Japanese combative art. Karate is, however, by strict definition not Japanese at all. Its roots are in the indigenous fighting methods of Okinawa, a tiny island archipelago south of Japan proper.

Karate was introduced to Japan in 1922 and has been adopted as one of that country's pugilistic arts. Some important distinctions, however, separate it from the native Japanese disciplines.

The fighting arts of Japan—at least their modern derivations, including karate—have become familiar in the twentieth century to enthusiasts on a truly international scale. They have offered thousands of practitioners a way of life characterized by the *Gojo* or "Five Virtues" propagated by the Confucian philosophy that is the foundation for all these methods: benevolence, knowledge, justice, trust, and etiquette.

Simultaneous to the worldwide popularization of the Japanese Ways (the various Martial Arts of Japan), though, has been the gross misinterpretation and misrepresentation of these disciplines. Abroad and even in their native country the martial Ways of Japan have been distorted and diluted during our age. The culprits here are numerous: a modern bastardization based upon sporting applications; various cultural dissonances that render them difficult to export and flourish in societies at present; and most important, the frailties and indulgences of ego that have tempted modern practitioners to pursue these Ways for all the wrong reasons. This contortion of values is so extreme it threatens the very existence of the martial Ways.

It will be revealed in the twenty-first century whether the martial Ways of Japan can survive. Each Way's methods and philosophies may serve as a marvelous metaphysical structure to contain and nurture the human spirit of individual students; this will afford a meaningful place for these Ways in the future. Or, they will become hopelessly warped and misused, serving not as instruments of peace and spiritual cultivation, but as tools for gratifying humanity's most venal desires: fame, power, and egotism. Perhaps it is up to individuals, such as the reader of this book, to decide which future will be realized for these worthy and noble Ways.

What exactly is meant, in the context of the Japanese combative disciplines, by martial art?

This is a crucial question. Normally, when people talk about martial arts they mean fighting arts. This is a misled way of thinking, however. In discussions about combative skills in Japanese culture, the fighting arts need to be distinguished from the martial arts. Not all fighting arts are martial arts.

A martial art is one that was practiced by a member of a professional warrior class, a martial person. In Japan, that meant the samurai. The martial arts were skills the samurai used in battle. People who were not professional military men, like merchants or farmers, did not practice martial arts in Japan. Since they were not involved in combat on the battlefield, they had no use for them.

Did the original Japanese martial arts have anything to do with self-defense?

The samurai had no concept of self-defense as people today think of it. It was not his job to defend himself. He was employed by his lord, much the same way a knight was in the service of his lord in feudal Europe.

The samurai's task was to further the political or economic powers of his lord. He went out to fight and to be aggressive in some circumstances. He had to be willing to die to promote his lord's interests. Obviously, he would try to save his own life in a fight. But he could not always be defensive. Often he had to go on the offense to try to antagonize an opponent and draw him into a fight. This is not what people think of in terms of self-defense today.

So what is an example of a fighting art that is not a martial art?

Karate is a method for fighting developed by the nonwarrior classes in Okinawa. It is a fighting art, but it is not a martial art.

The martial artists in old Japan, the samurai, never saw karate. And if they had, they would have had no interest in nor need for it. They had no reason to try to kick someone, for instance, when they were constantly armed with high-quality, lethal weapons.

What about judo, aikido, and kendo—are they martial arts?

No. They are fighting methods that developed after the age of the samurai was over. Based upon older martial arts, like jujutsu, aikijutsu, and kenjutsu, they are more properly called martial Ways.

In Japanese, *Way* translates as *do* (pronounced "dough"). It means "a path" or "a road." *Jutsu* is a word that means "skills." Very broadly and generally speaking, an art that ends with the suffix -jutsu refers to one of the battlefield arts of the samurai. An art that ends with the suffix -*do* is one of the more modern versions. This is where the words *bujutsu* (martial art) and *budo* (martial way) come from.

What is the real difference between a -jutsu form of fighting and a -do form?

As noted earlier, a bujutsu, or martial art, is one that has application in the warfare of the feudal period in Japan. A budo is an art that is more concerned with moral development, aesthetic form, and physical fitness, all in that order.

Isn't self-defense important in the budo?

Self-defense, in terms of solving physical confrontations like muggings or attempted assaults, is considered a by-product of training in most forms of the budo. The main goals concern perfecting the characters of the participants.

Of course, some schools of budo emphasize self-defense training and advertise themselves that way. But this is not in harmony with the philosophies of the individuals who developed the martial Ways in early modern Japan.

If a person wanted to learn the real thing in terms of fighting, would he or she have to study one of the older bujutsu?

That depends upon what is meant by "the real thing." If a person needs to know how to ride a horse in battle, or swim while wearing armor, or fortify a castle, that person might want to study one of the bujutsu. But those are skills few people have use for today.

Furthermore, the schools of the bujutsu (they are called *koryu* or "old schools") that still exist today are quite rare and small. They are never commercial enterprises. Most often, they are composed of one teacher and a few students, training very quietly. They don't attract a lot of attention in Japan.

If I wanted to join a koryu, how would I go about doing it?

Move to Japan. Only a handful of people are qualified to teach the bujutsu outside of Japan. Furthermore, it is virtually a necessity to be able to speak and read Japanese to study at one of these ryu. And you would almost certainly have to befriend someone already practicing in the school.

Some of the ryu that have accepted foreigners have been badly used. The foreigner studied for a few years or months, then returned home and promptly began advertising himself as a "master." For that reason, most of the koryu are quite reluctant to admit people without checking them out first.

How do these classical bujutsu schools differ from a modern martial Way?

They differ in many ways. There are no belt ranks in the bujutsu, for instance. Practitioners may be graded by a series of

A performance of the art of naginata, at the Tokyo Budokan, in 1972.
Photo courtesy of Dave Lowry.

menkyo, or licenses, given directly by their teacher. A bujutsu never has any sporting element nor any kind of free sparring. Training is confined to predetermined sequences of attack and defense, or kata.

Also, instruction in the bujutsu is almost always limited. Most bujutsu have only a few dozen practitioners active in them.

How many schools of the bujutsu are still extant in Japan?

There are about three hundred schools of the bujutsu in Japan. That's not a lot, considering the thousands and thousands of modern budo schools active there.

Turning to the more popular modern budo like karate-do, kendo, judo, and aikido, which one of these is the most popular?

In Japan, most male students practice kendo or judo during their school years, so these budo are probably the most popular, in terms of numbers, there. Worldwide, karate is probably practiced by more people than any other martial Way.

Are those budo—karate-do, kendo, aikido, and judo—the only forms of the budo?

No. There are several other budo forms. *Naginata-do* is the budo of using a long, bladed halberd. It is especially popular with women in Japan.

Jukendo is the art of fencing with a bayonet. A mock wooden rifle with a padded tip is used, along with heavy armor of the sort seen in kendo. *Kyudo* is the martial Way of archery. *Iaido* is the martial Way of drawing and cutting with the sword.

All of these budo have followers around the world, along with organizations and ranking committees that oversee them.

How much does the average Japanese know about the budo or the classical martial arts of Japan?

On the average, not much. Unless a person is involved or has friends or relatives involved, the martial arts and Ways of Japan don't play much of a role in everyday Japanese life.

Judo, karate, and kendo tournaments are regularly televised nationally. But many Western martial artists are disappointed when they go to Japan expecting everyone they meet to be an authority on these arts and Ways.

Many older Japanese have negative feelings about the budo, since these Ways were used to fuel the intense nationalism that led Japan into World War II. They may consider the martial Ways to be extremely right-wing or excessively brutal.

A typical kendo practice in Japan.
Photo courtesy of Dave Lowry.

Some younger Japanese have no interest in the budo because they represent "old-fashioned" ideas.

How about in the United States? What is the prevailing attitude toward the martial Ways in the West?

Unfortunately, because of violent movies featuring martial Ways, many Westerners have serious misconceptions about the budo. They may assume that those who are involved in the budo suffer from machismo complexes or are brutal or aggressive.

Also, many martial artists in the United States and elsewhere in the West promote themselves as "deadly killers" and publically behave in vulgar, attention-getting manners. These types receive a great deal of notoriety, especially in the press.

The student practicing the budo must be patient in dealing with the general public and in demonstrating that the image of the martial Ways depicted in films is not at all an accurate one.

What should I expect from my budo practice?

People come to the budo dojo with many preconceived ideas about what they will get out of their training. Some believe they will be able to defend themselves against possible violent encounters. Others imagine they will achieve a happier, more fulfilled lifestyle. Still others hope for some kind of mystical experience.

Any preconceived notion the beginner has can be an obstacle in the learning process. Instead, you should ask the teacher at the dojo toward what goals he or she is striving. This will give you a good indication of what to expect.

In general, however, consistent practice and learning in any of the budo should in time promote your physical and mental health.

How long will it take before I begin to notice the benefits of budo practice?

You will probably notice some of them fairly soon, especially the physical benefits. Stamina and coordination often increase markedly after practicing a budo for only a few months.

Other benefits are much more subtle. It may take some years before you notice a change in your personality. You might find yourself dealing with stressful situations more easily, or you might find you have more energy or a more positive attitude. You may discover you are more tolerant of others and have an easier time getting along with them.

These are cumulative effects, but they do not come quickly. The budo are not a quick form of psychotherapy nor a twelve-step program. They require a sincere and prolonged commitment to achieve real change in a person's life.

Are the budo dangerous? Should I expect to get hurt?

For the most part, the budo involve a certain element of risk. They are fighting techniques, however modified for modern times, and they are dangerous. Serious injury in the budo, however, is extremely rare.

If you are training in a good, legitimate dojo, the training process is carefully monitored. You should feel uncomfortable at times and challenged in your practice. But you will never be deliberately exposed to unnecessary danger.

You should expect bruises, sprains, and abrasions—the same sort of injuries you would receive playing a vigorous sport regularly, for instance. On the average, however, the martial Ways are not as dangerous as skiing or many other popular activities.

How much of the budo are mental and how much are physical?

The Japanese have traditionally believed that a person's physical abilities continue to increase until about the age of forty. At that point, the mental faculties all begin to mature. So training in the dojo often is geared toward the building of physical skills for younger people, and the refining of mental powers for those who are older.

For instance, a fifty-year-old black belt may not be able to kick as hard or as fast as a twenty-year-old. But the older black belt, if having trained longer, will have an advantage in timing, in setting up the opponent for an opening, and in mentally outmaneuvering the opponent. The older black belt will often have an advantage because the years of experience provide greater insights into strategy.

No matter what a person's age, though, the mental challenges presented by the budo will always be as great as the physical ones, and often even more so.

Why are the mental challenges as great as the physical ones in the budo?

Engaging in a serious practice of any of the budo is difficult. It is initially hard because of the physical demands.

In karate, for instance, the body must become accustomed to stances and movements that are often painful, stretching and building muscles not normally used in daily life in the modern world. It doesn't take long to build up strength, endurance, and flexibility to meet these demands, however. The difficult part comes in motivation and the willingness to continue on.

The budo can be boring. The student must go over and over the basics, and continue practicing them even though it seems that they are perfect. Most people do not have the patience for this. They are mentally geared toward instant solutions and progress that can be seen and felt quickly. That is the nature of modern society.

By comparison, the budo are much slower. It can be hard to summon the enthusiasm to go to the dojo week after week, even year after year, knowing the same things need to be practiced again and again.

What is the most difficult aspect of learning a budo?

Most experts would agree that the most difficult part of teaching lies in relaxing the student. The power in the budo is not a static kind. Instead, it requires fluidity and suppleness, which is accomplished through relaxation and good posture. If you stiffen up, your posture suffers. Relax, and bones, muscles, and connecting tissues like tendons and ligaments can all align and work together smoothly.

Beginners tend to be stiff and rigid. They may have a considerable amount of power in muscle mass, but their stiffness prevents them from delivering it to the target. In the budo, the body contracts and tightens only for a brief moment—just at the point of impact or in the focus of a throw or another technique. Beginners, however, often begin focusing their energies long before that crucial moment.

The expert stays completely relaxed until the very second of making focus. That's why older martial artists, if they have trained well, can keep up and continue their practice long after younger and stronger exponents are exhausted. The more experienced practitioner uses energy more wisely and relaxes constantly.

What's an example of an expert's focus compared to a beginner's?

If you practice karate, you are familiar with a step-in punch, usually called *oi-zuki*. If you practice aikido, you may call it *mune tsuki*.

Either way, step forward with your right leg and make a punch with your right hand. Now do it slowly. You will see that your fist begins to tighten and your leg muscles begin to squeeze before the focus of the punch. This is wasted energy.

If you think of the punch as done through the count of ten, you will see that you begin to tighten and contract muscles at about the count of five or six. The expert, however, doesn't begin this process until at about nine and three quarters. No wasted energy—and the power goes directly to the target without any stiffness slowing it down.

This process of learning to relax takes years to perfect. There are no shortcuts—just long years of committed training.

How long does it take to get a black belt in any of the budo?

Usually a well-meaning question, this is also one of the most ignorant. If you want a diploma from Oxford, you can find an example of one in a book, photocopy it, and write in your own name. You've got your diploma. But do you have the knowledge and learning of an Oxford grad? Hardly. Likewise, black belts are readily available through martial arts supply companies. Buying one and wearing it is easy.

No matter how many times they are told differently, the general public continues to believe that the black belt is the sign of the expert. It is not. In the budo dojo, black belts are given to students as signs of recognition that they are serious about their study. These students have been recognized as ready to begin real training. All the ranks up through black belt are symbols of the process of learning to become a student.

To answer the question, though, in most budo forms, it takes about four to five years of sustained practice to earn the first level of black belt.

Why is there such an emphasis on all the colored belts? Why have ranks at all?

Now these are good questions to which there are several answers.

The bujutsu, the classical martial arts of feudal Japan, were only practiced by professional warriors. They had no need for ranks. The fact that they survived a battle was proof that they knew their stuff. They didn't need to wear a colored belt to demonstrate their skills.

The budo, however, are practiced by people from all walks of life. Many of them, it was decided, needed some kind of symbol to encourage them to continue in their practice. They needed something to provide motivation; thus the kyu/dan system of colored and black belts.

A second reason is that with the masses of people training in a budo, the teacher and seniors need a way to make a quick identification of skill level. The colored belt is a good way to do that.

Another reason is that many budo dojo are commercial operations and require money to stay open. Testing students and awarding a series of colored belts is a good way to raise revenue for the dojo.

Does that mean I shouldn't be proud of my green or purple or brown belt?

No, of course not. You were probably proud of being able to say your ABC's when you were younger, and you should have been. For a child, that's a big step in learning to communicate. But looking back at your education now from a more mature and wider perspective, you can see that learning to recite letters was actually a small step in the learning process.

Be proud of your accomplishments in ranking, but keep them in perspective.

How, then, can the quality of a martial artist be judged?

Generally speaking, a martial artist should be judged by his commitment to practice. A so-called master may strut around with a black belt and a fancy, decorated uniform. But how often does he actually practice? Is he still training and trying to perfect himself? Or does he try to convince others that he has completed the Way?

Also, a martial artist can be judged by her loyalty to her teacher, dojo, and budo; citizenship; treatment of others; and courtesy and civility, especially under difficult or stressful circumstances.

It would be nice to be able to judge a martial artist by the belt worn. But it doesn't work that way. Consider it in another sense:

Karate master Gichin Funakoshi (far right, with back to camera) leads a class of Strategic Air Command personnel, who were making an intensive study of Japanese martial Ways, circa 1958. This was the first and most extensive training in these arts given to foreigners. In the center of the photo is the late Isao Obata, one of Funakoshi's most senior disciples.
Photo courtesy of Dave Lowry.

How can you tell whether someone is a "good Christian" or a "good Buddhist"? Being a good member of any faith is a matter of living it every day. It isn't a goal you can reach; it is a lifetime of effort. The same is true of the budo.

Wait a minute! What about considering a martial artist's skill in techniques? Isn't a budoka who can break ten boards better than one who can only break one? Isn't a budoka who can defend himself against a roomful of attackers better than one who stumbles trying to fight against just one?

Sure, in some cases these are true. But they are still a very limited way to judge the caliber of a budoka.

The introduction to this chapter discussed the values of the budo. The founder of Japanese karate, Gichin Funakoshi, said that the "ultimate aim of karate was not in victory or defeat, but in the perfection of the character of the *karateka*." Does it sound like he was interested in how many boards his students could break?

The physical skills of the budo are very important. But they are only the tip of the iceberg. It's what lies beneath these skills that is most vital. The values of the budo are found primarily in the Confucian values of justice, compassion, trust, etiquette, and wisdom.

If not physical, what are the attributes that characterize the successful budoka?

It's understandable that you don't understand. You are beginning to see that these martial Ways are much more sophisticated and run deeper than a sport or any similar kind of physical activity or hobby. They are not easy to grasp, and so you have to do a lot of thinking along with your training.

Take, for example, one of the most senior experts in karate right now, Morio Higaonna. Higaonna-sensei is an incredibly powerful man, fully capable of killing a human with a single blow. An expert in the hidden techniques found in the kata, his performances are astounding. He is admired the world over by karate practitioners and has thousands of students. By any standards, he is a remarkably good and respected martial artist.

Now, suppose that a tragedy occurs in Higaonna-sensei's life: an accident leaves him paralyzed from the neck down. More helpless than a baby, would he still be a great budoka?

Not if he were measured only by his physical skills. But the serious martial artist would continue to admire, respect, and learn from Higaonna-sensei—not for his physical abilities, but for his spirit, character, and positive attitude about life. These are the attributes that mark the successful budoka.

Are the physical aspects of the budo inessential to being a good budoka?

Not at all. The physical training in the dojo is absolutely essential, not as an end to itself but as the means to attaining character and spirit. You cannot think or philosophize your way to expertise in the budo. You get there through perspiration and hard training. But don't confuse the physical realm of the budo—the process—with the goals.

The founders of the budo were a rather wise bunch, weren't they?

They certainly were. They saw, in the classical martial arts of the samurai, a lot of potential value, not just for the Japanese, but for people of all backgrounds and nationalities. They were able to synthesize many of these arts' techniques and use them to communicate some very profound ideas.

The leaders of most of the modern budo lived during an interesting time period in Japan. Karate's Gichin Funakoshi, judo's Jigoro Kano, and aikido's Morihei Uyeshiba were all born during the twilight of Japan's feudal period. But they matured while Japan was being strongly influenced by the West; their budo reflect this.

A logical order in the teaching, curriculum, and organization of their budo forms demonstrates Western influences. The older,

classical martial arts were taught on an individual basis. There is a saying, "ten students, ten different arts." In other words, a bujutsu teacher would instruct different students in different ways, depending upon the inherent abilities and temperament of each student. This made for intense, personalized training.

It also meant that only a few people could learn at a time. By using Western educational concepts, however, the founders of the budo could allow large numbers of people to train. This permitted the budo to grow and eventually be exported to the rest of the world. Those who follow the budo today owe these men a debt that can never be repaid.

How can I decide which budo I would like to follow?

Think of the various budo as different routes up the same mountain. The route you choose will be the one agreeable to your temperament and personality.

Before you begin practicing a budo, it's a good idea to observe as many of them as you can. Even after having begun your practice, do not categorically refuse to consider chances to train in other budo forms. If you are training in aikido, for example, don't pass up an opportunity to see a kendo demonstration. You may find that your interests and perspective change even while you continue with your practice.

If you are smart, you will not look for a specific budo; instead, you will look for a specific teacher. If you find a good teacher, one you respect and whose teaching abilities match your learning style, you should practice with that teacher regardless of the form of budo.

What are kata, and do all of the budo have them?

Kata means "shape" or "form" in Japanese. All the budo have them. All the arts of Japan, including the tea ceremony, flower arranging, and the martial arts and Ways, have kata as a central precept.

Kata, the idea of a set form, is endemic in Japanese civilization. In the budo, kata consist of predetermined movements—sequences of action that may be thought of as the grammar of combat. Some kata may be practiced solo; others are done in pairs, with an attacker and a defender.

Isn't a kata more like a dance than a method to learn to fight? If the movements are predetermined, what does the budoka do in a spontaneous situation where an attacker does not move the way the kata is designed?

The method of learning to fight through a perfection of the kata was the sole way the samurai learned to fight. That alone should make

critics think twice before condemning kata as a mere dance.

The kata certainly are predetermined sequences of movements. But after having learned them, the budoka may be challenged in a way through kata training that he will never encounter in other practice methods. For instance, his partner in the kata may suddenly change the timing of attack, or the partner may move from one kata to another midway through the action.

In arts like karate, where solo training in the kata predominate, a partner might be used to fill the role of the attacker. Suppose the first movement of the kata is a step forward, for example. In a practice session, however, the attacking partner may decide to begin her movement while standing off to the side. The kata exponent must change the direction of the kata to meet this attack.

There are numerous ways in which the kata are manipulated so that the practitioner learns to adapt to a wide variety of conditions. The kata are the grammar of a budo. Once the rules of grammar have been thoroughly learned, the budoka can create his own "sentences" spontaneously.

Do the kata play a role aside from learning to fight?

The role of kata, as previously noted, plays an enormous role in Japanese daily life.

Traditionally, the Japanese have believed that outer form is as important, if not more so, than inner feelings.

This sounds odd, but consider a situation where you are under pressure. Perhaps you are facing a stressful situation at work or school, or maybe you are under the threat of a violent attack. At times such as these, the face you show may be critical in your performance.

Kata teaches the budoka to maintain this outer form, no matter what the situation. This is a very long process, one that must be conducted by a good teacher. But it is unquestionably a goal of the serious budoka to study and penetrate into the inner meanings of the kata.

It was noted earlier that karate is not a martial Way in the same sense as judo, kendo, or aikido, since it is not derived from one of the martial arts of the samurai. How was it created?

Karate is a combative method devised by Okinawans. Okinawa is now a part of Japan, but it was a separate country during much of the feudal era. A crossroads for most of the Pacific, Okinawa acquired many different nationalities, who contributed to the development of its fighting art.

Is karate purely Okinawan, or is it the result of these outside influences?

Okinawan karate is most likely about 40 percent native in its origins and 40 percent from Chinese influences. The remaining 20 percent may be traced to other Southeast Asian combative arts.

Does Okinawa have fighting arts other than karate?

Yes. Prior to the influences from China and other sources, the Okinawans appear to have favored grappling techniques in their fighting. Several forms of grappling and wrestling-type combative arts are native to Okinawa. Some of the techniques of these arts are hidden within the karate kata.

Is it true that karate was developed because the Okinawans had no weapons and had to fight the samurai?

Not really. This makes for romantic stories of beleaguered peasants defending themselves against the cruel samurai. Actually, there are very few authenticated episodes of that nature. The Okinawans fought one another, for the most part.

Although Okinawa is a small island, it is broken up into villages and regions that had intense rivalries. Karate found much of its practical historical application in the altercations between these different groups.

Judo was the first budo mass marketed to the United States. Yet its popularity now seems eclipsed by other martial Ways. What happened?

There are many opinions on this, of course. Because it was introduced first, judo became familiar to more Americans. So when other

The late Kyuzo Mifune, the last tenth dan in Kodokan judo, performs a demonstration of the art in Tokyo, as part of the 1964 Olympics, when judo made its debut as an official Olympic sport.

Photo courtesy of Dave Lowry.

martial arts like karate and aikido were demonstrated here, they possibly seemed more exotic and became more popular.

Another reason might have been that judo was split organizationally by several different groups, each of which claimed to truly represent it. The intense infighting between these organizations drove many judoka away from that martial Way.

Doubtless one reason judo lost some of its popularity was, surprisingly, its inclusion as an Olympic sport. Such an emphasis on competition led to a rapid disintegration of judo technique and the adoption of cruder,

The founder of aikido, Morihei Uyeshiba (left), and his son, Kisshomaru, who succeeded him as Doshu (Leader of the Way) when Uyeshiba died in 1969. This photo was taken in 1968, in Tokyo.

Photo courtesy of Dave Lowry.

wrestling-type strategies where physical force superseded skill.

Today, many Japanese judoka have become dismayed over what they perceive as the corruption of their Way and are working to restore its integrity.

What were the goals of judo, according to the founder, Jigoro Kano?

Kano was quite specific in his expectations for judo. He wrote, "Judo is the way to the most effective use of both physical and spiritual strength. By training you in attacks and defenses, it refines your body and your soul and helps you make the spiritual essence of judo a part of your very being. In this way, you are able to perfect yourself and contribute something of value to the world."

Kano saw judo as a *kyoiku*, a method for educating the spirit, mind, and body. The judoka who have heeded his words and ideas have discovered within judo a true and valuable martial Way.

What is the best martial Way for children?

Judo, unquestionably. If it is properly taught and supervised, judo will teach them balance, coordination, self-control, and an awareness of the physical, mental, and emotional aspects of their personalities that encourage a healthy maturation in young people. It also allows youngsters to expend their energies in a safe way: "fighting" in situations where injury is reduced to a minimum and self-confidence is constantly built.

Judo does not involve the rapid contractions of muscles seen in karate practice or the joint manipulation in aikido. These are two very fine budo forms for adolescents and adults but are really inappropriate for children below puberty.

Which is the most recently developed of the modern martial Ways?

Aikido. Of the "big three" of the Japanese budo, karate's Gichin Funakoshi, judo's Jigoro Kano, and aikido's Morihei Uyeshiba, Uyeshiba was the youngest and the last to die. He began to formulate his system of budo before World War II, but it did not start to mature into its present form until the late 1950s.

Why are there so many variations and schools of aikido?

The founder of aikido, Morihei Uyeshiba, was in a constant and ongoing process of refining his budo, right up until he died in 1969. Different students studied with him at different times, and when they began to teach, their instruction was influenced by the partic-

Aikido's Gozo Shioda (bowing) meets U.S. Senator Robert Kennedy, when the latter was visiting Japan in 1963. Shioda later performed an aikido demonstration for Kennedy.
Photo courtesy of Dave Lowry.

ular stage Uyeshiba was in when they were with him.

After his death, different senior students believed different aspects of his budo should be emphasized. They founded their own aikido systems to reflect this.

Aikido is often juxtaposed as a soft budo, while karate is perceived as a hard one. Is this an inaccurate way to think of aikido?

Yes. All budo deal with, in one way or another, the control and release of energy.

Aikido does this in such a way, blending with or redirecting the force of an attack, that it appears soft. It can be extremely powerful, however. It is not uncommon for *aikidoka* to be thrown so hard when taking the throws of experts that they are stunned or even knocked unconscious, even though they are using correct methods for falling safely.

Aikido also involves joint-locks and manipulations that can be extremely effective. It is true that some aikido teachers prefer to concentrate on less-aggressive forms of practice. But the potential for energy and force in aikido is every bit as great as for any other budo form.

What is the oldest of the modern budo?

Kendo. The pursuit of swordsmanship, not as a practical means of combat but rather as a spiritual and aesthetic discipline, has its origins in the early eighteenth century.

What are some of the reasons to study kendo?

Kendo is the most aerobically challenging of the budo. It builds considerable endurance and stamina. Kendo also continues to place a strong emphasis on etiquette and other matters that lend it more of a martial feeling. Thus, kendo can be an excellent way to also nurture spiritual strength.

Kendo is also a valuable budo to study because, as a percussive form of combat (as opposed to judo or aikido), it affords the practitioner the opportunity to actually make contact with an opponent (unlike karate). This feature permits the practitioner to get a real sense of power transmission and focus that are much harder to feel in a budo like karate.

Kendo also has strong ties with Japan's past. The *kendoka* has access to attitudes, training methods, and traditions that can lead to a mature understanding of budo philosophy.

Why don't more people outside of Japan practice kendo?

Kendo is the most expensive of the popular budo. A set of protective armor can run close to $1,000. This prevents many would-be enthusiasts from entering training.

Also, there are not many qualified kendo sensei in the United States, which has further limited its growth. But kendo continues to gain popularity in the United States, and many American kendoka have competed successfully in international tournaments.

I often hear or read the term classical martial art. What exactly is a classical martial art or Way?

Classicism is defined as having an adherence to the standards of simplicity, restraint, and

The late Yuji Omori (right) demonstrates the art of iai (sword drawing) as a special exhibition held as part of the Meiji Centennial in Japan, in 1967.

Photo courtesy of Dave Lowry.

proportion, which are considered to be valid in both a universal and timeless sense. This definition may be applied to all kinds of art, including the martial arts and Ways.

A classical budo or bujutsu is one in which standards have been set that exponents are expected to meet. In other words, in a classical martial discipline, *how* you do something is as important as *what* you do.

The word *classical* is also applied to arts formulated during a period of intense creative development. The era in Western music in which Bach, Haydn, and Handel were all composing at the same time was a moment of classicism for that form of art.

In Japan, the Muromachi era (ca. 1336–1600) was a period of warfare that saw the birth of nearly all of the bujutsu systems;

martial arts luminaries like Musashi Miyamoto, Yagyu Munenori, Itto Ittosai, and many others were all alive and active. Fighting methods codified and developed at this time may be called classical martial arts.

What does the word traditionalist *mean when applied to certain martial artists?*

The word *traditionalist* really doesn't mean much at all. At least one martial arts movie star, for instance, has been referred to as a tra-ditionalist, simply because he wears a plain white training uniform!

This word is often used in a pejorative sense by some who criticize "old-fashioned" methods. Others prefer to call themselves tra-ditionalists because they hope such an appel-lation will afford them a connection with the past in the martial arts, which they do not in fact have.

In very general terms, a traditionalist in the martial Ways recognizes that as individu-

Jesse Kuhaulua, the first American-born sumotori to rise to the middle ranks of professional sumo, throws an opponent from the ring in 1974. Kuhaulua, who wrestled under the name Takimiyama Daigoro, retired from professional sumo competi-tion ten years later and currently operates a stable for training other sumotori in Tokyo.
Photo courtesy of Dave Lowry.

als we are links in a chain that stretches far back into the past and has limitless potential for the future. The strength of the links that are forged after us will depend on how firmly we are connected with those before us. Lose the connection to the past, the traditionalist believes, and you risk losing everything important for the future.

How often should I expect to use my budo training?

If you are training seriously, you should expect to use it every day. You should be able to use the principles of the budo in your personal and professional relationships: in the way you treat others and in the way you conduct yourself. If you are not employing your martial Way on a daily basis, it is a clear sign that you are not practicing hard enough or with enough sincerity.

How long will I have to work on my budo practice before I will have perfected it?

Until the day you die. The budo is a journey that takes a lifetime to complete. It is, at its heart, a Way to follow for the rest of your life.

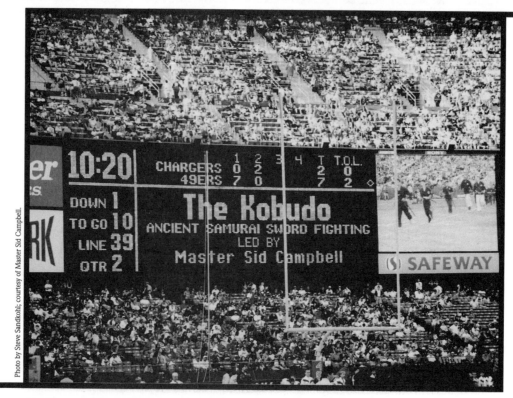

Americans, more than any other culture, have popularized the martial arts on an unprecedented scale. Here's one reason why. Master Sid Campbell and his students of Oakland, California, enter the field to perform an Okinawan martial arts demo in 3Com Park during the halftime of a San Francisco 49ers pro football game. Master Campbell's was one of six martial arts troupes performing before some sixty thousand spectators in attendance that day.

AMERICAN MARTIAL ARTS

Despite the fact that many people picture Asians when they think of the martial arts, there are actually more Americans practicing the two major martial arts, karate and taekwondo, than there are Japanese and Koreans practicing them in their native countries. In international competitions, Americans have become world champions or have placed prominently in just about every variety of world-class martial sports.

The American versions of the martial arts have proved themselves to be highly popular and effective. Yet controversy surrounds the American approach. Controversy because traditionalist factions for the most part do not respect or recognize newly consolidated styles. However, in merging the best parts of various martial arts, Americans only repeated what the Asian masters themselves had done before them. That is, they combined techniques from various Asian fighting disciplines to create new eclectic styles that fit their own personalities and physical characteristics.

Americanized martial arts as an entity only really started to gain momentum in the late 1960s and early 1970s. At that time, Americans had practiced the martial arts for only about a dozen years or so (outside of Hawaii) when these early practitioners began converting them into a unique blend of traditions, practical self-defense, and modern sport. American karate, as it came to be called, isn't actually a style as much as it is a way of physically and psychologically approaching the martial arts.

One thing is sure. It was and still is the Americans who have, more than any other culture, popularized the martial arts the world over. Hong Kong movies notwithstanding, the

American entertainment industry has taken the martial arts to the world's masses. The mass acceptance of Asian martial arts started in 1966 with the debut of television's *The Green Hornet* show, costarring the inimitable Bruce Lee, compounded astronomically from 1971 to 1974 with the immensely popular *Kung Fu* TV series, and continued right up to the recent Saturday morning animated martial arts TV heroes like the Power Rangers.

Martial arts trends that start in the United States, through pop culture entertainment or otherwise, have had a delayed but consistently huge impact on martial arts in foreign countries all over Europe and South America. What successfully originates in America almost always influences martial arts markets across the Western world.

Furthermore, America has been the world's most fertile ground for planting and spreading the martial arts through public instruction, a discovery not lost to the thousands of Asian martial arts teachers and masters who have immigrated to this country. In fact, each year since the mid-1970s, America has outpaced the entire world in number of active martial arts schools and students. Some eighteen thousand schools teach the martial arts in the United States today. According to a "Business Change Report," in 1994 martial arts instruction was the second-fastest-growing

occupation in the entire United States, eclipsed only by computer networking services.

America has, quite simply, set the standards for the world's contemporary approach to martial arts.

Kenpo karate pioneer Ed Parker, Sr. (d. 1990) is universally acknowledged as the Father of American Karate. Parker Americanized traditional martial arts techniques and concepts by replacing them with modern, eclectic applications more suited to the mind-set and physical characteristics of Americans.

Photo courtesy of Lee Wedlake.

When did the term American karate *first appear?*

The exact date is uncertain, but as early as the mid-1960s several well-known karate instructors like Peter Urban (New York City) and Ed Parker (Los Angeles, California) were calling their approach American karate. In fact, Parker is often cited as the Father of American Karate.

What exactly is American karate?

Karate is a Japanese word meaning "empty hand." But in the United States, karate has become a generic, catchall term referring to any striking-type martial art from Shotokan (the first modern karate style) to taekwondo (the popular Korean martial system). Thus, many martial arts teachers in America, even those from a Korean background, use the word *karate*.

The American approach to martial arts training has typically been to take elements from several disciplines and combine them into an eclectic method. Karate pioneer and actor Chuck Norris, quoted in *The Development of American Karate* by Jerry Beasley (Bemjo Martial Arts Library, 1983), states, "American karate is a conglomeration uniting all styles together. . . . We utilize all ideas in our system and the techniques con-

America has set the standards for the world's contemporary approach to martial arts. Retired World Heavyweight Kickboxing Champion Joe Lewis (center), appearing here with his chief protégés, Florida's Jim Graden (right) and John Graden, introduced some of the greatest technique innovations used throughout the martial arts today.

Photo courtesy of the John Graden Archives.

tinue to improve in quality because they are much more versatile."

American karate is thus an approach to the martial arts rather than a specific style.

Is there such a thing as American taekwondo?

Taekwondo has been practiced in America since 1956, before the formation of the

International Taekwondo Federation or the World Taekwondo Federation, the two leading organizations. These organizations were both founded in Korea, and neither uses the word *karate* in reference to their martial art. When they were formed, karate and taekwondo were practically indistinguishable. The early pioneers of taekwondo in America did not practice the newer, so-called Olympic style of taekwondo.

Today, like the practitioners of American karate, these martial artists and their descendants combine techniques from various systems to create an eclectic approach that's frequently called American taekwondo. If you watched an American taekwondo practitioner and an American karate practitioner sparring in an American tournament, you probably couldn't tell them apart.

Is there such a thing as American kung-fu?

Some practitioners use this term, but by and large the kung-fu stylists have maintained their connections (at least linguistically) to China and have been reluctant to embrace the term *American kung-fu*. However, many American kung-fu instructors take the eclectic approach found in American karate and American taekwondo.

Even if American karate isn't really a style, aren't there specific styles of American karate?

Yes, but there are far too many to name them all here. The two oldest and most recognized are kenpo, founded by Ed Parker, and American *goju*, founded by Peter Urban. Other well-known systems are Hawaii's kajukenbo (a combination of the names karate, judo, jujutsu, kenpo, and Chinese boxing), and *won hop kuen do*, founded by Al Dacascos, America's first national kung-fu champion.

Some styles, like Parker's kenpo, are widely practiced in the United States while many others are taught in but a single school.

Are there varying styles of American taekwondo?

Many of America's taekwondo practitioners study styles started in this country. Some well-known examples are Grandmaster Jhoon Rhee's taekwondo, created by the Father of American taekwondo (Rhee was the first to introduce Korean martial arts to the United States); Songahm taekwondo, created by Haeng Ung Lee; and Nam Seo Kwan taekwondo, founded by Keith D. Yates.

Also, many of the American taekwondo pioneers of the 1960s and 1970s today use

(Left) Grandmaster Jhoon Rhee, the father of taekwondo in America, teaches a class in Dallas, Texas, in 1966. Photo courtesy of Keith D. Yates. (Right) Grandmaster Rhee performing a demonstration with his students in Washington, D.C., his base of operations, in 1990. The performance was held at Capitol Hill in conjunction with the President's Council on Physical Fitness. Photo courtesy of Grandmaster Jhoon Rhee.

the word *karate* in place of taekwondo. For this reason, and because of the pervading influence of the Olympic taekwondo movement, there are probably fewer American taekwondo styles than American karate styles.

What is the best martial art style taught in America?

That is an impossible question to answer, not only because different styles emphasize different techniques and strategies, but because it really is true that, as the old saying goes, "The individual makes the style, the style doesn't make the individual." In other words, a supremely gifted athlete is going to be good no matter what style he or she practices.

Most experts will also agree that your teacher's ability is probably more important than the particular style you practice.

How do I go about finding a good karate teacher?

The same way you would go about finding a good teacher in any activity. If you want to find a good music teacher or tennis coach or art instructor, you ask for references. You check the Better Business Bureau. You examine each teacher's qualifications and educational background, and, perhaps most important, you watch each one teach.

Do they have a way of communicating and teaching that would enable you or your child to learn? Do they seem like someone you can relate to and someone you would enjoy training under?

For more information on finding a good school and a good instructor, see Chapter 15.

You cite qualifications. Is there an organization that certifies all martial arts teachers in America?

While there are some large martial arts organizations, there is no single governing body for the martial arts in the United States. Even within the same organization, the qualifications of different teachers can vary widely. And while some associations might have grandiose names—and claims—it is possible they could be nothing more than the "official" certifying group for merely one person: the person who created the association.

One independent group is the American Council on Martial Arts (ACMA). The ACMA, in conjunction with the Cooper Institute for Aerobics Research, a prestigious, international certifying organization based in Dallas, Texas, has developed a certification course that is style-independent and concen-

trates on topics like educational theory and exercise physiology. More information about the ACMA can be found at www.napma.com.

The bottom line is, while certification from an organization can be entirely legitimate, you still have to personally talk to the teacher and decide for yourself how qualified he or she is to fulfill your needs as a student.

What rank is considered a Master level in most American martial arts schools?

Again, this varies, but a person is usually considered a master instructor at the fifth- or sixth-degree black belt.

But there should be more to the equation than just rank. Maturity and teaching ability, for example, would certainly be expected of a master. Americans, it seems, are enamored with titles and often misuse them in the martial arts. Be suspicious of instructors in their mere twenties running around with *Master* embossed on the backs of their uniforms.

Are commercially run schools better than classes taught at YMCAs or community recreation centers?

A commercial school has certain advantages. For example, classes are usually held every night instead of just once or twice a week. On the other hand, the commercial school owner has to make a profit just to keep the doors open. The instructor in a YMCA or a recreation center sometimes teaches for personal enjoyment rather than to make a living.

Again, it comes down to the individual teacher and to what you want out of your training. One suggestion: don't decide on a class just because of convenience or price. The best teacher you can find is worth a few more minutes in the car and a few more dollars per month.

What about so-called black-belt courses or black-belt clubs in some schools?

Stay away from schools that guarantee you a black belt for a certain fee. No legitimate instructor will promise you a black belt for a set price. You have to earn it.

Many schools have found, however, that special clubs for students willing to commit to eventually becoming a black belt actually increase their motivation and their odds of achieving that goal. These clubs offer special patches, uniforms, or extra classes and have proven to be especially effective with kids.

Is it easier to earn a black belt in America or in Asian countries?

There are critics arguing on both sides of this question. Some veteran martial artists note that black belts are often earned in just a couple of years in Korea or Japan, while it usually

African-Americans have also redesigned martial arts techniques to suit their particular body styles. Two important African-American kenpo karate pioneers are (left) Steve Muhammed and (right) Jerry Smith, cofounders of the Black Karate Federation of Los Angeles.
Photo courtesy of the John Corcoran Archives.

takes longer—three to five years, on average—in the United States.

Others rightly point out that Asians usually train more seriously than most Americans and can therefore advance more quickly. Also, Americans won't tolerate the demands and austere methods of traditional Oriental training.

But, as previously discussed, requirements vary so much from school to school—in Asia as well as in America—that it is hard to say where the requirements are really easier.

What's the youngest age at which a person can earn a black belt in America?

In the early days of karate in America, most instructors would never consider awarding a black belt to anyone under the age of seventeen. Today, however, with more and more kids taking martial arts, many children have the technical knowledge and physical skills necessary for a black belt. Therefore, many schools have lowered the age requirements to thirteen or, even in some cases, as young as nine.

Emotional maturity is still an important part of being a black belt, however. So extremely young black belts should be an exception rather than the rule.

Can a child really defend her- or himself against an adult who wishes to do the child harm?

In most cases, a child does not have the physical size and thus the strength needed to inflict pain on an adult attacker. However, a good teacher will make sure the younger students learn and practice certain techniques that can be exceptions to this rule. Such blows are kicks to the knees and fingers to the eyes. Of course, screaming for help and running are often the best self-defense against a molester or kidnapper.

What is the percentage of children in the average karate or taekwondo class in the United States?

Beginning in the 1970s, as martial arts training became safer due to the invention of foam-rubber sparring pads, more and more children started taking lessons. Then in the 1980s with the impact of the blockbuster *Karate Kid* movies, followed by the advent of television shows featuring both real-life and animated martial arts heroes in the 1990s, kids flocked to martial arts schools in record numbers.

In most schools today, the number of children exceeds the number of adults, and has been estimated to be as low as 52 percent and as high as 80 percent of student enrollments.

Americans typically don't stick with the martial arts very long. Can someone really benefit from just a few months of training?

There are two sides to this issue. Many experts maintain that it only takes a simple technique to stop a potentially dangerous situation. So if you learned something in a couple of months that could save your life, then of course it was worth it. Critics say, however, that a person with a few months' training "learns just enough to get himself killed in a real fight."

Also, inadequate training, above all, stunts a person's potential growth in other important areas. The martial arts teach much more than techniques—things like self-discipline, self-control, and habits of physical and mental fitness—that it seems a shame to quit after just a short time.

Hasn't the American approach watered down the character-building benefits of training by its overemphasis on sport?

That might be the case in some very sport-oriented schools, but the vast majority of American martial arts teachers are very careful to include emphasis on things like self-discipline and respect for others. In that regard, American karate has retained the higher values of the more traditional systems.

If you are especially concerned about this, ask your potential or current teacher his or her attitude toward character-building in the classroom. And, as has already been said, watch how that person teaches.

Is that why the martial arts have been touted as good for children?

Definitely. American parents have come to recognize the advantages of an activity that increases their children's concentration abilities and demands that they develop self-control. Child psychologists often even recommend karate classes for kids with attention-deficit disorders, because it helps them develop the ability to focus on a single task. That is also why belt colors are important goals for kids. They can work on short-range, achievable goals as they progress and develop their skills.

Several programs in American public schools have shown that karate training gives students a sense of belonging to a group and actually decreases their chances of becoming involved with drugs and gangs.

Do karate students learn to use weapons?

In many schools, weapons like the long staff (called a bo) or the nunchaku are a part of the curriculum. Other instructors, however, prefer to exclusively teach empty-hand techniques. If you are interested in learning some weapons techniques (usually known as kobudo—"ancient warrior ways"), check with your teacher to see if it's a part of his or her curriculum.

Are karate weapons legal in America?

The laws vary from state to state, but it's generally safe to assume that you cannot carry a samurai sword or even a pair of nunchaku around with you or in the front seat of your car. Put your training weapons in your bag and carry them in the trunk of your car to and from class.

Where did the emphasis on board-breaking come from?

According to martial arts historian Keith D. Yates in his book, *Warrior Secrets* (Paladin Press, 1985), "Karate master Mas Oyama first demonstrated karate to American audiences during a tour of the U.S.A. in 1952. The Americans seemed more amused than impressed until Oyama began his barehanded breaking of boards and bricks. Although breaking is a very small part of a karate education, there are still those who think that is all we do and they expect you to be able to smash through several inches of wood or concrete."

Is it hard to break boards and bricks?

Yes and no. If you have never practiced it before and haven't received any instruction from a competent teacher, then you could end up really hurting yourself. With proper technique and a little practice, however, anyone, even kids, can perform simple board breaks. Children's bones are softer than those of adults, so special care should be taken by

instructors when teaching board-breaking to younger students.

Bricks and concrete are much more difficult and should only be attempted by someone with a lot of experience and practice.

Bruce Lee once made the now legendary remark, "Boards don't hit back." So why practice breaking boards at all?

Some instructors agree with him and don't spend much time, if any, on this aspect of the martial arts. Breaking a board, however, can be a good confidence-builder. After all, board-breaking looks good in a demonstration showing what a martial arts blow can do.

Who was or is the most famous martial artist in the world?

That lofty status is closely contested between two people, both Americans. Even though many people may think of Bruce Lee as the most famous martial artist in the world, there is one man who was probably even more famous: Elvis Presley. While Elvis might win the fame game, there's no contest in terms of technical skill. The incomparable Bruce Lee was superior on a scale requiring light-years' measurement.

Presley started studying Chito-ryu karate while stationed in Germany in the 1950s. He obtained the rank of black belt in this system before leaving the U.S. Army. Throughout his adult life, he studied various styles of karate as well as taekwondo. His instructors included kenpo karate's Ed Parker, taekwondo's Kang Rhee, and for just three weeks, kickboxing world champion Bill Wallace.

Presley always said that karate was his favorite interest second only to his music. Anyone who has seen his stage and screen performances would have noticed his incorporation of karate moves. He also financed some commercial martial arts ventures, including a martial arts documentary that was only partially completed.

In view of his Hollywood film success in recent years, Hong Kong action star and martial artist Jackie Chan has rocketed to global popularity. He is already cited as the best-known Chinese person in the world and could ultimately tie or even surpass both Lee and Presley in fame.

Do I have to be in shape to take up the study of martial arts?

It certainly helps. You will do exercises in class to improve your conditioning, flexibility, and strength. Most instructors will let you start out slowly and work your way into shape. So it is best not to put off signing up until you get into shape by yourself—you could be waiting a long time.

As a student, do I have to wear those white pajamas?

The karate gi (pronounced *ghee*) is fashioned after kimono-like work clothes from Okinawa and Japan. The modern Olympic-style taekwondo schools use a V-necked pullover top called a *tobak* (pronounced *toe'bock*).

Most schools wear these traditional uniforms. However, some Americans prefer to work out in shorts and a T-shirt. In certain situations nothing is wrong with that attire, but you lose a certain amount of the Asian flavor or mystique when you wear, say, a Chicago Bulls T-shirt in a martial arts class.

Do I have to have the ability to kick head-high in order to become a black belt?

No. In fact, some styles don't advocate kicking to the head at all, because it leaves you so vulnerable to a counterattack. Other styles maintain that being able to perform high kicks helps your ability to do any kicks, even the lower and more practical ones. The flexibility and balance needed for those high kicks can't help but improve your overall martial arts skills.

Two of the most influential entertainment icons in American martial arts are (left) Chuck Norris, the first American martial arts film star, and Ernie Reyes, Sr., from San Jose, California, who pioneered professional live performances in his field. Photos courtesy of the John Graden Archives.

No matter which style you take, an instructor will not prevent you from advancing just because you may have a physical limitation that prevents you from high-kicking.

Will physical limitations prevent me from attaining the black belt?

Obviously, each teacher has to make up his or her own mind about how to handle indi-vidual situations. There have been numer-ous cases in America where students with physical disabilities have shown amazing perseverance and have been awarded black belts.

Why do martial artists yell?

There are three good reasons for the *kiai* (spirit shout.) First, it gives you more power, similar to the burst of focused power a football player or weight lifter achieves with grunts and yells. Second, a proper kiai tightens the abdominal muscles and forces the air out of the body, preparing you to absorb any accidental punch or kick that might hit you. Third, if loud enough, it scares the attacker, allowing you to run or strike.

What are the main benefits of studying the martial arts?

Physical fitness, already cited, is one big benefit. Another is self-defense. Outside of carrying a gun around with you, the martial arts are perhaps the best means of self-defense ever devised. And while someone can take your gun away from you, they can't take your martial arts skills away and use them against you.

Some people see karate tournaments in movies, on TV, or even in person and decide they like the competition aspect. Martial sports are fine endeavors for those who might take a little longer to develop athletically, because they are individual rather than team activities. If you lose a match, you aren't "letting the team down."

Many people also take up the martial arts because of the intangible benefits of increased concentration, self-confidence, and character-building.

America is one of the most violent societies in the world. Don't martial arts teach a violent response to confrontation?

Actually, it's just the opposite. Studies have shown that if you have the confidence to defend yourself, you are much less likely to participate in a confrontation. All martial arts instructors tell the students the first thing to do is to avoid a fight, even if that means running away. Running or talking your way out of a confrontation is using your martial arts training.

Should I hold back when defending myself in a real fight for fear of later legal repercussions?

There's an old saying in America, "I'd rather be judged by twelve than carried by six." It means that you'd rather be tried by a jury of your peers for the crime of manslaughter than laid to rest by coffin-bearers.

The most important thing in a self-defense situation is your life and the lives of your loved ones. For that reason, you should do whatever you feel you need to do to protect yourself. Remember that if you don't finish the fight, your attacker probably will. Also, remember that he could have friends lurking in the shadows. You don't have time to "take it easy."

On the other hand, after the danger is over and your attacker is lying on the ground, you cannot legally walk over and cause him any further harm. Get out of there and call the police.

Would I learn how to defend myself against guns and knives in a martial arts class?

While weapons defense is a part of the curriculum in most martial arts schools, it is usually reserved for the more advanced students. Training for confrontations with guns and knives is extremely serious and should only be undertaken by those with a clear mastery of basic empty-hand self-defense.

Needless to say, you do not want to have to try to block knives and bullets. Do everything in your power to make the assailant(s) leave you unharmed. That includes giving up your purse, wallet, fancy shoes, gold watch, money, and whatever else they demand. There is nothing you can put on your body that is worth your life!

What kind of karate techniques should not be used in a no-holds-barred fight?

Any fight where the loser can be knocked out or injured (whether in a formal contest or in a parking lot) is not a place for sport tech-niques. Front-leg round kicks and backfists are examples of techniques that may score in a tournament, but are of little value when you are facing an attacker who is intent on tackling you and slamming you to the ground. Suddenly, knees and elbows—techniques outlawed in sport karate—take on new importance.

What are the best places to strike an attacker in an actual fight?

Assuming that you are in a fight for your life and not just a schoolyard scuffle, you should attack the eyes and the throat. These are the places that you can stop someone with just a finger strike. The groin is also a vulnerable target for a kick. However, you risk getting your kicking leg grabbed if you are not careful.

Are Tae-Bo and any of the other American martial arts–based fitness programs really effective means of self-defense?

Although these exercise routines are great ways to get into shape (and certainly promote the visibility of the martial arts), no one can truly learn effective self-defense without an extensive study of things like the stages of an attack, specific target areas, and psychological factors.

Are "quickie" self-defense programs that barely cover any of the just-mentioned topics a waste of time?

They are not a waste of time, because they do help make the participants aware of the dangers and give them some idea of how they can take control of a dangerous situation. But who has a better chance in a real street fight, a person who has trained for months or years in realistic-type situations or a person who sat through a two-hour seminar on self-defense?

You simply have to train with a knowledgeable instructor for a longer period of time in order for your reactions to become second nature.

Will American open martial arts competitions ever make it to the big time, like baseball or boxing?

It has been almost forty years since the first open martial arts competitions took place in the United States. These tournaments started off small, being held in YMCAs and high school gyms. No one participated except the competitors and instructors. The media didn't even know about karate as a sport—and didn't care. In spite of names like the United States Championship and the All-American Championship, participants rarely came from farther than neighboring states. The judges were the black-belt competitors themselves.

With a few notable exceptions, in the twenty-first century the situation is much the same. Tournaments with grandiose names are held in the meeting rooms of local motels or hotels. The only people in attendance are the competitors and their parents, who double as spectators. Judges are any black belts who volunteer. There is currently almost zero coverage of the sport in the mainstream media.

While pro wrestling has found an ever-increasing audience, martial arts events like the Ultimate Fighting Championship have been pushed aside for reruns of old National Football League (NFL) games.

For now, karate tournaments are only as interesting to the general public as skeet shooting or kayaking—meaning, not much. Maybe a new generation of martial arts stars can take the competition world to the next level.

Will the U.S. government ever regulate the martial arts?

Some aspects of the martial arts are regulated. The government recognizes some organizations as authorities over martial sports. The United States Taekwondo Union in Colorado Springs, Colorado, for example, is the recognized U.S. governing body for Olympic-style taekwondo competition.

State or federal governments, however, will probably never regulate martial arts instruction, because too many instructors are against it. There have been movements by some states to try and license martial arts teachers, but an outcry and organized opposition from the martial arts community itself has prevented any legislation from being enacted.

The state of New Jersey holds the all-time record for defeating proposed bills to regulate martial arts. Seventeen attempts have been made in the past twenty years, and all seventeen bills have been defeated.

What is the perceived problem with government regulation of martial arts?

The common rebuttal is, "How could a bureaucrat tell an experienced martial artist how to do or teach a proper front kick?" Although government would probably not get this detailed in any kind of regulation, it is certainly true that the approaches of different martial arts have so much variation that there could never be across-the-board consistency in teaching methods. The subject is far too controversial for everyone from all styles to ever agree on a standard method of regulation.

How far can the martial arts evolve in America?

The martial arts are not merely static physical activities or even finalized sporting events. They are, indeed, art forms, and as such will never stop changing and evolving. Since the arts themselves will never grow stale for the individual, they can and must always remain growing and therefore exciting lifetime activities.

Fit For a King

ELVIS'S CUSTOMIZED KARATE GI

Up to his death in 1977, Elvis Presley had the most expensive customized karate gis in existence. Where are they now?

Elvis Presley, pictured here with Master Kang Rhee, one of his main instructors, was a legitimate black belt whose martial arts involvement spanned nineteen years. The customized gi he's wearing cost $500.

Photo by Wayne Carman; courtesy of Master Kang Rhee.

Two of Elvis Presley's personal karate uniforms and belts, complete with bloodstains, were purchased by John Graden, this book's coauthor, in 1997. As part of the acquisition, Graden also procured Presley's official seventh-degree black-belt rank card, constructed of metal, issued by his main instructor, the late Ed Parker.

The first gi is Elvis's sweat-and-blood-stained, white training uniform along with his frayed original black belt. The second is one of the King's flamboyant demonstration uniforms and his oversized, custom-made, red-white-and-black belt. This belt is embroidered with "Elvis Presley" on one side and "Tiger," Elvis's martial arts nickname, on the other.

As he did with his performance wardrobe, Elvis had a duplicate copy of his customized gi made. That one sits on prominent display in his trophy room at Graceland, now a popular tourist attraction, in Memphis, Tennessee.

John Graden (center), this book's coauthor, and his models display the King's martial arts wardrobe. Shelly Watkins (left) models Elvis's demonstration uniform and customized belt, and Karen Englebright shows off Elvis's workout gi and original black belt. Graden holds Elvis's gi pants.

Photo by Images and Impressions; courtesy of the John Graden Archives.

The two customized uniforms reportedly originally cost Elvis about $500 each, at a time when the best gi on the market cost about $50.

Taekwondo in South Korea: the spectacular mass board-breaking demonstration at the opening ceremonies of the 1988 Olympics in Seoul, watched by an estimated worldwide TV audience of one billion viewers. Taekwondo was introduced as an official demonstration sport at the Seoul Olympics.

KOREAN MARTIAL ARTS

Commonly the first image that comes to mind when thinking of the Korean martial arts is the devastatingly beautiful kicks of tae-kwondo. Although these kicks have come to define the modern Korean martial arts, a rich martial history dates back for centuries in Korea and has been drawn upon as new systems of martial arts have continued to evolve in modern-day Korea.

From 1909 until the end of World War II, Korea found itself under the brutal rule of the occupying forces of Japan. Prior to this annexation Korea had been living its Yi dynasty (1392–1909). This period of time is known as Korea's "age of enlightenment." During these centuries, the arts and philosophies flourished. They were much more important to the Korean populace than the pursuit of warfare. Due to this cultural mind-set, Korea was easily over-powered by Japan at the beginning of the twentieth century.

During its period of occupation, Korean culture took a devastating blow. The Korean people were commonly forced into the service of the Japanese Imperial Army or put to work by the Japanese aristocracy in demeaning occupations. More than simply physical labor, the Japanese occupying forces attempted to anni-hilate Korea's culture altogether. This entailed the destruction of many ancient Korean Buddhist temples, the burning of all textbooks written in the Korean language, and the instant destruction of any ancient Korean manuscripts that were found. The Korean people were even forbidden from speaking their own native language while in public.

It is believed that during this period of occupation many of the Korean founders of modern Korean martial arts learned their technical foundations through the practice of Japanese karate, most probably the specific styles of Shotokan or *shudokan*.

Korea was liberated in 1945, at the end of World War II, when the United States and the Allied forces drove the Japanese military from its control over the Korean Peninsula. With this new independence came a fervor on the part of the Korean citizenry to never allow another government to control their country again. Along with a massive Korean military development and armament came the advent of several new systems of Korean martial arts. These styles were developed as methods to not only protect the average citizen, but also aid in the overall protection of their homeland.

With this new focus on personal freedom and cultural liberation, the modern Korean martial arts were born. Many new styles rose from the ashes of a devastated Korea.

This chapter will explore the fascinating world of the Korean martial arts and how, throughout the past fifty years, these styles have drawn upon their ancient heritage, redefined the applications of self-defense, and spread across the earth to substantially influence the entire world of modern martial arts.

THE ANCIENT KOREAN MARTIAL ARTS

What is the basis of the Korean martial arts?

As is the case with all ancient civilizations, the formalized art of warfare on the Korean Peninsula can be traced back to the dawn of civilization.

What was the first form of hand-to-hand combat devised in Korea?

The first form of hand-to-hand combat historically proven to have existed in Korea is *su bak*.

When was su bak developed?

Dating the origin of this system of martial arts relies predominantly upon legend. Korean historians often place su bak's development during the legendary rule of King Tan'gun, in approximately 2333 B.C. Though this may have been the case, no historical data substantiates the fact that su bak existed during this ancient time. There are, however, historic records of su bak's existence during the fourth century A.D.

What are the historic records documenting the existence of su bak?

There are paintings in the Kak Je Tomb historically dated to the fourth century A.D., which depict two martial artists sparring.

What fighting techniques did the fourth-century Koreans use?

It is difficult to decipher what actual fighting techniques were employed at this time since the tomb paintings are quite vague. Nevertheless, the paintings establish the fact that this system of self-defense did exist at that time.

What was su bak?

It was a hard-style form of hand-to-hand combat, which also employed the various weapons of the era including the sword, staff, lance, and bow and arrow.

Who practiced su bak?

It is known that su bak was commonly practiced by the warrior classes who inhabited the Korean Peninsula during the fourth through sixth centuries A.D. No doubt su bak was used in response to the continued wars that took place on the Korean Peninsula during this time period.

What happened to su bak?

During the late Three Kingdom period, in the seventh century A.D., practitioners of su bak began to go their separate ways. Su bak became fragmented and differing schools came into existence.

Were there other ancient schools of Korean martial arts?

Yes, when the schools of su bak began to fragment, a new system of Korean martial arts was formed. It was named *yu sul.*

What was yu sul, who practiced it, and what happened to it?

Yu sul was a softer grappling art. With the birth of yu sul, two very different schools of martial thought were on the Korean Peninsula. One used the hard, straightforward attacking methods based in su bak, which predominantly embraced striking techniques, and the other used the softer, manipulative defenses of yu sul.

Yu sul declined and eventually vanished from the Korean Peninsula. By the end of the seventh century A.D., there was no longer any historical evidence that it was being practiced.

Many Korean martial artists refer to the ancient system of martial arts known as tae kyon. What was tae kyon?

Su bak evolved and eventually became known as *tae kyon*. Tae kyon was written in the Chinese characters for "push shoulder."

What happened to tae kyon?

Tae kyon was the immediate successor to su bak. Thus it was a very aggressive, hard-style system of martial arts. When peace came to the Korean Peninsula, due to the unification of the Three Kingdoms, there was little use for tae kyon among the common people. Thus the martial arts became unpopular with the Korean masses. As such, tae kyon fell into rapid decline and was only practiced by the military.

Who were the famous Korean Hwa Rang Warriors?

The Korean term *Hwa Rang* means "flowering youth." The Hwa Rang were an army of highly trained Buddhist warriors who were first envisioned by King Chinhung of the Korean Peninsula kingdom of Silla, in approximately 576 A.D.

Why and how were the Hwa Rang formed?

Three warring kingdoms existed on the Korean Peninsula. The Hwa Rang were organized as a unit of exceptional warriors in order that the kingdom of Silla might triumph over its neighbors.

The Hwa Rang were made up of young, talented noblemen. They were trained in all forms of martial warfare, as well as the spiritual and meditative aspects of Buddhism. In addition, they were also trained in the fine arts. It was believed that by providing a unique, expansive education to an individual, he would become a superior warrior.

What martial art training did the Hwa Rang undergo?

The martial art instruction program of the Hwa Rang included developing their bodies by climbing rugged mountains and swimming in turbulent rivers during the coldest months of the year. They trained their bodies in all the forms of hand-to-hand and weapons combat that were known at the time.

What weapons did the Hwa Rang use?

The Hwa Rang were taught to unyieldingly use the sword, staff, hook, spear, and bow and arrow.

Did the Hwa Rang develop their own form of martial arts?

Yes. In addition to su bak, the Hwa Rang are believed to have invented the martial art system of foot fighting named *su bak gi*. This is believed to be the ancient basis for the extensive use of kicking techniques employed in modern Korean martial arts.

What happened to the Hwa Rang?

After the Hwa Rang defeated the armies of the neighboring kingdoms and the invasive Tang Chinese, the mind of the Korean people began to rapidly shift from aggressive actions to more philosophical thoughts. Consequently, the Hwa Rang fell into decline.

For the next few centuries, they became known more as a group specializing in healing, Buddhist philosophy, and poetry than as a warrior troop. By the end of the seventh century A.D., they became almost nonexistent.

When one thinks of the Korean martial arts, images of the devastatingly beautiful kicks of taekwondo are commonly what first come to mind. Here Lee Reyes of San Jose, California, demonstrates impeccable form in his execution of a dazzling flying split kick.

Photo courtesy of the John Graden Archives.

THE MODERN KOREAN MARTIAL ARTS

Taekwondo and the Kwans

What is the most widely practiced Korean martial art in the world today?

Taekwondo, a diverse and complex discipline, is by far the most popular Korean martial art in the world today in terms of number of active practitioners. It is certainly the most widely practiced martial art in the Western world. Tai-chi chuan is, overall, the world's most popular martial art practiced today because of its tens of millions of devotees in China alone.

What exactly is taekwondo?

Taekwondo roughly translates as "hand-foot way," meaning the "way of the fist and foot." The Korean word *tae* refers to the hand or fist. The Korean word *kwon* means "foot" or "kick." And *do* means "way" or "the way of." The term *taekwondo* is also commonly presented in two other variations: *tae kwon do* and *taekwon-do.*

Taekwondo is a Korean martial art well-known mostly for its extensive arsenal of kicking techniques. Essentially it is a discipline of mind, spirit, and body molded through a systematic training regimen that allows an individual to refine his or her training through competition with others, while preserving the competition with oneself as its most valuable tool.

Are kicks the only weapon that taekwondo stylists use?

No. Although kicks are a defining element to this system of self-defense, taekwondo employs a wide range of offensive and defensive techniques.

How did taekwondo originate?

What is known today as taekwondo originated in 1955 when several schools or *kwans* of the modern Korean martial arts came together and merged under one banner. It was not until 1961, however, that the leaders of the various kwans fully formalized into one body. This affiliation became known as the Korea Taekwondo Association and General Hong-Hi Choi was elected its inaugural president.

What is a kwan and how is it related to the martial arts?

The Korean word *kwan* can be loosely translated as "school." More specifically, a kwan is a school of martial arts. Collectively, the kwans were schools of martial arts that were formed in post-1945 Korea at the end of World War II, when the country gained its liberation from Japan. There were originally five major kwans that were soon joined by four more. (See the accompanying sidebar and diagram at the end of this chapter for detailed information about the original kwans.)

Why weren't kwans formed earlier in Korean history?

Because the Japanese military forces occupying Korea forbade the indigenous Koreans to practice martial arts unless they were in the service of the Japanese military.

Where did the original kwan founders study the martial arts?

They were all influenced, to varying degrees, by the Japanese martial arts. Many were forced into service in the Japanese military, where they were exposed to the hard-style Japanese systems. Some, like General Hong-Hi Choi, had lived in Japan prior to forced service in the Japanese army, where they became black belts in Shotokan karate.

Why are these systems considered Korean if the founders all studied the Japanese martial arts?

Because they were founded in Korea by Korean citizens. Each founder drew upon his heritage of ancient Korean martial arts, and each integrated the overall mind-set, if not various techniques, from tae kyon into his system of self-defense.

Where did these founders obtain their knowledge of tae kyon?

From ancient manuscripts and from a few Korean Buddhist monks who secretly passed down the system during the Japanese occupation.

How were the kwans related to the origins of taekwondo?

In the period between 1945 and 1947, the five main schools of martial arts that would later combine to become taekwondo were opened. Around the mid-1950s, the leaders of the various schools started to feel the need for a common name for what they were teaching. Several names were proposed; among them was the name taekwondo.

In 1965 the Korea Taekwondo Association was formed and the name taekwondo became official. General Hong-Hi Choi, the man reported to have originally suggested the name taekwondo, was elected its inaugural president.

Do the kwans still exist?

Yes. According to one historian, in August of 1978, a proclamation finalizing the official closing of the kwans was signed by the nine kwans (plus the tenth, an administrative kwan). However, the kwans stubbornly have remained alive to this day, with many Korean and Western masters holding tight to their lineage.

When did taekwondo first appear in America?

Historian Keith D. Yates writes in his *Complete Book of Tae Kwon Do Forms* (Paladin Press, 1982), "In 1956, Jhoon Rhee introduced America to taekwondo in the city of San Marcos, Texas. At that time *karate* was the only term Americans related to, and Rhee (as well as other Korean instructors who soon came to this country) called his style 'karate' for several years until the name taekwondo gained wider recognition. By then the die had been set, however, and many taekwondo stylists (especially Americans) today still use the word *karate* when referring to their art."

What are the most important taekwondo associations that govern the art and sport today throughout the world?

The first, as previously cited, is the Korea Taekwondo Association, which is still in existence today.

In 1966, due to ongoing conflicts and ideological differences within the organization,

Grandmaster Jhoon Rhee, who introduced taekwondo to the United States, displays the remarkable physical benefits of a lifetime of martial arts training. At sixty-two years old, he possesses the physique of a man half his age—and the same strength and flexibility. In public demonstrations, he executes one hundred push-ups in one minute and performs, from a sitting position, a full leg split with his chest pressed against the floor.

Photo courtesy of Grandmaster Jhoon Rhee.

General Hong-Hi Choi resigned his post as president and founded the International Taekwon-Do Federation (ITF). Choi relocated to Montreal, Quebec, Canada, where he continues to govern his worldwide organization.

Dr. Un Yong Kim was elected the new president of the Korea Taekwondo Association. Believing that taekwondo was a genuinely Korean martial art and therefore its governing body should be based in Korea, Dr. Kim dissolved the relationship between the Korea Taekwondo Association and the ITF.

In 1973, the World Taekwondo Federation (WTF) was formed with Dr. Kim as its elected president. It is the governing body for Olympic-sport taekwondo and represents the only officially practiced system of taekwondo in South Korea. This organization was solely responsible for establishing taekwondo as an official Olympic sport.

What is the difference between the WTF and the ITF?

Though they are based on the same art, their emphases differ somewhat. WTF practitioners have streamlined the art and focus predominantly upon very linear, straight-to-the-point offensive and defensive techniques. ITF practitioners, on the other hand, practice the style as it was originally developed, embracing a more expansive system of self-defense.

One of the main differences between the two large governing bodies is that they each practice a different set of established patterns or forms, known in Korean as *poomse* (pronounced *poom'see*) but more commonly known by the Japanese word *kata.*

Are there other established taekwondo organizations in the world?

Yes, there are several. As taekwondo has continued to spread across the globe, several organizations have formed, each administrated by its own set of criteria.

What are some of the important American organizations and the styles they represent?

According to the popular book *The Complete Idiot's Guide to Tae Kwon Do* (Alpha Books, 1998), by Karen Eden and Keith D. Yates, the major organizations and styles, other than the WTF and ITF, include the Songahm style of the American Taekwondo Association (Little Rock, Arkansas); the Jhoon Rhee system of the Jhoon Rhee Institutes (Washington, D.C.); the Chayon-ryu style of the International Chayon-Ryu Association (Houston, Texas); and the Nam Seo Kwan style of the American Karate and Taekwondo Organization (Garland, Texas).

What is the Kukkiwon?

The Kukkiwon was known as the Korea Taekwondo Association Central Dojang until February 6, 1973, when the name was changed to the World Taekwondo Federation headquarters. The Kukkiwon, located in Seoul, South Korea, is the home of WTF Olympic-style taekwondo.

What is Olympic-style taekwondo?

Olympic-style taekwondo is taekwondo streamlined to its most essential elements. This streamlining took place under the direct guidance of the WTF in order that taekwondo could become an accepted Olympic sport. Taekwondo first appeared as a demonstration sport in the 1988 Olympics in Seoul, Korea, and achieved full-medal status in 2000 in Sydney, Australia.

In Olympic-style taekwondo competition, punches toward an opponent's head are prohibited. Only body strikes are allowed with the fist. Kicks, on the other hand, may be and are commonly targeted to any location on the opponent's body so long as they are delivered above the waist. These innovations were designed to enhance taekwondo competition as an almost purely kicking sport.

Many of the original practitioners of taekwondo harbor distaste for Olympic-style taekwondo. They believe it has robbed the art of many of its former self-defense-orientated techniques.

Do taekwondo devotees practice forms or just fighting?

One of the key elements to taekwondo as an art is its reliance upon forms. Forms, known in Korean as *poomse* in the WTF or *hyung* in the ITF, are highly organized patterns of movement using precise punching and kicking techniques against imaginary opponents. Put simply, it is shadowboxing with punches and kicks.

Why does taekwondo place such an important emphasis upon forms?

Taekwondo stylists believe that by practicing forms they gain an enhanced sense of body coordination. In addition, it is believed that the practice of forms increases the stylist's understanding of how offensive and defensive techniques are correctly executed.

The forms taught at a school are the encyclopedia of that school's techniques. They are practiced regularly and reinforced through thousands of repetitions until they become ingrained.

How is a taekwondo class conducted?

A taekwondo class usually begins with stretching, leading to the delivery of various basic punches, blocks, and kicks. These techniques are delivered into the air but are mentally targeted toward imaginary opponents. In some cases, they are directed toward a mirror so the students can check their accuracy and form.

A taekwondo class then progresses onto the execution of forms. Upon the completion of the forms segment of class, partner-practice begins with various self-defense techniques and noncontact kicking drills with an opponent. The taekwondo class often culminates with sparring.

How long does it take to earn a black belt in taekwondo?

In Korea, it takes approximately one and a half years to earn the first-degree black belt. The training in Korea is quite vigorous, however, in comparison to the taekwondo training of other countries. It is not uncommon for a child to begin studying taekwondo by the age of five.

In other countries, the time required to reach the rank of black belt varies by school and by organization. Commonly, it takes approximately three years. These time frames are based on a student of normal skill who practices the art a minimum of three times per week.

Korean traditionalists equate the earning of the black belt to high school graduation. It denotes that the student has simply finished the basic beginner courses and is now ready to really learn.

Are black-belt certificates issued by the large taekwondo organizations, by the kwans, or by individual schools?

The answer is all three. Instructors affiliated with both a kwan and a large organization can issue black-belt certificates to the student from both.

Some instructors, however, feel that a large governing body such as the WTF or the ITF limits the scope of the martial arts that they are allowed to teach their students. In these instances, some instructors will forgo membership in one of these large governing bodies. Then the black-belt certificate will be issued singularly by the instructor's kwan.

In some cases, black-belt certificates are issued solely by the instructor of the school. Of course, individual black-belt certifications are harder to verify, especially if the original instructor is no longer in business.

Certification from a large organization is preferred, but ultimately your verification is your skill rather than a piece of paper.

Hapkido

What other martial arts were established in modern Korea?

In alphabetical order, hapkido, Hwarangdo, kuk sool wan, and tang soo do are the most commonly known and practiced. Also, a few lesser-known systems have come into existence in recent years.

What is hapkido?

Hapkido, meaning "the way of internal power," is unique among the modern Korean martial arts in that it emphasizes deflection as

Grandmaster Bong Soo Han of Santa Monica, California, sends a student flying with a hapkido throw. Grandmaster Han brought the Korean art of hapkido to the attention of the world through his spectacular kicks used in the fight scenes in the 1971 movie *Billy Jack* and its sequels. Hapkido is known for its extensive arsenal of joint-locks, throws, and advanced kicking techniques.

Photo courtesy of Grandmaster Bong Soo Han.

opposed to forceful blocking. Hapkido is known for its extensive arsenal of joint-locks, throws, and advanced kicking techniques.

Who founded hapkido, and where did he study the martial arts?

Hapkido was founded by Yong Shul Choi in 1945. Choi studied Japanese Daito-ryu aiki-jutsu while he was living in Japan during Japan's occupation of Korea. Choi's teacher was Sokaku Takeda, the thirty-second patri-arch of Daito-ryu aikijutsu.

Was hapkido the original name of this self-defense system?

No. The name went through several changes until it finally was formalized as hapkido in 1963. Among the previous names were: *yu kwon sul, yu sool, ho shin mu do,* and *bi sool.*

Has hapkido maintained its original tech-niques or has it evolved?

As is the case with all of the modern Korean martial arts, hapkido has gone through a long period of refinement. As the advanced kicking techniques of tae kyon were being rediscov-ered by the other leaders of the modern Korean martial arts, hapkido also began to integrate these advanced methods of offense and defense into its self-defense arsenal.

What is the essence of hapkido?

As hapkido Master Scott Shaw states in his book, *Hapkido: Korean Art of Self-Defense* (Charles E. Tuttle Publications), "Hapkido is not bound by many of the traditional formali-ties that limit the various other martial arts. In fact, it was developed in such a way that the practitioner may learn the various meth-ods of defense and then apply them in a unique and individual manner should the need arise."

What is hapkido's connection with Japanese aikido?

Like the founder of hapkido, Yong Shul Choi, aikido founder Morihei Uyeshiba also studied Daito-ryu aikijutsu from Sokaku Takeda (in Uyeshiba's case for seven years). For this rea-son many historians draw a comparison between the two systems of martial arts.

What is the difference between hapkido and aikido?

Though hapkido and aikido share similar ori-gins and, in some cases, possess similar tech-niques, a big difference in self-defense philosophy exists between the two styles of martial art. Aikido is a wholly defensive system of self-defense, whereas hapkido employs an extensive array of offensive techniques as well.

Was hapkido one of the original kwans?

Yes and no. Although hapkido was one of the first systems to be formalized on the newly liberated Korean Peninsula in the 1940s, it did not draw from the same original sources, namely the hard-style Japanese martial arts, as did the other kwans. Thus, it evolved separately.

Are forms practiced in hapkido?

Traditionally, no. The hapkido practitioner believes it is essential to move and react uniquely to each type of confrontational situation. For this reason forms are never employed; they hold the practitioner too closely to the belief that one specific movement must follow the last.

It must be noted, however, that over the years some hapkido teachers have added formalized patterns of movement to their specific hapkido curriculum.

What are the important organizations that govern hapkido?

There are three major organizations, all based in Korea: the Korea Hapkido Federation, the Korea Hapkido Association, and Ki Do Hae. In addition, a few smaller organizations are located in Korea as well as in other countries in the Western world.

How is a hapkido class conducted?

A hapkido class commonly begins with warm-up and stretching, followed by *ki* (internal energy) development exercises. The class progresses to kicking and punching drills. Then self-defense applications with a partner are practiced.

The advanced student of hapkido commonly trains with various weapons including the sword, staff, short staff, and cane during class sessions.

How long does it take to earn a black belt in hapkido?

Of all the systems born in modern Korea, hapkido is one of the most elaborate. For this reason, it takes approximately three and a half years to earn the first-degree black belt in this system. But it can also take up to five years.

Tang Soo Do

What is tang soo do?

Tang soo do is one of the original Korean kwans created in Korea in the 1940s. Tang soo do literally means "way of the China hand," which is the Korean translation of the original word *karate*. (The Japanese translation of *karate* was later changed to "way of the empty hand.")

The name *su bak do* was interchangeable with the early schools of tang soo do. This name was used as a means to draw upon Korea's ancient martial art of su bak. Therefore, su bak do means "way of the su bak warriors."

As one of the original kwans, was tang soo do part of the kwan merger that formed taekwondo in 1955?

Yes and no. The *chung do kwan* changed to the term *taekwondo*—according to Grandmaster Jhoon Rhee—but Hwang Kee, the founder of *moo duk kwan*, chose not to join. He wanted his system to remain free from domination by the politics of an organization.

Did Hwang Kee found tang soo do?

Yes. In his own book, Grandmaster Hwang cites that he originally named his system *hwa soo do* (art of the flower hand), but changed it to tang soo do in 1953.

After several years of trying, he got official permission to establish his art as *soo bahk do* (borrowing from the ancient Korean art of su bak) in December 1965.

Today, however, many still claim the heritage of tang soo do moo duk kwan, especially in the United States, and teach under that term.

Isn't there a branch of taekwondo also known as moo duk kwan?

Yes. Moo duk kwan means "school of martial virtue." Several of the original students of the Hwang Kee method of moo duk kwan broke away when the Korea Taekwondo Association was formed in 1961. They formed the branch of taekwondo known as taekwondo moo duk kwan, using the lengthy name to depict their merger of the two arts.

Overall, it is confusing. There is (1) the taekwondo moo duk kwan, (2) the soo bahk do moo duk kwan, and (3) the tang soo do moo duk kwan. This section will concentrate on tang soo do from here on.

How is a tang soo do class conducted?

Similar to taekwondo, a tang soo do class commonly begins with stretching. Then various punches, blocks, and kicks are performed—delivered into the air. From there the tang soo do class normally progresses to partner-orientated self-defense applications, followed by the performance of forms. In some classes, sparring follows these activities.

How long does it take to earn a black belt in tang soo do?

Tang soo do practitioners do not wear the black belt. Its founder, Hwang Kee, believed that black is the color that encompasses all other colors. Therefore, by wearing the color black, a practitioner sends the message that he or she knows all there is to learn about this art. Since this is considered humanly impossible, the tang soo do practitioner at this level wears a dark blue belt instead of the more conventional black belt.

Because tang soo do is very similar in style and technique to the original tae-kwondo, in Korea it takes approximately one and a half to two years to earn the first-degree blue belt. Outside of Korea, it commonly takes approximately three years.

Hwarangdo

What is Hwarangdo?

Hwarangdo is a modern system of self-defense founded by Joo Bang Lee. Lee was initially a student of hapkido, which explains the close resemblance between the two systems. Lee states that he then studied with a monk who taught him additional ancient methods of the Korean martial arts.

How is a Hwarangdo class conducted?

Similar to hapkido, Hwarangdo initially focuses upon warm-up stretching and ki-development exercises. It then moves on to self-defense applications. The advancing

Hwarangdo student then often trains with weapons.

How long does it take to earn a black belt in Hwarangdo?

Traditionally, the Hwarangdo practitioner wears a black sash as opposed to the more

Grandmaster Joo Bang Lee (center) of Downey, California, is the principal pioneer of modern Hwarangdo and the driving force behind its global expansion. Under his technical development, Hwarangdo has matured into an elaborate self-defense system featuring some of the most intricate techniques in all of the martial arts.

Photo courtesy of Grandmaster Joo Bang Lee.

conventional black belt. For training purposes, however, the traditional black belt is used.

As is the case with hapkido, Hwarangdo is an elaborate system of self-defense. As such, it takes approximately four years to earn the black sash.

Kuk Sool Wan

What is kuk sool wan?

Kuk sool wan, or kyuk-sool-wan, is a martial art of Korean origin that differs from many of the other Korean disciplines such as taekwondo, tang soo do or hapkido in its much more explicit emphasis on internal power and weapons' techniques—particularly the sword, for which there are eighty forms. The remainder of the system is just as overwhelming, reputedly encompassing over 3,600 techniques.

According to In Hyuk-Su, the most prominent exponent of the art in the United States, kuk sool wan is based on four concepts: circular movement, strikes to the 270 critical points of the body, joint manipulation, and form. At advanced levels, the external blocking, striking, and grappling components of the art are supplanted by more sophisticated internal energy techniques.

How is a kuk sool wan class conducted?

Kuk sool wan classes commonly begin with warm-up stretching and ki-development exercises. The class then proceeds to partner self-defense drills. The advanced students also practice weapons.

How long does it take to earn a black belt in kuk sool wan?

Like Hwarangdo, the kuk sool wan practitioner wears a sash as opposed to a belt. The traditional time to earn the black sash is approximately four years, depending on training time and training frequency.

Kumdo

Is there a specific school of swordplay in the Korean martial arts?

Yes. Korea has a modern system of swordplay called *kumdo*. *Kum*, is the Korean word for sword. *Do* means "the way of."

What is the history of kumdo?

Kumdo is a direct descendant of the Japanese sword arts of Iaido and kendo. Many modern practitioners of kumdo attempt to claim historic lineage to the ancient Korean sword arts. Traditionally this is not the case, since all kumdo movements can be witnessed in the various schools of Japanese iaido and kendo.

As time has gone on, however, many Korean martial arts scholars have been working with ancient Korean manuscripts such as *Moo Yeh Do Bok Tong Ki (Text of the Military Code for the Warrior)* and have attempted to integrate the techniques presented in these ancient warrior texts into the modern Korean martial arts.

Where is kumdo taught?

Initially, kumdo was taught as part of the curriculum among the early kwans. Thus, many of the Korean martial arts stylists who later congregated under the banner of taekwondo were schooled in this sword art.

With the advent of Olympic-style taekwondo, and the exacting rules that now define this art, kumdo is rarely taught to the modern practitioner of taekwondo. Thus to study kumdo, a stylist must seek out specific kumdo schools.

General

How many degrees of black belt are there in the Korean martial arts?

In most systems, there are ten. Traditionally, the first- through third-degree black belts are simply considered to be advanced students. Upon obtaining the fourth-degree black belt, one is considered an instructor. At the fifth-degree level, one is understood to be a master. The tenth-degree black belt is reserved for the founder of the system.

In some taekwondo systems—the WTF, for example—nine is considered the highest of the single-digit numbers and thus is the highest rank obtainable.

Who wears the red belt in the Korean martial arts?

In the Japanese martial arts, the red belt is commonly worn by advanced masters and founders of the various systems. In the Korean arts, however, the red belt is worn at the stage just before the black belt—the level where the brown belt is more commonly worn by other, non-Korean systems of self-defense.

Who are some of the best-known masters of the Korean martial arts?

In alphabetical order by last name, they are:

Hee Il Cho, a taekwondo grandmaster who has to date appeared on the covers of more martial art magazines worldwide than any of his Korean peers. He is renowned for his spectacular kicking expertise, particularly the complex spinning and jumping kicks.

Bong Soo Han, a hapkido grandmaster who brought the style to the attention of the world in such movies as *Billy Jack* and its sequels. He is a veteran actor and fight choreographer.

Dana Hee, the first American female to win the Olympic gold medal in taekwondo when it debuted as a demonstration sport in the 1988 Games. Today, she's a professional stuntwoman and actress who works in big-budget Hollywood films.

Chuck Norris, originally a tang soo do stylist who, after becoming a world champion in tournament competition in the late 1960s, launched a film and television career that made him a household name. He has starred in over a dozen films and in the hit TV series *Walker, Texas Ranger.*

Herb Perez, the first American male to win the Olympic gold medal in taekwondo when it debuted as a demonstration sport in the 1988 Games.

Jhoon Rhee, a taekwondo grandmaster who is renowned as the father of American taekwondo, having introduced the art in the United States in 1956. Headquartered in Washington, D.C., he also gained fame as a teacher of politicians and celebrities.

Philip Rhee, a taekwondo master who starred in the hit film series *Best of the Best.*

Master Scott Shaw, a hapkido master and author with the most extensive list of published works on the Korean martial arts and the ki sciences.

Keith D. Yates, an American taekwondo pioneer and master, author of nine books, and a regular columnist for five national magazines.

What is the most important aspect of the Korean martial arts?

Training is the element you need most to become competent in any form of martial arts.

Continued training not only teaches you essential elements of self-defense, but also brings to light a great deal about yourself. Through training, you come to define the qualities of your physical body and moral character. You continually learn where you excel and the areas that need further development.

What's the secret to success in training?

Continued training teaches you how to act instinctively in a confrontational situation. When you have trained and retrained to act according to the appropriate self-defense application in your martial art studio, you will know how to react instinctively on the street.

The Kwans of Korean Martial Arts

Much confusion reigns over the names, the numbers, and the subsequent roles of the following kwans (schools) in the formation of taekwondo. While not all of the existing kwans merged to form taekwondo on April 15, 1955, some that did sporadically seceded and then rejoined, adding to the historical confusion.

It is believed that at least four more kwans were established in the early 1960s. In the early 1970s, however, the Korea Taekwondo Federation, the government-sponsored sanctioning body, abolished the names of nine officially recognized kwans and assigned them simple numbers so that the name *taekwondo* would become singularly representative of most of the hard-style Korean martial arts.

Each of the following nine official kwans appear in **bold type**, as does any idiomatic similarity by which that school might be known. Under each kwan appears the name of its founder and the year it was founded.

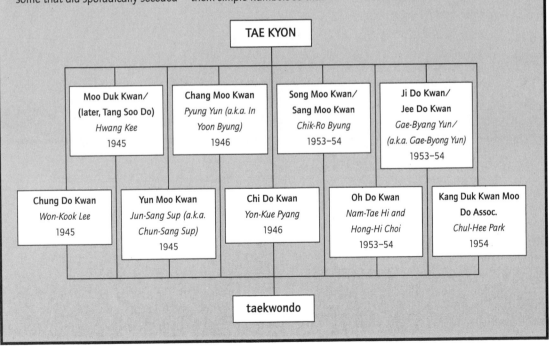

TAE KYON

| Moo Duk Kwan/ (later, Tang Soo Do) *Hwang Kee* 1945 | Chang Moo Kwan *Pyung Yun (a.k.a. In Yoon Byung)* 1946 | Song Moo Kwan/ Sang Moo Kwan *Chik-Ro Byung* 1953–54 | Ji Do Kwan/ Jee Do Kwan *Gae-Byang Yun/ (a.k.a. Gae-Byong Yun)* 1953–54 |

| Chung Do Kwan *Won-Kook Lee* 1945 | Yun Moo Kwan *Jun-Sang Sup (a.k.a. Chun-Sang Sup)* 1945 | Chi Do Kwan *Yon-Kue Pyang* 1946 | Oh Do Kwan *Nam-Tae Hi and Hong-Hi Choi* 1953–54 | Kang Duk Kwan Moo Do Assoc. *Chul-Hee Park* 1954 |

taekwondo

The gentle, slow-motion exercises of tai-chi, as demonstrated here by David Dorian-Ross, have made it the world's most popular martial art. Millions of Chinese in China alone rise every morning at dawn to practice tai-chi, and the 1990s saw a tremendous surge of interest in it by America's senior citizens seeking to improve their health.

CHINESE MARTIAL ARTS

Almost everyone has heard of the late martial arts film legend Bruce Lee. In fact, Bruce Lee was responsible for introducing Chinese kung-fu to most of the Western world. Between his famous movies, including *Enter the Dragon*, and the cult classic TV series *Kung Fu* featuring David Carradine, the American public began to develop a passion for the Shaolin Temple and its exotic, mysterious martial arts based in China. Yet, even though this entertainment explosion began in the late 1960s and early 1970s, many people today are still unaware of the realities of the Chinese martial arts styles and have developed many misconceptions about them.

Western pop culture, in recent decades, has experienced a fair share of Chinese martial arts integration. From a musical group with the name of a famous mountain associated with the internal arts (the Wu-Tang Clan) to a true American icon (G.I. Joe with the kung-fu grip), Americans have been exposed to the Chinese martial traditions from a very early age. In keeping with the wide diversity of kung-fu (or *wushu*, as it is now commonly called), the 1990s saw a tremendous surge of interest from America's seniors in the gentle style of tai-chi.

Tai-chi got its first mainstream boost from an unexpected scientific endorsement. On May 3, 1995, the *Journal of the American Medical Association* (AMA) released findings of thorough studies that indicated that seniors' regular practice of tai-chi reduced the incidence of loss of balance and subsequent falls. The AMA–documented study concerning tai-chi was done at Emory University. Indeed, tai-chi has become so popular since then that many non-Chinese martial arts schools and even fitness gyms have incorporated tai-chi programs into their existing curriculums.

Mark Salzman's bestselling book, *Iron and Silk,* brought readers into the training halls and more important, presented the training experiences of an American in China. Every teenage boy's dream of learning from a Chinese master was visible in the book's film adaptation, which made Salzman's teacher, Master Pan Qingfu, a celebrity in martial arts circles. When the U.S.A. Wushu Kungfu Federation hosted the Third World Wushu Championships in Baltimore in 1995, one of the most-sought-after autographs was Master Qingfu's.

In the past few decades in America alone, numerous top masters from China have opened schools and produced a second generation of teachers, with a third and even a fourth generation of quality students. A person no longer needs to travel across the Pacific to study real kung-fu.

Nevertheless, in recent years, Americans have gone to the motherland of kung-fu, China, to study and even just to compete. And several athletes have won medals there in competition against others from across the globe. A chosen few have been lucky enough to visit and train at the legendary Shaolin Temple, thus fulfilling the dreams of so many TV fans who have longed to walk on rice paper.

What follows here is a basic overview of the sometimes mystical, always provocative world of Chinese martial arts.

What is the difference between kung-fu and karate?

Kung-fu is the popular term for the martial arts of China, while karate came from Okinawa and Japan. Although there are many similarities, the styles look very different when practiced. Generally, kung-fu styles favor a circular approach, while karate styles subscribe to a more linear method.

Which came first, kung-fu or karate?

The Chinese styles have a very long history, stretching back over two thousand years. In fact, the family trees of many Okinawan and Japanese karate styles can be traced back to older arts practiced in China.

Some of the names of various Okinawan and Japanese schools and routines are direct indications of Chinese origin. The name of Shorinji kempo, a popular Japanese style, for example, means "Shaolin Temple boxing."

If a karate student and a kung-fu student were to fight in competition, who would win?

So many factors are involved in any form of competition that it is impossible to answer

The Chinese styles have a very long history, stretching back over two thousand years. Due to their ancient heritage, the Chinese martial arts, overall, encompass the practice of more weapons than do any other arts. Here National Forms Champion Willie Johnson of Laurel, Maryland, employs the sword and shield.

Photo courtesy of Willie Johnson.

that question. Karate practitioners might argue that their side is less involved and uses clearer, practical techniques. Kung-fu artists might counter that their wider arsenal of techniques gives them the upper hand.

In the ring, all things being equal, it is usually the better fighter, not the better style, who wins the match.

Are there belts in kung-fu?

Traditionally, most Chinese styles did not use belt-ranking systems. Since the late 1900s, and especially in Western countries, colored sashes or cotton belts have become very common in many schools. Ranking has been a welcome addition to the modern Chinese martial arts.

How many kung-fu schools are there?

It is estimated that there are over 2,500 Chinese martial arts schools in the United States alone. An even greater number of schools incorporate some style of Chinese martial art into their curriculum. In recent years, many non–Chinese-style schools have employed tai-chi instructors as adjuncts to their existing programs.

Why do kung-fu practitioners salute with an extended fist and palm?

This "bow" is different from that commonly used by other martial artists. The fist symbolizes strength and physical power, while the palm means control and mental discipline. Together the hand forms signify the unity of yin and yang—mind and body.

Can anyone learn kung-fu?

Anyone can learn kung-fu of some style or school. The diversity of the Chinese martial arts instruction ranges from very hard, vigorous movements to the soft, internal actions of tai-chi or chi-kung. There is a form of kung-fu training to suit everyone, from full-contact fighters to grandparents.

How many styles of kung-fu are there?

There are over 180 documented styles of Chinese martial arts, which fall under a few central categories. The Shaolin school, the wudang school, and the *emei* school are each unique and varied in their respective approach to training, performance, and application. The most common distinction is "external" versus "internal" styles.

Did kung-fu originate at the Shaolin Temple?

The Shaolin school is one of the most well-known martial arts institutions in the world. However, not all forms of kung-fu began there. In fact, legend has it that the Shaolin martial arts were initiated by Shikamunyi (Bodhidharma), a Buddhist monk who came from India to China bringing with him the teachings of the Chan (Zen) sect.

Do kung-fu practitioners actually fight in practice or competition?

As with other martial arts, some teachers emphasize drilling techniques, some performance orientation, and others fighting applications. Many schools enter fighting competitions exclusively, while others may only engage in fighting in class. A few schools completely shun free-fighting in both training and sport competition.

What do kung-fu students call their teachers?

Several terms are used to refer to instructors: *Sifu, Laoshr, Guanzhang, Jiaolien,* and *Dashr* are all commonly used. *Sifu* is by far the most popular term used in the United States, while in China, *Laoshr* is more prevalent.

Why do kung-fu practitioners wear shoes?

Chinese practitioners have usually practiced in their typical attire. In addition to loose-fitting clothing, light and somewhat flexible footwear were used. In modern times, light sneakers and sweats have become common in China, while many schools in America use the traditional black kung-fu pants.

What is the most popular style of kung-fu?

Tai-chi is the world's most practiced style, not only of kung-fu, but of any other martial art. Millions of people in China practice the slow-motion exercises of tai-chi on a daily basis. Especially since the 1990s, tai-chi has become increasingly popular throughout the Western world.

Why is tai-chi performed so slowly?

Because tai-chi is one of the internal styles, the emphasis is on correct alignment and the flow of internal energy. Attention must be paid to each aspect of every movement, and slow-paced practice helps accomplish that. There is an old saying, "The *yi* (intent) leads the *qi* (energy) to *li* (action)."

Does a person have to be really flexible to practice kung-fu?

As in any physical activity, enhanced range of motion is obviously an asset. Training for some styles of kung-fu, like the colorful drunken form in which the practitioner purposely appears unstable, requires a great deal of stretching. However, too much flexibility without adequate levels of strength and power can be detrimental to a student's development.

What is the difference between kung-fu and wushu?

Kung-fu means "time and effort" and is a popular term for martial arts practice, although the Chinese use it to describe high-level skill in almost any endeavor. *Wushu* means "martial techniques" and is a more appropriate term for martial arts. The Japanese word for the characters *wushu* is *bujutsu*.

Other names for Chinese martial arts are *wu gong* (martial skills, exercises), *kuo shu* (national technique), and *wu yi* (martial art, high-level skill).

What is the difference between kung-fu and tai-chi?

Tai-chi is a term for the Chinese philosophy of yin and yang. Tai-chi chuan is one of the traditional Chinese martial arts and thus is a type of kung-fu. Frequently, *tai-chi* and *kung-fu* are terms used to separate the internal and external styles of wushu, respectively.

How long does it take to earn a black belt or black sash?

Schools that use a ranking system usually require at least three to five years to reach the black-belt level. Kung-fu means both time and effort, so the amount of time is not really the most important factor. Some schools completely shun the belt- or sash-ranking system.

Does a real kung-fu master have to be Chinese?

Many practitioners of non-Chinese heritage are quite good at Chinese martial arts. At this time, however, most of the true masters of Chinese wushu are Chinese themselves.

Are weapons used in kung-fu or wushu?

Dozens of weapons are practiced in wushu. Some styles only use one or two, while other

Since the early 1970s, Chinese wushu troupes from mainland China have toured the world giving spellbinding live presentations of their national art. These performers combine martial arts and gravity-defying acrobatics, as demonstrated here by this troupe member in Orlando, Florida, in 1997. Photo courtesy of Rebecca Lee.

schools have many weapons in their arsenals, and sometimes several routines for each weapon.

For many practitioners, the weapons performance is the highlight of kung-fu demonstrations, especially the complex and breathtaking multiperson weapons routines. When performed with expert precision at full speed, these routines, although prearranged, take on the appearance of real combat. As such, a single mistake or miscalculation could seriously injure a participant.

What are some types of wushu weapons?

The primary weapons are the staff, spear, broadsword, and straight sword. Others can be grouped into single weapons like the tiger fork, double weapons like the deer-horn knives, and flexible weapons like the nine-section whip chain.

Some styles employ weapons unique to that method, like the big broadsword of *bagua* boxing, which usually measures over four feet long!

Are the weapons used in kung-fu the same as in karate?

Some of the weapons are the same and many are similar, but generally both arts have many unique weapons. The most basic kung-fu weapon, the staff or cudgel, is similar in many aspects. Yet it is constructed from different types of wood, has a different taper, and, of course, uses a different method of technical performance.

Far more schools in the United States offer karate and taekwondo instruction than schools offering kung-fu classes. Why aren't there more kung-fu schools?

Most of the Chinese martial arts schools in the United States are located in cities with large Chinese populations. However, in recent years more and more kung-fu schools

Dozens of weapons are practiced in wushu. The primary weapons are the staff (as used here by Brian Leung of Madison, Wisconsin), spear, broadsword, and the straight sword (as demonstrated by Scott Sheeley of Bellefontaine, Ohio). Photos courtesy of, respectively, Brian Leung and Scott Sheeley.

have opened throughout North America. As time goes on, students from these schools will move to other parts of North America and establish their own schools.

Is there a national kung-fu association?

Three major groups promote Chinese martial arts in the United States: the U.S.A.–Wushu Kung-Fu Federation, headed by Anthony Goh; the U.S. Chinese Kuoshu Federation, led by Huang Chien-liang; and the United Kung-Fu Federation of North America, directed by Wai Hong.

Can girls and women be competent at kung-fu?

Girls and women can be not only competent, but also expert. Some of the foremost exponents of various styles of kung-fu are women. Notably, the grandmaster of the sun style of tai-chi is Madame Jian Yun Sun of Beijing, China. One of the grandmasters of zha-style boxing is Madame Jurong Wang from Shanghai, who now lives in Houston, Texas.

Some of the top female teachers in the United States include Shuyun Fu, Gini and Lily Lau, He Weiqi, Zhang Lingmei, and Bow Sim Mark—all women recognized as masters in their respective arts.

Is tai-chi a real martial art?

Many exponents of tai-chi practice it for its proven health benefits. The *Journal of the American Medical Association* listed results of studies showing the wonderful effects of regular tai-chi practice on seniors' ability to balance. But the fundamentals of tai-chi retain their martial purposes, including striking, kicking, grappling, and joint-locking. The techniques of real tai-chi are very much applicable in combat, both for the bare-handed and the weapons forms.

Does tai-chi have a religious connection?

Tai-chi has been linked to Taoism because of its name. However, historical reference shows tai-chi originated with the Chen family in the Henan province and was not related to any religious practice or belief. Because tai-chi is a great method for developing self-awareness, it is practiced by people of many spiritual beliefs and traditions.

Some of the foremost exponents of various styles of kung-fu are women. Women also compete in wushu forms divisions. Here National Forms Champion Anne Hsu strikes a pose during her grand championship performance at the New England Open Nationals in Boston, Massachusetts. Photo courtesy of Rich Baptiste.

What is chi-kung (a.k.a. qigong)?

Chi-kung means "energy skills" and is a traditional method of health-building and preservation in China. While it is not itself a martial art, most kung-fu styles use some type of chi-kung training. The internal styles like tai-chi, pa kua chang, and hsing i chuan especially use chi-kung methods as part of basic training and power development.

Qigong translates as "breath (or energy) skills," although *exercise* is also an acceptable translation.

Do my moves have to look good to work?

There is a Chinese saying, *"Hao kan bu hao yong,"* which means, "If it looks good, it is useless." You should not concentrate on the appearance of your movements, but on the method of the techniques you are performing. Practically speaking, though, martial intention should produce correct movements, which, incidentally, look great!

Do kung-fu practitioners meditate?

Many teachers include meditation in their training programs. It is definitely an optional element at most schools. Quite a few competitive athletes use some form of meditation as a regular part of their regimen, especially close to and during tournament time.

Was Bruce Lee really a kung-fu master?

Bruce Lee was famous not only for his ability on screen, but as the founder of jeet kune do, a system of kung-fu theory and application based on Lee's personal training experience.

Chi-kung means "energy skills," and is a traditional method of health-building and preservation in China. While it is not of itself a martial art, most kung-fu styles, especially the internal varieties, use some type of chi-kung training as part of basic training and power development. Allan Ondash of Courtdale, Pennsylvania, shows the extraordinary strength he has acquired through his training. Photo courtesy of the John Graden Archives.

He started his martial arts training as a student of the famous Wing Chun–style grandmaster Man Yip, of Hong Kong.

Is kung-fu something a disabled person could do?

Certainly some forms of kung-fu training are suitable for persons with disabilities. Many styles can adapt their training process to accommodate physically challenged students, and wushu training should be of great benefit to most disabled persons.

However, there are also some forms of training that could be especially harmful and dangerous for the disabled to even attempt. The careful supervision of a truly qualified instructor is absolutely essential.

Does kung-fu have any special body-conditioning exercises?

Many styles use some type of conditioning method for various reasons. Most common are the *pai shen* techniques, which feature slapping one's body with some degree of force to condition it for impact during combat. In addition, sandbags, weights, liniments, and a spectrum of other methods are found in the kung-fu culture.

What is the iron hand?

The so-called iron hand or iron palm is an extensive conditioning program to toughen the hand and enable a practitioner to use the hand as an awesome weapon. Some fantastic feats are possible through this exotic training method, particularly as applied to the bare-handed breaking of objects. However, many risks are involved with training incorrectly and without the right kind of medicine applied to the hands during this conditioning process. This should definitely be done only under the direct supervision of a well-qualified, experienced teacher.

Are the real methods of wushu kept secret by the true masters?

Certainly the advanced techniques and theories are not taught to anyone right off the street. Any wushu instructor, even one without an extensive background, will not teach everything openly nor, more important, too quickly. If a master has the ability to teach very dangerous methods, that teacher is especially ethically bound to teach such techniques to only a select few.

Is there a strict moral code in Chinese wushu?

The Chinese martial arts community welcomes those whose skill levels are good and who demonstrate high standards of ethics and conduct. Those whose technical level is lacking but have good character will be encouraged and should develop physical ability in time. But someone who displays a lack of morality will be shunned, no matter what skill level he or she might have.

Does a person have to speak Chinese to understand kung-fu?

While it's not necessary to be fluent in Chinese to learn or even become competent at kung-fu, it would certainly be helpful to understand the theories and concepts of a martial art in its original language and context. Oftentimes, the popular translations of some forms, movements, and even basic training exercises are incorrect.

Are there kung-fu competitions?

Yes. In North America, several exclusively kung-fu tournaments are conducted every year, and some large-scale competitions are held every two years. Most are very well-organized and attended, since for years kung-fu athletes had to compete as the minority in open martial arts events populated by karate and taekwondo stylists.

Every year, the number of participants at the all-Chinese-style events has grown larger.

What is the difference between northern and southern kung-fu?

This is another common way to classify the multitudinous kung-fu styles. The northern styles were developed in the north of China, and the southern in the south. The two systems developed this way due to indigenous geographic, ethnic, and cultural factors.

The northern styles tend to emphasize leg work, while the southern styles stress upper-body techniques. Relative to this distinction, there is a saying in China, "The Northern Kick subdues the Sea Dragon, the Southern Fist beats the Mountain Tiger."

What is the difference between internal and external styles?

The internal styles emphasize the natural use of the body to produce *jing*—total body energy that stems from the intrinsic energy called chi. The external styles emphasize correct alignment as well, but rely on the use of muscular strength called li.

At some point in training, however, the end result should be the same: a powerful, agile body with clear technique behind the efficient application of force.

Why do some kung-fu styles use acrobatic feats like high jumps and tumbling? Is this really kung-fu?

Yes. Many of the more gymnastic-oriented movements are evasive tactics smoothly integrated with the strikes and blocks of kung-fu. Some external styles, especially those from northern China, use high kicks, jumping, and tumbling movements as a regular part of training. These movements obviously require a great deal of basic training for strength and flexibility, and help the students maintain their spatial awareness in all types of positions and circumstances.

In addition, the more difficult tumbling techniques instill a certain degree of courage and self-confidence along with the enhanced body awareness and development.

Why do kung-fu practitioners sometimes strike themselves when they practice?

This is an example of the *pai shen* technique, done to condition the body to absorb strikes. Also, appropriately striking the body helps the student to focus power correctly and gauge how much force a given technique generates. Striking one hand against the other or slapping a kicking foot, etc., especially helps children learn how to do the movements well.

Does kung-fu have throwing and grappling techniques?

Although most people first think of the various weapons and unique hand formations like those used in boxing forms (like the eagle-claw fist), wushu has a decided level of grappling skills within each style and form. The skills of *shuai-jiao* (Chinese wrestling) are very similar to Japanese judo. The Chinese skills of *qinna* (or *chinna*) are very similar to jujutsu in the application of their controlling, choking, and joint-locking techniques.

Can kung-fu be practiced outdoors?

Actually, many (if not most) of the practitioners in Asia regularly train outdoors. Those who do tai-chi especially like to be outdoors when practicing, in order to enjoy the fresh air and enhanced feeling of body awareness. Of course, some styles should be practiced only on a proper surface to ensure safety and prevent injury.

What is all the talk about "animal styles" in kung-fu?

In traditional kung-fu, a number of styles have techniques based upon the movements of animals (even insects) during combat. According to orally transmitted legends, the founders of these styles each studied a particular animal as it engaged in mortal combat with the same or other animals. The founder then converted certain animal movements to human applications in the form of fighting techniques.

Also, one category of competition in formal martial arts competitions in China is called *xiangxingquan*, or "imitative boxing." The routines in this division include eagle-claw boxing, praying-mantis boxing, monkey boxing, tiger boxing, snake boxing, *ditang* (tumbling) boxing, and drunken boxing.

What is drunken kung-fu?

Despite its humorous name, drunken kung-fu is not an exhibition performed by an inebriated practitioner. The movements and techniques of the drunken style are, however, designed to replicate the stumbling, weaving, off-balance body movements of a besotted individual for the purpose of deceiving a foe.

Essentially, the drunken style is the sparring concept of broken rhythm applied to centuries-old, classical kung-fu techniques. While a practitioner appears to lurch uncontrollably, in reality he or she is very much under control, executing blocks, strikes, and kicks with grace and precision before once again lapsing into the weaving gait of an overindulger.

Aside from the singular system itself, variations and portions of drunken kung-fu appear with regularity in numerous other kung-fu systems—sometimes as a novelty, at other times as an advanced empty-hand or weapon form within the larger style.

What will I learn in a kung-fu class?

As a student just getting started in kung-fu training, you may expect to practice many basic exercises for conditioning, work on stances and elementary movements like punching and kicking, and then acquire some fundamental fist forms. Usually, you then proceed to self-defense applications, weapons training, two-person forms, and free-sparring. Even then, almost every school will continue to emphasize the basic elements.

What is the highest rank a person can achieve in kung-fu?

The highest level of ability does not depend on, and may not be reflected by, someone's ranking. Many traditional teachers avoid the ranking system entirely. The best thing to do is to work hard over a long period of time without inactive intervals. That is the only way to achieve kung-fu (skill).

Which famous celebrities study kung-fu?

Unquestionably, due to the vast popularity of their films, the most famous kung-fu practitioners of recent times are Jackie Chan and the late Bruce Lee. Former national Chinese wushu champion and actor Li Lianjie (a.k.a. Jet Li) has also become an international celebrity since his striking debut as a villain in *Lethal Weapon IV*.

Dozens of other wushu practitioners are well-known entertainment and sports figures, including vocalist David Lee Roth, basketball legend Kareem Abdul-Jabbar (Bruce Lee's friend and student), actor Marc Singer of *Beastmaster* fame, and beach volleyball star Karch Kiraly.

On his way to winning one of three consecutive Ultimate Fighting Championship (UFC) titles, Royce Gracie (bottom) grapples with Ken Shamrock. The UFC, a concept inspired by the Gracie family in the early 1990s, was the original series of events that created the so-called "no-holds-barred" competitions.

7

BRAZILIAN JIU-JITSU

Brazilian jiu-jitsu became *the* style of the 1990s because it universally changed the way of thinking and training throughout the martial arts world. For decades, jiu-jitsu had been treated like the illegitimate stepson of the martial arts family. Martial arts films had put the strikes and kicks of the so-called percussive arts in vogue, and grapplers and their grappling arts suffered an acceptance crisis with the general public.

That all began to rapidly change in the mid-1980s with the arrival in the United States of Gracie clan members of Brazilian jiu-jitsu fame. Part of this legendary clan's fame was an alleged undefeated status in one-on-one public challenge matches against all comers. Although some critics disputed that undefeated status, the Gracies immediately challenged all comers from all martial disciplines in their new country and won every single challenge match. These guys definitely could put their skills where their mouths were.

In the early 1990s, the Gracies took this challenge one giant step further. With business partners, several Gracie brothers created the Ultimate Fighting Championship (UFC), a series of freestyle elimination contests pitting martial artists from all disciplines against each other. As close as one can get to a no-holds-barred competition, this event marked the birth of "reality fighting."

The first UFC played exclusively on pay-per-view TV and generated the highest ratings ever for a martial arts event in that medium. Further, the UFC events drew increasingly larger numbers of pay-per-view TV viewers with each subsequent program, grossing millions of dollars per event in the process. And just as important, Royce Gracie won the championship title of the UFC events before retiring, proving that the Gracies' expertise lived up to their own claims. And this was against all comers of all sizes of all fighting arts.

Technically, the impact of Brazilian jiu-jitsu was felt worldwide. In fact, it revolutionized the way the martial arts are being taught today. Martial arts school owners who had previously taught a percussive art exclusively started adding jiu-jitsu and grappling programs to their curriculums.

The Gracies' global fame made them more successful than perhaps anyone could have imagined. A January 1997 survey of the top U.S. schools, conducted by *Martial Arts Professional* magazine, found that the main Gracie Jiu-Jitsu Academy in Torrance, California, was the single most financially successful martial arts school in the entire United States. Based on square footage, number of active students, and annual gross, the Gracies' Torrance school, at two million dollars a year in total revenues, outgrossed the second-place U.S. school, Fred Degerberg's academy in Chicago, by more than double!

With the subsequent immigration to the United States and elsewhere of the best Brazilian jiu-jitsu fighters and instructors—such as the Machado brothers, cousins of the Gracies—more and more martial arts students today are participating in this proven, renowned style of combat.

The information in this chapter is based on interviews with John Machado, a Gracie cousin and retired Brazilian jiu-jitsu champion, who teaches his clan's art in Rio de Janeiro, Brazil, and Redondo Beach, California.

Rickson Gracie, who is currently considered the best fighter in the Gracie family. To date, Rickson has been invincible in both jiu-jitsu matches and no-holds-barred contests, and was also a champion in sambo competition. In Brazil, he is considered the "terror" of the rings.
Photo by and courtesy of Andre Lima.

Where did Brazilian jiu-jitsu originate?

Many martial arts historians recognize jiu-jitsu as the first established martial arts system, originating in India some two thousand years before Christ. It spread to Asia and eventually proliferated in feudal Japan.

In 1914, Esai Maeda, (a.k.a. Count Koma), chief of the Japanese immigration colony, went to Brazil, where he transmitted his art to a family named Gracie.

Who is the Gracie family?

The Gracie family is responsible for the creation and development of Brazilian jiu-jitsu. The older brother, Carlos Gracie, learned Japanese jiu-jitsu, then created the Brazilian version and taught it to his younger brothers.

The new style was consequently taught to their children, then to the grandchildren, and so on. This family is extremely large in number today and divided into different clans. (See the sidebar at the end of this chapter, Who's Who in the Gracie Family.)

What is the relationship of the Machado brothers to the Gracie family?

The Machado brothers, Carlos, Roger, Rigan, Jean-Jacques, and John, are one of the clans originating from the Gracie family.

They learned the art with one of Carlos Gracie's sons.

What is the difference between Brazilian jiu-jitsu and the other martial arts?

Brazilian jiu-jitsu is a simple art with which one can defeat a much bigger opponent while fighting mostly on the ground. Therefore Brazilian jiu-jitsu starts where most of the other martial arts end—in the clinch.

The five Machado brothers pose with their most famous student, Chuck Norris, who has earned a black belt in Brazilian jiu-jitsu under their instruction. (Kneeling, left to right) Roger, John, and Jean-Jacques Machado. (Back row, left to right) Carlos Machado, Chuck Norris, and Rigan Machado.
Photo by and courtesy of Andre Lima.

Rorion Gracie displays a vintage copy of the Brazilian *O Globo* newspaper that features a story about his father, Helio, teaching a prominent politican. Photo by and courtesy of Andre Lima.

What does Brazilian jiu-jitsu have that the other martial arts do not have?

Brazilian jiu-jitsu emphasizes takedowns (falls) and ground techniques, which usually finalize a real fight.

Is anything missing in Brazilian jiu-jitsu?

Like any other martial art, Brazilian jiu-jitsu has room for development. Brazilian jiu-jitsu needs improvement in the takedowns, kicks, and punches in order to become a complete art.

What brought about the controversial Gracie challenges against other martial arts and martial artists?

In Brazil, at the beginning, there was a strong resistance by society, especially by the Japanese community, against accepting and recognizing Brazilian jiu-jitsu. After several failed attempts, the most effective way found by Carlos Gracie and his brothers to introduce the art was through challenges to others to engage in no-holds-barred fights.

This became the form of advertising the effectiveness of Brazilian jiu-jitsu, and it worked.

When exactly did these challenges start?

Between the 1930s and 1950s. It was an accepted practice at that time.

How many jiu-jitsu practitioners are there in Brazil today?

It is estimated that over 100,000 people practice jiu-jitsu in Brazil today.

Is there any kind of national organization in Brazil?

Yes, it is called Federacion Brasileira de Jiu-jitsu (Jiu-jitsu Brazilian Federation), and it has organized many competitive events.

Is there a U.S. federation for Brazilian jiu-jitsu? How about a world federation?

The Machado brothers founded the American Federation of Brazilian Jiu-jitsu with the intention of organizing the sport in the United States. It is a neutral organization formed to promote the well-being of the sport, and it is open to participation by all jiu-jitsu practitioners, not only those who learn Gracie jiu-jitsu.

The Jiu-Jitsu International Federation, of which John Machado is vice president and his cousin Carlos Gracie, Jr., is president, was founded in 1996. Their goal is to gain acceptance for jiu-jitsu as a future official Olympic sport.

Have there been any international competitions?

Yes. Pan-American and world championships have already taken place. These essential promotional events are necessary before applying for Olympic acceptance.

How many countries already participate in Brazilian jiu-jitsu international competitions?

At the time of this writing, there were nine countries: Brazil, the United States, Australia, Canada, the United Arab Emirates, France, Switzerland, Netherlands, and Germany.

But international competition is growing tremendously.

Why is Brazilian jiu-jitsu so popular in the world today?

According to John Machado, each and every martial art is important and has its place in the evolution of time. The 1990s were the decade of Brazilian jiu-jitsu.

Brazilian jiu-jitsu is enormously popular now because it completes all the other arts. Jiu-jitsu gives a person the weapons to successfully finalize a fight, regardless of the person's martial art. Its large and rapid popularity is a consequence of its simplicity combined with efficiency.

Is Brazilian jiu-jitsu exclusively a grappling art or does it also emphasize strikes?

Brazilian jiu-jitsu itself is basically only about grappling and torsions. Nevertheless, students in a number of Gracie jiu-jitsu schools are encouraged to also learn strikes in order to be more complete martial artists.

Which country generates the best jiu-jitsu fighters in competition?

Evidently, because of the larger number of practitioners in this martial art's native country, Brazil is the leader. Due to the serious work, dedication, and interest from Americans in learning the sport aspect, the United States is a close second.

What is the sequence of rank belts in Brazilian jiu-jitsu?

The color sequence begins with white, followed by blue, purple, brown, and finally, black. The color sequence is different for those under sixteen years of age. This sequence is white, yellow, orange, then finally, green. The young practitioner will continue the sequence from blue to black belt only after reaching age seventeen. A student cannot earn the black belt before age eighteen.

How does a student progress from one belt to the next? Is it determined by a period of study or a testing of skill?

The belt is given to the student per his or her efficiency. Time has its influence, but the change of belts is based strictly on efficiency. Some schools use testing; others use only observation to award ranks.

How long does it normally take to earn the black belt in Brazilian jiu-jitsu?

With technology, intensive training, and different methods of training, the time from white to black belt has been greatly reduced.

Today, it is possible to achieve the black belt in Brazilian jiu-jitsu in five years.

Who is the world's highest-ranked master in Brazilian jiu-jitsu?

Carlos Gracie was the highest-ranked until 1994, when he died. At the time of this writing, his brothers Helio and Gastao are the highest-ranked exponents. They both carry the red belt, which means each has been a black belt for over fifty years.

How many Brazilian jiu-jitsu practitioners are there in the United States today?

There were an estimated 15,000 students training at Brazilian jiu-jitsu schools by early 1997. However, adding the people who train in Brazilian jiu-jitsu through videotapes and seminars, the number might surpass 50,000.

Are many women training in this art?

The number of women practicing Brazilian jiu-jitsu has been growing tremendously every year. Brazilian jiu-jitsu is very useful for women, due to the extensive level of self-defense techniques from on the ground that are taught in the system. Ground techniques are very efficient in real self-defense situations, and women who are attacked are usually taken to the ground immediately.

Which famous martial artists have trained in Brazilian jiu-jitsu?

Some of the more prominent martial artists who have trained with the Machado brothers are film stars Chuck Norris and Steven Seagal; Richard Norton, the Australian martial artist and actor; Dan Inosanto and Master Richard Bustillo, Bruce Lee's ex-students; kickboxing world champion Kathy Long; and Bob Wall, who worked on several Bruce Lee films. Renowned grappling master Gene LeBell regularly exchanges techniques with the Machados at their school.

What attracts these seasoned martial artists to the practice of Brazilian jiu-jitsu?

Besides all of the exceptional technical qualities of this art, what has attracted these personalities and others to the Machado brothers is, according to John Machado, the way they transmit their knowledge of Brazilian jiu-jitsu. They teach their art based on simplicity, respect, seriousness, efficiency, and friendship.

Were the Machado brothers champions in Brazil?

Yes. They were undefeated champions in their respective divisions before moving to the United States.

John Machado (top) of Rio de Janeiro, Brazil, applies a Brazilian jiu-jitsu grappling technique to his brother Jean-Jacques. The five Machado brothers, cousins of the Gracies, were undefeated champions in their respective divisions before most of them migrated to the United States.
Photo by and courtesy of Andre Lima.

What is the Machado brothers' opinion of the UFC?

They see both positive and negative aspects. The positive side of the UFC, according to John Machado, was that it showed everyone the importance of the ground techniques found in Brazilian jiu-jitsu and grappling, in a confrontation with very few restrictive rules.

The negative side is that the UFC gives an image of violence to Brazilian jiu-jitsu, and it stimulates a big rivalry among all styles of martial arts.

Why are no-holds-barred events so popular?

Observing fights seems to be part of the human instinct, especially when it is as close to the real thing as a contest could be.

Numerous governmental authorities, in Canada and in the United States in particular, have worked intensively to ban no-holds-barred tournaments because of the sport's brutal nature. What do proponents think about this official opposition?

John Machado is partly in favor of it yet at the same time, partly against that opposition. If no-holds-barred events are banned, he thinks the government would then have to ban all other kinds of activities in which there is a similar level of violence. This would include professional sports like football, TV programs, movies, and so on.

Machado believes that whomever wants to watch or participate in these events should be able to do so freely at their own discretion.

Which are the basic techniques taught to the beginner in Brazilian jiu-jitsu?

The first thing is to learn how to defend oneself. The student is taught the "lever technique" in self-defense. That means the student should not defend her- or himself with the use of power alone but with leverage.

After learning defense, escape, and the smooth transition from one movement to the other, the student will learn how to control and how to finalize the movements, so as to end a confrontation efficiently and effectively.

Is there any kind of philosophy in Brazilian jiu-jitsu like there is in other martial arts?

Machado jiu-jitsu has a philosophy. First of all, peace above everything: peace of mind, peace in the school, peace at home, and peace everywhere else. Second, strength in training. The school is known as a school of champions, and they intend to maintain that tradition through strong training practices.

How long does it take for someone to be able to defend him- or herself by using Brazilian jiu-jitsu techniques?

In about six months, the student has already memorized the basic movements and is able to take great advantage of the art in a self-defense situation. Sometimes, seminar participants who have trained in other martial arts show remarkable progress after just one day of intensive training.

Do Brazilian jiu-jitsu competitors wear any kind of protective equipment?

Protection for the knees, elbows, wrists, ears, and mouth are permitted at the option of the contestant. The conventional gi is the only mandatory piece of equipment.

How is a Brazilian jiu-jitsu match conducted?

There is only one round per match, and its duration varies according to each color belt. The durations are five minutes for the blue belt, seven minutes for the purple belt, eight minutes for the brown belt, and ten minutes for the black belt.

A victory may be accomplished by submission or by points. Points are awarded according to the finalization of some movements: escape from certain lock positions, strategic transitions, and who maintains the most control during the contest.

What are the categories of competition?

The categories of competition are as follows: above sixteen years of age is the adult category; above thirty is the master category, which is subdivided into separate divisions for each additional five years of age—from thirty to thirty-four, from thirty-five to thirty-nine, and so on.

There are also ten weight divisions plus an open category where a person fights against anybody else from any other weight division.

There are also belt categories.

What is the future of Brazilian jiu-jitsu in the United States?

The United States is already a strong center of Brazilian jiu-jitsu today and could very well become the biggest center of the art in the future. Overall, there are more martial arts practitioners in the United States than anywhere in the world, and Americans who train in the martial arts have a propensity for seeking out the most effective systems.

Further, in the United States everything is in favor of the development of the sport of Brazilian jiu-jitsu: accessible sources of good nutrition, high technology, training accessories, superb weight-training programs, and more.

Who's Who in the Gracie Family

There has been an enormous amount of confusion about who is who among the Gracies due to the huge number of family members, all of whom, for generations, have studied their ancestral art of jiu-jitsu. Further confusion has resulted because so many family members have names starting with the letter *R*. This sidebar should help to clear up all the confusion and set the record straight.

Originally from Scotland, George Gracie arrived in Brazil in 1801. In 1914, Esai Maeda, also known as Count Koma, chief of the Japanese immigration colony, went to Brazil and soon became a very close friend of George's grandson, Gastao Gracie, a Brazilian scholar and politician. Back in Japan, Maeda was known for being an unbeatable and very famous jiu-jitsu champion. As a proof of friendship, he taught the art of jiu-jitsu to Gastao's oldest son, Carlos Gracie.

Gastao—had eight children, five boys and three girls: Carlos; Osvaldo; Gastao, Jr.; George; Helio; Helena; Mary; and Ilka.

Carlos—the one who had learned jiu-jitsu directly from Count Koma, taught this martial art to all four of his brothers. In 1925, they opened the first jiu-jitsu academy in all of Brazil, in Rio de Janeiro.

Helio—Despite his slight frame of 140 pounds, Helio, the youngest of Carlos's brothers, studied the most. Based on the traditional Japanese jiu-jitsu, Helio developed new techniques and created a new formidable system: Gracie jiu-jitsu.

For the last seventy years, the Gracies have dedicated their lives to their unique form of self-defense. With an extraordinarily large number of family members involved in this art, a strong line of successors has been established to maintain the tradition of the Gracie dynasty.

THE FIRST GENERATION

Carlos—had twenty-one children with five different wives (one at a

Helio Gracie, patriarch of the Gracie jiu-jitsu clan, has ushered his art into the world arena. With an extraodinarily large number of family members involved in his art, a strong line of successors has been established to maintain the tradition of the Gracie dynasty.
Photo by and courtesy of Andre Lima.

time, obviously). He died on October 7, 1994, at ninety-two years of age.

Osvaldo—died young and didn't have children.

Gastao, Jr., had a son, Gastaozinho, who dedicated himself to teaching Brazilian jiu-jitsu and gun-shooting.

George—had only female children; he died in 1991.

Helio—had nine children.

Note: From the five brothers who started careers in Brazilian jiu-jitsu, only Carlos, the oldest, and Helio, the youngest, were the ones who developed the art.

THE SECOND GENERATION

Carlos Gracie had twenty-one children. They are, from oldest to youngest,

Carlson was the best fighter of the family during the 1960s, unbeatable in countless no-holds-barred challenges. Today he owns one of the biggest Brazilian jiu-jitsu schools in all of Brazil, in Copacabana, Rio de Janeiro, and is a very respected teacher nationwide, having trained a large number of champion students. One of his two kids, Carlson, Jr., presently competes.

Robson, a great fighter, is today the president of the Rio de Janeiro Jiu-jitsu Federation. His three sons, Renzo, Ralph, and Raian, are good fighters as well. Renzo is an outstanding participant not only in Brazilian jiu-jitsu competitions, but also in no-holds-barred challenges in Brazil. He briefly visited the United States to make several instructional Brazilian jiu-jitsu videos.

Geysa—details unknown.

Rosecler—details unknown.

Sonja lives in the United States.

Rolls was to many people the best family fighter of all time, surpassing even Rickson. Rolls also competed in other styles, like Greco-Roman wrestling, becoming a champion of all the competitions in which he participated. He died in a tragic hang-gliding accident over the beaches of Rio de Janeiro.

Reyson—details unknown.

Oneika lives in the United States.

Reylson has two schools, one in Rio de Janeiro and the other in Las Vegas, Nevada, where his blackbelt sons, Rodrigo and Ceasar, assist him. Reylson, an eighth dan, is the highest-ranked Gracie member living in the United States.

Rosley—details unknown.

Rolange lives in the United States. He has seven children, none of whom train in Brazilian jiu-jitsu.

Rocian—details unknown.

Carlien—details unknown.

Clair—deceased; details unknown.

Carley was the first family member to bring Gracie jiu-jitsu to the United States and teaches the art in San Francisco.

Carlos, Jr., is the president of Brazil's National Jiu-Jitsu

Who's Who in the Gracie Family
(continued)

Federation. He is also an excellent instructor, having a very successful school in Rio de Janeiro. He taught Brazilian jiu-jitsu to all five Machado brothers, who presently live and teach in the Los Angeles suburb of Torrance, California.

Karla is the only female family member who trained in the art up to the rank of black belt.

Crolin has three children and teaches Brazilian jiu-jitsu in the south of Brazil.

Reila—details unknown.

Rillion is another outstanding family fighter. Presently he runs a school with his brother Crolin in the south of Brazil.

Kirla—details unknown.

Helio Gracie had nine children. They are

Rorion moved to the United States in 1981. Truly a master in the art of advertising and promo-tion, he's the person responsible for the worldwide popularization of Gracie jiu-jitsu. When younger, Rorion was a great fighter. He has seven children.

Relson teaches Brazilian jiu-jitsu classes in Hawaii.

Rickson is considered by many people to be the very best Brazilian jiu-jitsu fighter of all time. He learned a lot from his cousin, Rolls, whom he considers a brother. Rickson has always been invincible in Brazilian jiu-jitsu matches, in no-holds-barred contests, and in street fights, and was also a champion in sambo competition. In Brazil, he is considered the terror of the rings.

Recently, Rickson has partici-pated in major open champi-onships in Japan. On the first two occasions, he reportedly trounced all his opponents with ease.

Royler is a national lightweight Brazilian jiu-jitsu champion in Brazil. He owns a school in Rio de Janeiro and has won several no-holds-barred challenge bouts.

Royce teaches at his brother Rorion's school in Torrance, California. He has become very famous in the United States for his early victories in the UFC events, where, weighing only 180 pounds, he had to face and defeat oppo-nents weighing as much as 300 pounds.

Rherika—details unknown.
Ricci—details unknown.
Robin—details unknown.
Rolker teaches Brazilian jiu-jitsu in Brazil.

There are some other curious facts worth mentioning about the prolific Gracie clan:

- Helio and his first wife, Margarida, raised the first eight children of Carlos. Carlos's wife had died and it became impos-sible for him to raise the chil-dren alone.
- The last of Carlos's wives, Lair, with whom he had six children, has a sister named Luiza who, despite not directly belonging to

the Gracie family, had her five sons learn Brazilian jiu-jitsu. All of them became outstanding fighters. They are the Machado brothers (Carlos, Roger, Rigan, Jean-Jacques, and John), and today they all live in the United States. They first drew widespread attention by training Chuck Norris in Brazilian jiu-jitsu.

- In such a family, so large and full of peculiarities, perhaps it's no surprise that the names should also be special. All of Helio's children's names begin with the letter *R*, and the names of almost all of Carlos's children begin with the letter *R*, *K*, or *C*. The reason for this is simple. Carlos believed that the sounds of those letters have a certain magic power. "They are strong letters," he used to say.

Jackie Chan is a physical genius who has left audiences around the world laughing at his kung-fu comedy fights, and has equally astounded them with his daredevil stunts, which he performs personally. In this scene from the 1985 film *The Protector*, he leaps from a roof and in midair kicks his adversary.

JACKIE CHAN

8

It took Hong Kong legend Jackie Chan sixteen years and four attempts to crack the U.S. market and prove that he is indeed one of the world's biggest stars. Not until the February 1996 reissue of Chan's box-office hit *Rumble in the Bronx* did mainstream Americans discover him. But he was already a worldwide cult star to martial artists and savvy filmgoers who marveled over the death-defying stunts he always performed himself without using stunt doubles.

Jackie Chan is a physical genius who defines the word *action*. He's a human dynamo who has left audiences around the world in stitches over his kung-fu comedy fights and equally astounded them by his daredevil stunts. It can be safely stated that very few of the world's film industry stars have equaled the accomplishments and successes that Jackie Chan has achieved. He is that prime example of the time-honored success story: the individual who is born into poverty, works hard, develops his or her talents, strives for achievement, suffers setbacks, and ultimately becomes a huge success.

A multifaceted talent, Chan is also a one-man industry in Hong Kong: an actor, comedian, kung-fu master, acrobat, stuntman, singer, humanitarian, writer, director, and consummate filmmaker. His unique and inventive filmmaking style has endeared him to film critics the world over and has helped raise the Hong Kong movie-making standards to new and improved heights. He has helped give the term *Hong Kong action film* a new worldwide respect, along with millions of new fans.

As a performer, Jackie Chan bounces across the screen with a reckless ease. He defies death and gravity with his courage and awesome athletic abilities while showing off, having fun, and almost winking at the audience. His upbeat screen characters hide the serious perfectionist he is when it comes to his craft. In his quest to please his audience with constantly bigger and better stunts, Jackie has sustained innumerable bruises, cuts, burns, sprains, and broken bones. One particular stunt in Yugoslavia almost killed him. Yet, to this day, he still personally performs ever greater and more dangerous stunts with each new film.

Jackie is a throwback to the physical comedians of the silent-film era, who would put themselves in harm's way to thrill or get a laugh from the audience. Like those great early stars, Jackie understands the universal appeal of film and also knows what his audience expects from him. His willingness to put his life on the line for his art has helped raise him to superstar status.

Jackie Chan is the world's greatest action star of our time.

When and where was Jackie Chan born?

Jackie Chan was born in Hong Kong on April 7, 1954. At birth, Jackie was given the name Chan Kong Sang.

Where was Jackie raised?

Although Jackie was born in Hong Kong, his family moved to Canberra, Australia, shortly afterward. His father worked as a chef for the American embassy and his mother worked as a maid, but they were still very poor. As a result, they brought Jackie, their only son, back to Hong Kong at the age of seven and enrolled him in the famous China Drama Academy.

The academy educated children in the arts of the Peking Opera and paid for their room and board. In return, the children performed in Peking Opera shows for the academy.

When did Jackie begin studying the martial arts?

Jackie began studying the martial arts while attending the China Drama Academy. The academy, also known as the Opera Research School, was already world famous for producing some of the finest martial arts performers in the world.

What else did Jackie study while attending the China Drama Academy?

Jackie not only studied the martial arts, but also had to learn reading, writing, gymnastics, acrobatics, acting, mime, singing, and many other performing-arts skills required of Peking Opera performers. Jackie remained with the school for ten years.

Jackie began studying the martial arts while attending the China Drama Academy in Hong Kong. There he also had to learn reading, writing, gymnastics, acrobatics, acting, mime, singing, and many other performing-arts skills required of Peking Opera performers. Jackie remained with the school for ten years.

nineteen-hour days of training. The students' masters were hard and strict, and discipline was often handed out in beatings and canings.

In interviews, Jackie has admitted to having a love-hate relationship with the academy and would not recommend parents to send their children there.

Which other Hong Kong action stars did Jackie meet while studying at the academy?

The young Jackie met and formed lifelong friendships and working relationships with fellow academy students Sammo Hung (in recent years, star of the American TV series *Martial Law*) and Yuen Biao. Sammo (otherwise known as Samo) was the oldest, Jackie was in the middle, and Biao was the youngest. All three went on to become Hong Kong cinema stars and have worked together on numerous occasions. Hung made an award-winning film that chronicled their lives at the academy, entitled *Painted Faces* (1988).

What were conditions like at the China Drama Academy?

Although the academy had maintained a fine tradition of turning out elite performers, living conditions were bleak and harsh. The students were put through exhausting

Who was Jackie's martial arts teacher at the academy?

Although Jackie had a number of teachers, including Yuan Hsiao Tien (a.k.a. Simon Yuen, who was an actor and stuntman with some three hundred film credits to his name), his primary instructor was Sifu Yu Chan Yuan. Yuan was a martial arts master, as well as a legend in the Peking Opera. He was credited as being a fine teacher and a very strict disciplinarian.

What was the name of the Peking Opera group with which Jackie toured?

Jackie, Sammo Hung, and Yuen Biao were all part of a group known as Qi Xiao Fu (The Seven Little Fortunes). This was the academy's troop of players who toured throughout Southeast Asia and performed Peking Opera shows. The group was formed when Sifu Yu Chan Yuan chose seven of his finest students to perform.

What nickname did Jackie Chan receive as a teenager?

Because he had a very large nose at a very young age, Jackie was given the nickname Big Nose.

Which martial art styles did Jackie Chan study at the academy?

Jackie studied a number of traditional northern Shaolin kung-fu systems, as well as various southern Chinese kung-fu systems. Among these styles were *chang chuan*, pray-ing mantis, white eyebrow, the drunken style, and the traditional Shaolin animal styles.

Jackie has also studied Korean hapkido, taekwondo, and many diverse weapons.

Did Jackie ever appear in films as a child actor?

One year after joining the academy, Jackie made his film debut in *Big and Little Wong Tin Bar* (1962). Taiwanese actress Li Li Hua was impressed by the young Chan and cast him as her son in the film.

Jackie went on to appear in *The Love Eternal* (1963) and *The Story of Qui Xiang Lin* (1964), under the stage name Yuan Lou.

By which other names is Jackie Chan known?

Jackie is also known as Chen Gangsheng, Chen Long, Sing Lung, Chan Lung, Yuan Lou, and Chen Yuan Long.

How did Jackie Chan begin his adult career in movies?

After graduating from the Chinese Drama Academy at the age of seventeen, Jackie went to work for the Shaw Brothers Studios, one of Hong Kong's biggest film-production companies. There he took the screen name Chen

Yuan Long and began working as an extra and stuntman.

After two years of determination, hard work, and a number of bumps and bruises, Jackie was promoted to stunt coordinator and began devising and arranging the stunts and fights for various Shaw Brothers' motion pictures.

For a complete Jackie Chan filmography, visit http://www.movieworld.com.hk on the Internet.

Did Jackie Chan ever work with Bruce Lee?

Jackie worked with Bruce Lee on several films. As a stuntman, Jackie appeared in Lee's greatest hit, *Enter the Dragon* (1973). He played one of Han's guards in Lee's famous battle with the guards in the secret, underground opium factory scene.

In *The Chinese Connection* (a.k.a. *Fist of Fury*), Jackie was the stunt double for the leader of the Japanese dojo when Bruce Lee kicked him through a wall and into the garden.

What was Jackie's first starring role?

After several years of working as an extra, a stuntman, and a stunt coordinator, Jackie was discovered by a producer who happened to be on a set where Jackie was working. Jackie

was teaching some of the performers how to fight and die dramatically for the camera. The producer liked his approach and signed him on to star in *The Little Tiger of Canton* (1971). This film is also known as *Master with the Cracked Fingers* and *Snake Fist Fighter*.

Which famous Hong Kong director adopted Jackie as his godson?

Jackie was adopted by director Lo Wei, the famous Hong Kong filmmaker who directed the Bruce Lee films *Fist of Fury* (a.k.a. *The Big Boss*) and *The Chinese Connection*. Jackie was brought to Lo Wei's attention by Jackie's friend and manager, Willie Chan. Lo Wei had just set up a new production company, and recognizing Jackie's talent, quickly adopted Jackie as his godson and signed him to a multipicture deal.

Is it true that Jackie Chan was being groomed as Bruce Lee's successor?

This is true. The untimely death of superstar Bruce Lee left a large hole in the Hong Kong film industry that many eager producers and stars scrambled to fill. Lo Wei groomed Jackie to be "the next Bruce Lee" and even changed his name to Sing Lung (which means "potential dragon").

Jackie starred in a sequel to Lee's *The Chinese Connection* entitled *New Fist of Fury* (1976), and went on to do a number of dramatic kung-fu films for Lo Wei and his company. Many of these films, however, were only marginal successes.

Although Jackie Chan is known as a comedic actor, did he ever do any dramatic film work?

Most of Jackie's early work for Lo Wei involved dramas. *New Fist of Fury*, *Shaolin Wooden Men* (1976), *To Kill with Intrigue*

Jackie Chan created and popularized the comedy kung-fu film genre starting in 1978 with two back-to-back movies: *Snake in the Eagle's Shadow* and *Drunken Master* (a.k.a. *Drunken Monkey in a Tiger's Eye*).
Photo courtesy of United Artists Corporation.

(1977), *Killer Meteor* (1977), *Spiritual Kung-Fu* (1978), *Snake and Crane Arts of Shaolin* (1978), and *The Magnificent Bodyguards* (1978) were all traditional, dramatic kung-fu films.

Were Jackie's early films box-office hits?

Although many critics and fans recognized Jackie's talents, his films were only moderate successes. Jackie realized that he would not succeed if he allowed himself to be compared with the late Bruce Lee. Consequently, he altered his fighting style, steered himself toward comedy, and made his characters hardworking, likable, and noninvincible Everymen with whom the audience could readily identify. Thus began Jackie's meteoric rise to superstardom.

Who is credited with creating the comedy kung-fu film genre?

Jackie Chan is credited with popularizing the comedy kung-fu film. In 1978, Lo Wei, who had Jackie on contract, loaned him out to Seasonal Films. There, Jackie, producer Ng See Yuen, and director Yuen Woo Ping collaborated on two films, *Snake in the Eagle's Shadow* (1978) and *Drunken Master* (a.k.a. *Drunken Monkey in a Tiger's Eye*, 1978).

Jackie put his new formula for success to the test. Both films were comedies, and both were huge successes at the box office. This success signaled the beginning of the long-running comedy kung-fu genre in Hong Kong.

What makes Jackie Chan's fights so unique?

Jackie is blessed with an enormous inventive physical genius when it comes to creating ever newer and ever more mind-boggling screen fights. He transforms a simple implement like chopsticks, for example, into a tool for fighting for a small sliver of food, or a lady's dress into a fiercely rotating weapon to undo a villain. These everyday objects that he converts into weapons can include a lawn chair, a wooden bench, or even a refrigerator. He often finds an object on the set that he likes and coordinates an entire fight sequence around it.

Further, Jackie does not plan his fights in advance, which, he says, drains his fights of "electricity." Instead, each move is blocked out on the spot.

No other film star anywhere in the world, martial arts or otherwise, can match Chan's fight-scene genius.

What film marked Jackie Chan's directorial debut?

Jackie's directorial debut was *The Fearless Hyena* in 1979. Jackie directed and starred in this comedy kung-fu epic, which became the

Jackie is blessed with an enormous inventive physical genius for creating ever newer and ever more mind-boggling screen fights. He transforms a simple implement like chopsticks, for example, into a tool for fighting for a small sliver of food, or a lady's dress into a fiercely rotating weapon to undo a villain. Photo courtesy of New Line Cinema.

second-highest grossing film in Hong Kong that year. Jackie was also the writer and martial arts fight choreographer.

This movie was a turning point in his distinguished career. It marked the first time he was given creative control over his films.

What was Jackie Chan's first U.S. film?

Jackie made his U.S. film debut in 1980 with *The Big Brawl*, directed by Robert Clouse (who also directed Bruce Lee's *Enter the Dragon*). Although the film was a minor box-office success, it failed to live up to the producers' high expectations. So Jackie returned to Hong Kong.

What other early films did Jackie make for the U.S. market?

After the moderate success of *The Big Brawl*, Jackie appeared in *The Cannonball Run* (1981), *Cannonball Run II* (1984), *The Protector* (1985), and *Rumble in the Bronx* (1995).

Although *Rumble in the Bronx* was originally made for the Hong Kong market, New Line Cinema decided to release the film in the United States in February 1996. The company upgraded the soundtrack to increase the picture's appeal to an American audience. It was a solid hit, grossing $32 million. Based on this movie's success, Miramax, chiefly a U.S. arthouse film distributor, released a reissue of Jackie's *Supercop* (a.k.a. *Police Story III: Supercop*, 1992), which grossed around $14 million against stiff summer-1996 competition.

This one-two punch at the box office set Jackie's career in motion in the United States, previously the only market in the world where he was not a recognized star.

For what film did Jackie Chan learn to roller-skate?

Jackie learned to roller-skate for the racing scene in *The Big Brawl*. He also put his skat-ing skills to good use in *Winners and Sinners* (1983), where he races through traffic and under a moving trailer truck. Jackie also learned how to use a skateboard for scenes in *Wheels on Meals* (1983) and *City Hunter* (1993).

Jackie constantly seeks to learn new physical skills for use in his films.

Has Jackie Chan always played the hero in his films?

Although Jackie prefers to play the hero, he played the villain to star Jimmy Wang Yu's hero in the 1977 film *Killer Meteor*. This marked the first and last time Jackie played a bad guy.

Which American film role did Jackie turn down because he did not want to play a villain?

Jackie turned down the role of the lead Yakuza villain in the 1989 action-thriller *Black Rain*, starring Michael Douglas. He felt that his audience would never accept him as a bad guy.

Is it true that Jackie is a perfectionist when he works?

Jackie works hard and wants to give his audience everything he has. As a result, he works tirelessly and relentlessly to get a scene right. For example, he once performed 328 takes to get a "fan-fighting" sequence correct for his 1980 film *The Young Master*.

His manager, Willie Chan, claims that Jackie once did over a thousand takes to get a scene right for his film *Dragon Lord* (1982). That final take lasted less than two seconds on screen!

With which other famous Hong Kong film directors has Jackie worked?

Jackie Chan has worked for directors Lo Wei, John Woo (*Hand of Death*, 1975), Sammo Hung (*Wheels on Meals*, 1983; *Winners and Sinners*, 1983; *Twinkle, Twinkle Lucky Stars*, 1985; *Dragons Forever*, 1988); Tsui Hark (*Twin Dragons*, 1992), and Stanley Tong (*Police Story III: Supercop*, *Rumble in the Bronx*, and *Police Story IV: First Strike*, 1996).

John Woo has since become one of Hollywood's premier action directors. His major credits include *Broken Arrow* (1996), *Face/Off* (1998), and *Mission: Impossible 2* (2000).

With which American directors has Jackie Chan worked?

Jackie has worked with American directors Robert Clouse (*The Big Brawl*), Hal Needham (*The Cannonball Run*, and *Cannonball Run II*), James J. Glickenhaus (*The Protector*), Arthur Hiller (*Burn Hollywood Burn*, 1997), Brett Ratner (*Rush Hour*, 1998), and Tom Dey (*Shanghai Noon*, 2000).

Who were some of Jackie Chan's American film influences?

Jackie is a fan of the American silent film comedies and has enjoyed the work of Buster Keaton, Charlie Chaplin, and Harold Lloyd. Jackie pays homage to these comedians by re-creating some of their classic bits in a few of his films.

Which film is considered to be the major turning point in Jackie's career?

1983's *Project A* is considered the turning point, for several reasons. Jackie directed and starred in this large-scale and high-budgeted comedy adventure, which also featured, for the first time, a number of exciting and death-defying stunt sequences. This type of action, mixed with kung-fu battles, would become the main staple and trademark of Jackie's films from that point on.

Project A remains one of his best and most profitable box-office hits and marks the point where Jackie broke from the traditional kung-fu films. His decision to add high-caliber stunts to his films may have come from working on the U.S.–made *Cannonball Run* films and being exposed to the world of high-risk Hollywood stunts.

In which films did friends Jackie Chan, Sammo Hung, and Yuen Biao appear together?

The three lifelong friends and associates have appeared in *Project A*; *Winners and Sinners*; *Wheels on Meals*; *My Lucky Stars*; *Twinkle, Twinkle Lucky Stars*; and *Dragons Forever*.

Which American kickboxing legend did Jackie fight in several of his films?

Jackie fought against kickboxing legend Benny "The Jet" Urquidez in *Wheels on Meals* and *Dragons Forever*. Both were excellent fight sequences, but Jackie's battle with Urquidez in *Wheels on Meals* is considered by many to be one of the finest fight scenes ever filmed.

With which other famous martial artists has Jackie worked with?

The following noted martial artists have all appeared in Jackie's films at one time or another:

Gary Daniels, Pat Johnson, Shih Kien (the villainous character Han in *Enter the Dragon*), Yasuaki Kurata, Michiko Nishiwaki, Australian Richard Norton, Wang Ing Sik (the Japanese fighter in *Return of the Dragon*), Chen Sing, James Tien (who appeared opposite Bruce Lee in *Fist of Fury* and *The Chinese Connection*), retired U.S. national karate champion Keith Vitali, retired U.S. world kickboxing champion Bill "Superfoot" Wallace, Michelle Yeoh, Jimmy Wang Yu, and Simon Yuen (one of Jackie's former kung-fu teachers).

Does Jackie Chan really perform all of his own stunts?

Jackie indeed performs all of his stunts himself, no matter how dangerous they are. He feels that he would be cheating his audience if he did not do so. His willingness to please his audience and come up with bigger and more exciting stunt sequences has cost the action star, as well as his stunt people and other actors in his films, a large number of injuries over the years.

In which film was Jackie critically injured?

While filming the opening action scene in the 1986 film *Armour of God*, Jackie made a long jump from a castle wall to a nearby tree limb. The branch broke, and Jackie plunged about

Jackie's sensational battle with American world kickboxing champion Benny "The Jet" Urquidez in the 1983 film *Wheels on Meals* is considered by many to be one of the finest fight scenes ever filmed. The two fought again in the 1988 film *Dragons Forever*.

Photo courtesy of Benny Urquidez.

forty feet and struck his head on the ground. He was rushed into emergency surgery and made a miraculous and quick recovery in a matter of days. His conditioning and recovery astounded the Yugoslavian doctors. They nicknamed him Superman.

As a result of the injury and surgery, Jackie has a small, plastic-filled hole on the right side of his head. In fact, he often jokes about it with media representatives.

What other injuries has Jackie sustained during his career?

Aside from the usual bumps, bruises, sprains, cuts, and scrapes, Jackie has broken his legs, his nose, his jaw, his hands, and fingers, and has broken bones in his shoulders. He has also received burns while performing several different fire stunts.

What is unique about the closing credits of many of Jackie's films?

The closing-credit sequences of many of Jackie's films showcase the outtakes that did not make it into the final movie. These outtakes feature the usual flubbed lines, but also include a number of stunt and fight sequences that went painfully awry. They usually end with Jackie or his stunt people bleeding, writhing in pain, or being loaded into an ambulance!

American director and stuntman extraordinaire Hal Needham (*The Cannonball Run*) used this outtake technique at the end of his films, and this may have influenced Jackie to do the same with his pictures. Once Jackie began using this device as a signature, however, Hollywood filmmakers picked up on the concept and it's now commonly used at the end of many pictures.

Who are Jackie Chan's stunt people?

Jackie Chan's stunt team is composed of a very talented group of Hong Kong martial artists, acrobats, and stunt people who are known as Jackie Chan's Stuntmen Club. They are fiercely loyal to their employer and it shows—they are routinely called on by Jackie to risk life and limb in order to create the ultimate stunt and fight sequences.

Jackie has also employed European stunt-driving legend Remy Julienne (who worked on a number of the stunt-laden James Bond films), to coordinate many of his films' car chases and crashes.

What was Jackie Chan's most difficult stunt?

Any number of stunts from any of Jackie's films could certainly qualify for this honor. But the superstar cites one particular stunt that made him the most nervous. In the finale of 1985's *Police Story* (a.k.a. *Police Force*), Jackie had to leap from a shopping mall ledge to a nearby pole and slide down seventy-five feet through a series of exploding lights and live wires. He then had to release the pole, fall through a wood-and-glass roof, get up, and finally apprehend the villain—all in one take!

The scene was shot in one take by virtue of the use of multiple cameras and was executed to perfection. This stunt reportedly cost Jackie's production company $500,000 to execute and naturally is one of the most exciting sequences in the film.

Does Jackie Chan have trouble securing insurance to cover his film productions?

Due to the dangerous nature of the stunts in his films and his track record of injuries, Jackie has found it impossible to find anyone in the world to insure him—not even Lloyds of London, which typically insures high-risk subjects or objects for a premium price. As a result, Jackie pays for all of the medical bills and needs of his performers and crew.

Is there anything that makes Jackie more nervous than performing death-defying stunts in his films?

According to Jackie, doing love scenes makes him more nervous than doing stunts. He also keeps them to a minimum in his films because he claims that they would upset his female fans.

Which film is considered to be Jackie Chan's version of Raiders of the Lost Ark?

Jackie's 1986 box-office smash, *Armour of God*, is considered to be his version of *Raiders of the Lost Ark*. In the film, Jackie

Jackie Chan is the only action star in the world who performs his own stunts without using a stunt double—a choice that has cost him innumerable injuries and once almost killed him. In this scene from the 1995 movie *Rumble in the Bronx*, he desperately hangs onto a moving vehicle.
Photo courtesy of New Line Cinema.

plays a soldier of fortune known as The Asian Hawk, who is sent on a dangerous mission to recover valuable artifacts. The film resembled *Raiders'* style of high adventure, but Chan's inventive comedic touches and action sequences keep it unique.

Which films has Jackie Chan directed?

Jackie has directed *The Fearless Hyena* (1979), *The Young Master* (1980), *Dragon Lord* (1982), *Project A* (1983), *Police Story*

(1985), *Armour of God* (1986), *Project A II* (1987), *Police Story II* (1988), *Mr. Canton and Lady Rose* (a.k.a. *Miracles*, 1989), and *Armour of God II: Operation Condor* (1991).

Which of Jackie's Hong Kong films cost the most to make?

Jackie's 1991 epic, *Armour of God II: Operation Condor* is his most expensive film to date, costing over eighty million Hong Kong dollars to make. This box-office hit was a sequel to his 1986 film *Armour of God* and took over one year to make. It was filmed in four countries and boasted some of the biggest production values ever found in a Hong Kong action film. His 1995 film *Thunderbolt* is also said to have cost roughly the same amount, though some sources claim it was even higher.

What are some of Jackie Chan's most financially successful films?

Just about all of the films that Jackie has made from the 1980 film *The Young Master* on to the present day have done very well at the Asian box office. However, some of Jackie's biggest blockbusters include *Project A*, *Project A II*, *Armour of God*, *Armour of God II: Operation Condor*, *Police Story*, *City Hunter, Drunken Master II, Thunderbolt,* and *Rumble in the Bronx*, which boasted the biggest holiday opening ever in Hong Kong.

Rumble in the Bronx broke many Asian box-office records and became a hit film in the United States as well. Because of its worldwide success, it is Jackie's most successful film to date.

Of his American-made films, the 1998 film *Rush Hour* has been the most successful to date, earning more than $142 million in the United States and Canada alone.

How many films are in Jackie's popular Police Story series?

To date, there have been four entries in Jackie's successful *Police Story* series: *Police Story* (1985), *Police Story II* (1988), *Police Story III: Supercop* (1992), and *Police Story IV: First Strike* (1995).

In which films has Jackie portrayed China's legendary folk hero Wong Fei Hung?

Jackie Chan played the legendary kung-fu master Wong Fei Hung (1847–1924) in both *Drunken Master* (1978) and *Drunken Master II* (1994). Wong Fei Hung (a.k.a. Huang Fei Hong), who is one of China's most popular folk heroes, has also been played over the years by Hong Kong film stars Kwan Tak Hing, Ku Feng, Gordon Liu (a.k.a. Liu Chia Hui), and Jet Li (who played the character in *Once upon a Time in China*, parts I and II).

Which American film honor did Jackie Chan receive in 1987?

In 1987, Jackie's film *Police Story* was chosen to be one of the films screened at the prestigious New York Film Festival.

Which U.S. city honored Jackie Chan with a day named after him?

The city of San Francisco honored the star by proclaiming September 6th, 1986, to be Jackie Chan Day.

On which popular American TV shows has Jackie appeared?

Jackie has appeared on the TV shows *Live with Regis and Kathie Lee* (ABC), *The Tonight Show* (NBC, with Jay Leno), *The Late Show with David Letterman* (CBS), and the *Dinah Shore Show* (CBS). He was also profiled on ABC's newsmagazine show *Prime Time Live* and on *The Incredibly Strange Film Show* (Showtime cable).

In how many films has Jackie appeared?

It would be difficult to accurately count the number of films Jackie has appeared in, especially considering the numerous movies he appeared in as a stuntman and an extra. As of 2000, Jackie Chan has had starring roles in seventy-six films and has made appearances in dozens of others.

Have any of Jackie's films ever reached number one at the U.S. box office?

Two have reached number one in the United States. Jackie's worldwide blockbuster *Rumble in the Bronx* was released in the United States on February 23, 1996, and reached number one at the box office for several weeks. So did his 1998 film *Rush Hour*.

Was Rumble in the Bronx *actually shot in the Bronx—the tough New York neighborhood?*

While some footage was shot in New York City (mostly shots of some of the more recognizable sites), most of the film was actually shot in Vancouver, British Columbia.

Is it true that Jackie Chan is also a singer?

Jackie was trained to sing Chinese opera while at the Chinese Drama Academy. He occasionally sings pop songs, which wind up in many of his movies. He sang one of his more memorable songs for the closing credits of *Armour of God*.

Is Jackie also involved in charity work?

The busy superstar donates much of his time and money to charity work. In 1987, he founded the Jackie Chan Charitable Foundation, to provide money to a variety of different charities and scholarships. He has also been at the forefront of the Hong Kong film community's stand against organized crime in the movie and entertainment industry.

To which other organizations does Jackie belong?

Jackie has been an executive committee member, vice president, and president of the Hong Kong Directors' Guild, an executive member of the Hong Kong Stuntmen's Association, honorary president of the Hong Kong Society of Cinematographers, vice president of the Hong Kong Performance Artist Guild, and president of the Hong Kong Motion Picture Association.

Has Jackie Chan ever won any awards for his work?

Jackie has won a number of worldwide awards for his work, including Member, Most Excellent, Order of the British Empire (1989, British Government), Best Actor (1989, Hong Kong Artist Guild), *Des Insignes de Chevalier des Arts et des Lettres* (1990, France), Best Actor (1992 and 1993, Golden Horse Awards, Taiwan), and the MTV Lifetime Achievement Award (1995, MTV, USA).

Jackie and his stuntmen have also won five awards for Best Action Direction at the Hong Kong Film Awards.

Is Jackie Chan the number one box-office star in the world?

Jackie Chan has been Hong Kong's number one box-office draw for close to twenty years. In light of his popularity in Asia and the rest of the world, his loyal and growing following in the United States, his numerous films and the tens of millions of dollars they have generated, many feel that Jackie Chan is the number one box-office star in the world.

In addition to the 1995 *MTV Movie Awards*, where Jackie was honored with a Lifetime Achievement Award, Chan has won a number of worldwide accolades for his outstanding body of film work.

Meditation, a common practice in most martial arts, is a method to promote mind and body relaxation.

THE HIGHER VALUES OF MARTIAL ARTS

9

The abundance of physical benefits derived from martial arts training is universally recognized today. The self-defense benefit by itself certainly is enough to justify martial arts training, given the alarming prevalence of criminal assault and violence today. But new practitioners of the martial arts will quickly discover how much they develop internally, too, as a natural consequence of their physical training.

When you begin martial arts training, you are about to embark upon perhaps the biggest mental and spiritual changes of your life; it's inevitable. Your mind and spirit will be learning to work together harmoniously to bring about the necessary changes to make you a more "complete" human being.

With your training, you will begin to know your body very well—everything from turning it into a self-defense weapon to increased vitality and good health. Conversely, things like insufficient sleep and improper eating habits will become very evident to you. Overall, you will be imbued with a wonderfully fresh zest for life.

One of the greatest advantages of martial arts training will be the sharpening of your mind caused by a heightened increase in concentration and sensory awareness, as well as a lower level of anxiety. You'll also develop a spiritual awareness (not in the religious sense), and the spirit is the life force of our very being.

Thousands of martial arts instructors believe that the intangible benefits of the martial arts can cure some of society's ills, especially the problems plaguing our youth today. Jhoon Rhee, the Washington, D.C.–based master who introduced Korean taekwondo in the United

States, laces a logical argument with a startling analogy:

"What is more important," Rhee asks, "your children or your car? The answer is obvious. If we can do something to develop a child's leadership, wisdom, and character, we are going to become bigger than General Motors. That's because we in the martial arts are in the business of developing people. General Motors," Rhee concludes, "is in the business of developing cars!"

It is a fact that martial arts instructors can often instill wonderful qualities in children when parents and other authority figures cannot. Because of the technical powers the martial arts instructor has acquired and the highly regarded status symbol of the black belt, the instructor holds a very important position of influence with his or her students in general, especially the young students.

The instructor is the ideal role model that the students can hardly find elsewhere: someone physically capable of defending him- or herself, yet possessing a nonviolent nature and a gentle humility. Students usually emulate their instructors; therefore the more often than not the instructor can motivate students to achieve things they never thought possible. As a result, many young martial arts students with disciplinary, attention-span, and academic problems are transformed into successful achievers.

The martial arts, as you will learn in this chapter, are much more than mere kicking and punching. The longer you train, the more you'll change internally and the more you will realize the comparatively small role the physical aspect of the martial arts plays in your everyday life.

DISCIPLINE

How does martial arts training develop self-discipline?

Self-discipline comes about when you see the tremendous results your training gives you. It then becomes much easier to acquire the willpower you need to overcome personal obstacles. Martial arts themselves are "self-discipline." Training day after day, week after week, and year after year creates a physically disciplined pattern for you. Once you discover how you've accomplished this physical discipline, your mind can more easily adapt this quality to your daily life as well.

Does martial arts training develop discipline in children, even undisciplined ones?

Yes, martial arts, first of all, creates a disciplined environment. Children are told what to do, and they begin to take pride in the results that they witness in themselves. This

Thousands of martial arts instructors share the belief that the intangible benefits of the martial arts can cure some of society's ills, especially the problems plaguing our youth today. Veteran Tom Callos of Sparks, Nevada, is a nationally recognized expert who teaches martial arts instructors how to instill higher values in their young students. Children represent 52 percent of the martial arts student enrollment in the United States.

Photo courtesy of Tom Callos.

trains them to adopt this strategy, even in everyday life.

It is important for children to have patterns of discipline to follow. If not given patterns, children become overwhelmed and almost fearful of having to create their own patterns, or routines, in life. The martial arts gives them a positive pattern to follow and thus a sense of security, because this pattern basically never changes. Their training remains constant, even though other aspects of their lives may not.

How soon will a parent see the results of such discipline?

Results are always achieved on an individual basis. However, on the average, discipline surprisingly can be achieved very quickly, sometimes within a matter of weeks. With children, discipline becomes evident once they get set in the discipline pattern. That's why it's so important that parents get their children on a fixed schedule of martial arts class attendance and remain adamant about the continuance of their training as well.

In what ways is discipline achieved?

Discipline can be achieved even in the simplest ways. Martial arts training can bring a trainee's mind, body, and spirit together to achieve such accomplishments as learning to not talk back or to stick to a strict diet.

Children in martial arts classes begin to understand that there are rules both inside a martial arts class and also at home. A child learns that breaking these rules leads to a reprimand; abiding by them leads to praise and affirmation. This is a very simple formula, and it's also the basis of discipline to which most martial arts instructors strictly adhere.

How can I help to expedite discipline?

You help to expedite discipline by gaining enough confidence to take chances with yourself. You must learn to say no or yes appropriately when the right thing must be done. Your training can teach you this. Also, simply sticking with your training—never

quitting, never getting discouraged no matter what—will quickly bring about self-discipline.

It's also important, especially for children, to continue training even during training "lulls."

RESPECT

What kind of respect do the martial arts promote?

The martial arts promote two kinds of respect: self-respect and respect for others. You can't have one without the other: you cannot respect others if you do not first respect yourself.

Why is it important to first learn self-respect?

If you don't learn to respect yourself first, then it is impossible to show respect to others. Self-respect gets you in tune with your body, as well as your well-being. Through self-respect, you learn to take better care of yourself. You learn to continue, through training and programming, the necessary changes that make you a better individual.

The martial arts promote both self-respect and respect for others, even when they are antagonists. DeLand, Florida's Dr. Terrance Webster-Doyle, author of *Why Is Everybody Always Picking on Me: A Guide to Handling Bullies* and other similar works, is an expert in teaching children how to handle the "bully syndrome" without resorting to violence.

Photo courtesy of Dr. Terrance Webster-Doyle.

How is self-respect achieved through martial arts training?

One way to gain self-respect is by advancing through the belt-rank system. This tremendous feeling of accomplishment also enables you to learn to set and achieve both short- and long-term goals. Other ways include helping those lower-ranked than yourself accomplish your same goals, and by seeing the gradual improvement in your ability to more completely execute martial arts with excellence.

Does self-respect tie in with a sense of belonging?

Yes, belonging to a school, a federation, or an organization, where the same beliefs and teachings are upheld, will instill self-respect. There's always strength in numbers.

What is the significance of self-respect through board-breaking?

Board-breaking is one of the biggest confidence boosters in martial arts. Confidence is a major key to acquiring self-respect. Board-breaking symbolically teaches students to see through some of the toughest obstacles in life. They learn to take chances and to conquer personal fears. Finally, through individual effort, they learn to rely upon their inner strength and their ability to get through difficult times.

How does an instructor help students achieve self-respect?

An instructor helps students achieve self-respect by giving them credit, but only where and when it is due. Students must feel that they have earned all promotions and have worked very hard to get where they are.

Does an instructor who teaches demanding classes and challenging techniques instill or discourage self-respect?

A demanding instructor will definitely contribute to better self-respect in the long run. Classes must be challenging before they can be personally rewarding. A hard instructor also pushes students to reach their fullest potential.

Should students be commanded to show respect for others?

Children must be told to follow rules and guidelines and to show proper respect. Adults, however, must earn the respect of others. This respect can easily be earned by the instructor first by respecting the students as human beings. This, in turn, creates a mutual-respect situation.

Suppose it is difficult for me to automatically show respect to others?

If you cannot respect others who have earned their ranks and positions, then perhaps you do not feel very secure about your training in particular, or yourself in general. When you've learned to respect yourself, then it will become easy to show respect to others.

Is answering "Yes, ma'am" or "Yes, sir" important in showing respect?

Answering with respect shows that you acknowledge the other person's rank and accomplishments, very much like the military. We must remember that someday we, too, could be in that same position of seniority. Then, likewise, we will want to be treated respectfully.

Is vocalizing respect, by answering verbal commands and by bowing, so important?

Yes, because it moves you in the right direction. It maintains a strict and disciplined atmosphere that's necessary for martial arts training. It also sets a good example for those just beginning their training.

Should I extend my respect to someone whom I can physically conquer even if they're higher-ranked than me?

Yes, because he or she still possesses something that you do not: wisdom and knowledge. These are assets earned through a seriously committed effort. Even if that person cannot physically perform a technique better than you or even show you a tech-

nique, he or she can mentally show you how to achieve your own martial arts goals.

How can learning respect spill over into my everyday life?

Once you've gained respect and know how to freely give it, you'll feel like you stand apart from the ordinary person. It's a tremendous sense of pride. You begin to feel more confident about taking other risks and chances in your life outside of martial arts as well.

Is it important to have guidelines and standards to acquire respect?

Yes. There must be a hierarchy system, the leaders of which set the standards for others to follow. Otherwise, there will be no foundation for the gaining of respect. This is an especially important structure for children.

CONFIDENCE AND SELF-ESTEEM

How is confidence gained through martial arts training?

Discovering how your body, mind, and spirit can work for you in achieving goals—whether in martial arts class, at school, or on the job—is the backbone of martial arts training. The martial arts themselves are a process

It's amazing what the martial arts can do for a child's self-esteem, and within a reasonably short amount of time. This quality derives from consistent training.

by which you set goals and learn how to achieve them.

Does martial arts training really help children who have a low self-esteem problem?

It's amazing what the martial arts can do for a child's self-esteem, and within a reasonably short amount of time. This quality derives from consistent training. Even when a child doesn't see the results for her- or himself, the child must be encouraged to continue with the training. Eventually, it will manifest itself in surprising ways.

Why is structure so important in contributing to self-esteem in children?

Children expect to be told what to do; otherwise, they become fearful. Rewarding them when they're good and disciplining them when they're bad is a basic martial arts structure, which will help them develop a pattern of accomplishment.

Will my training give me the confidence to take more chances in life?

Martial arts successes can definitely be carried over into daily life. If, for example, you can see how you've accomplished breaking a board to earn your yellow belt, then why can't you go in and ask for a promotion at work? Understanding that you can accomplish what you set out to do is a great discovery achieved through consistent training.

When will I start to feel better about myself?

You should start feeling better as soon as you put on your uniform and take part in a class. Becoming part of a positive group that has the same goal in mind and is directed by a positive and anchored instructor is a great source of comfort for the soul.

HUMILITY AND DEVELOPING A GOOD ATTITUDE

What does having a good attitude have to do with the martial arts?

A good attitude is the only sign of whether the training is changing a student on the inside as well as on the outside. Internal changes are shown through attitude and appreciation. This attitude should also carry over into the student's daily life.

Why is it important to be humble?

Being humble is the first step to gaining true wisdom. Humility in your accomplishments makes it easy to be humble in your challenges as well.

What exactly does it mean to be humble?

Humility is realizing that we all have more to learn. We don't know it all, and we will never know it all when it comes to martial arts. Realizing that each promotion is just another beginning, regardless of rank, encourages a healthy and humble martial arts attitude.

What are the signs of practicing with humility?

A deep and constant appreciation for your instructor and your art, a willingness to never stop learning, and keeping a meek attitude in spite of your accomplishments all demonstrate sound humility.

DEDICATION AND PERSISTENCE

How do martial arts instill dedication and persistence?

The martial arts instill dedication and persistence by teaching that you can accomplish whatever you set out to do, simply by putting forth the time and effort. Success in martial arts is not an overnight achievement. Everyone starts as a white belt.

What are some examples of dedication and persistence?

Board-breaking teaches both qualities, since the student must keep trying until he or she has successfully mastered the board. Also, each and every advancement of rank proves that the individual has more dedication and more persistence. Those who fall short of promotions yet continue until they master the challenges set before them show the greatest amount of dedication and persistence.

How do these two qualities affect children?

These two qualities prove to children that no personal accomplishment comes easily. In the martial arts, nothing is handed over; all accomplishments are earned. And they cannot be earned without the necessary investment of time and effort.

Can adults achieve dedication and persistence?

Yes, because the more a person sticks with martial arts training, the better he or she gets at it. Compare a white belt's technique to a black belt's. The difference is that the black belt put in the time. Even when things got tough, the black belt persisted, learning how to overcome each challenge.

Will making mistakes hamper my dedication and persistence?

No, because your martial arts training should be teaching you to be patient with yourself as well. Go at your own speed until you get it right. Just don't give up! Not only in martial arts, but in life as well.

How can I become more dedicated and persistent?

First, you must become more patient with yourself. Don't set a time limit for yourself to achieve a certain level. Rome truly was not built in a day, as the old saying goes. You must first be a white belt before you can be a black belt. Second, learn to relax.

RELAXATION

How can I relax when I know I've got to fight in a competition?

You relax by not placing the emphasis on winning or losing. There are no losers when it comes to competitive fighting. Anyone who gets into the ring and fights has already won a major battle within him- or herself.

Will martial arts teach me to relax in my personal life?

Yes. You must realize that once you've learned to master your body, you've already mastered your mind, since right from the start the martial arts are more mental than physical. Also, understanding that great accomplishments were at first difficult for everyone sets an emotional pattern of patience and relaxation.

How can I use my training to help me relax?

Practicing forms is a great way to learn mind-over-body control. The martial arts will teach you to be the master of your mind as well as your body. They also teach correct breathing techniques—a proven physical way to learn how to relax. Finally, meditation, a common practice in most martial arts, is another method to promote mind and body relaxation.

CONTROL AND CONCENTRATION

Is good control achieved through martial arts training?

Yes, because you must learn how to judge your own distance to be effective in the martial arts. Judging distance helps teach good

control, and this is practiced through various sparring techniques. Coordination as well as the understanding of one's own strength are also learned through sparring techniques.

How does martial arts training instill good control and concentration in children?

Forms practice has long been known to bring about both of these qualities. Also, the instructor insists on these two important qualities in young students. When practiced repetitively, these qualities eventually become instinctive.

SPIRITUALITY

What does a person's spirit have to do with training?

The body, mind, and the spirit must all work together to make a person complete. Without spirit, a person's training would have no passion or intensity behind it.

Is having a strong spirit necessary?

Yes, because without it, all essential qualities that martial arts can bring about for a person cannot be achieved. Your spirit is the driving force behind making your training work for you. It's that extra push of power from within, demonstrated by a spirited yell when physical tasks are especially difficult. It's that voice within that drives you to continue, even though every muscle in your body aches.

Do martial arts make a person spiritual?

Yes, but not in a religious sense. It's only natural that when you've accomplished so much with your mind and body, you want to seek the same wholeness with your spirit. The realization that there's so much more than just the physical aspect of the martial arts moves us toward a spiritual path. Martial arts training itself is a very spiritual thing.

How can I learn to be more spiritual with my training?

One way that you can get in touch with your spiritual sense is to meditate before each class. Also, learn to push yourself beyond what you consider your limits to be—not just physically but in your life in general. Finally, always search and always reach for a higher understanding of yourself and your fellow man.

This chapter's author, karate pioneer Jim Harrison of Missoula, Montana, is a man who knows about fear and all of its ramifications. Harrison estimates he has engaged in over one hundred street encounters in his life. A number of them, during his three-year involvement in a special violence squad from 1959–61, were life-and-death confrontations.

10

FEAR AND THE FIGHT-OR-FLIGHT REFLEX

by Jim Harrison

Fear is a natural human emotion that causes a person who's facing imminent danger to have one of two completely opposite—but mutually instinctive—reactions. You either confront the danger head-on, or you run away to totally avoid it. This is the "fight-or-flight reflex."

Fear is a subject of particular importance to martial artists, yet one that has been inadequately addressed and perhaps even grossly overlooked in the field's collective literature. No matter how much of the martial arts you learn or how proficient you become at it, if the time comes for you to face a genuine life-threatening situation, you will experience the two-edged sword of fear—fight or flight—and will be forced to exercise one or the other.

When a person thinks he or she is being threatened, typically the heart pounds like a trip-hammer, and the person becomes short of breath, sometimes to the point of hyperventilation. There is a nausea, often described as "butterflies" in the stomach. Some individuals experience an inability to control their bowels. The degree of emotional and physical intensity varies with each person.

As undesirable as these powerful symptoms may sound, they actually are indicators that the body is ready to perform at its highest level. Both world-class athletes and people who freeze from terror under stress experience the same series of physiological reactions. What determines the success of the outcome is how rapidly the individual is able to either retain or regain control of his or her instrument, mind, and body.

Fear is stimulus-specific. Some people evidence few, if any, of the usual biochemical reactions (as cited above) to life-threatening circumstances. They are considered "fearless."

Yet, even these people have some particular personal situations in which they find it difficult to maintain their composure.

For example, some people are unperturbed by the sounds of gunfire, sirens, and screaming, yet become rubbery-kneed at the sight of a baby's soiled diaper. So the threshold of intense stress varies drastically from person to person.

This topic demands nothing less than straightforward answers from an indisputable expert. Therefore, we have approached one of the world's most fearless warriors, karate pioneer Jim Harrison of Missoula, Montana. This man truly knows about fear and all of its ramifications.

One of the icons of the notorious Blood-'n'-Guts Era of 1960s American karate, legendary fighter Jim Harrison has never pulled a punch in his life—whether in the ring, while running phony black belts out of town, or as a member of a St. Louis, Missouri, special violence squad. Harrison estimates he has engaged in more than a hundred street encounters in his life. A number of them, during his three-year involvement in the special violence squad from 1959 to 1961, were life-and-death confrontations. In this work, he was forced to kill eight criminal assailants and was shot a total of seven times. Incredibly, he survived!

In the early 1970s, as an anti-insurgency team member, Harrison helped lead a search-and-destroy (SAD) team in and out of communist Cambodia. Wounded, captured, and tortured, he and only one other team member were able to escape certain death, while leaving behind a toll of dead Khmer Rouge soldiers.

During competition in the 1960s, Harrison, who stood six feet tall and weighed only 165 pounds, fought in some three hundred judo matches—in the days of no weight divisions. He also fought in some five hundred karate matches, with bare knuckles and bare feet, during the time when a knockout scored only one point and the bout continued when the opponent was revived. Harrison was also the first U.S. light heavyweight kickboxing champion, a title he won in the third round after almost being knocked out himself by knocking out 185-pound Victor Moore, who remained unconscious for twenty minutes.

Although considered fearless by most of his peers, Jim Harrison readily admits to being scared before every match, gunfight, firefight, or battle. In this chapter, he clearly explains what fear is all about and how you can overcome it.

DEFINING FEAR

What exactly is fear?

One dictionary defines fear as "an emotion of alarm and agitation caused by the expectation and realization of danger." However, to fully understand a topic as important as fear, a more technical analysis is required.

A medical dictionary informs us that fear is "*a somatic* [part of the body] disturbance or expression of anxiety [stress], neurosis [nerves], or an anxious psychotic [mental disturbance], which may stimulate *hyperthyroidism*—an excessive condition of glandular secretion by the thyroid." This includes an injection into the nervous system of a *hyperadrenal*, another glandular secretion of hormones, chief among which are epinephrine and norepinephrine—"fight" and "flight" adrenaline, respectively.

This common human condition is what is known as the fight-or-flight reflex (or fight-or-flight instinct or response).

What is flight adrenaline and what does it do to a person?

Flight adrenaline (norepinephrine) is a hormone that's secreted by the adrenal gland when a human being—or any animal, but specifically mammals—anticipates danger. Flight adrenaline greatly increases a person's awareness and alertness.

In addition to making someone considerably more alert and sensitive to the immediate surroundings, it also increases peripheral awareness. To put it simply, it opens up the senses to detect danger. It allows—or actually forces—the person to tune in to danger or the possibility of danger.

Fear is a natural human emotion that causes a person who's facing imminent danger to have one of two completely opposite—but mutually instinctive—reactions: to either run away from the danger to totally avoid it, or to confront it head-on. This is the fight-or-flight reflex. Martial arts student Camille Bristow of St. Petersburg, Florida, displays both reactions in this sequence.
Photo courtesy of the John Graden Archives.

Flight adrenaline fine-tunes a person's receptive and responsive abilities. It especially increases the desire and ability to *avoid* danger, because there is normally less risk in avoiding danger than in confronting it.

An old Zen parable best illustrates the distinction between these two reflexes:

> A Zen master out for a walk with one of his students pointed out a fox chasing a rabbit.
>
> "According to an ancient fable," the master said, "the rabbit will get away from the fox."
>
> "Not so," replied the student. "The fox is faster."
>
> "But the rabbit will elude him," insisted the master.
>
> "Why are you so certain?" asked the student.
>
> "Because" answered the master, "the fox is running for his dinner and the rabbit is running for his life."

What responses does flight adrenaline cause in humans?

Flight adrenaline signals the body to be ready to run. It also enables humans to run earlier and much faster than normal. That's because it is much better to avoid danger than to confront it. In other words, it's better to flee than to fight.

Originally, before human brains evolved to where people could invent and develop auxiliary weapons, the only natural human weapons were teeth and nails, which were very weak weapons. People survived only by avoiding danger and fleeing—running away. Whether you believe it or not, people can actually run much faster when afraid.

Are the desire and ability to flee the only signs of flight adrenaline?

No. A secretion of norepinephrine can also send *false* signals. It will create butterflies in the stomach in mild and medium instances of fear, and nausea and even outright vomiting in more severe cases. It also makes a person feel weak in mild cases, falsely fatigued at medium levels, and sometimes outright exhausted in higher doses. Flight adrenaline can cause different levels of mental confusion, which hinder and curtail the decision-making process, in order to leave no other alternative but to run.

A hard jolt of norepinephrine does everything possible to convince a person that he or she is not capable of fighting.

What is fight adrenaline and how does it affect a person?

Fight adrenaline (epinephrine) is a hormone also secreted by the medulla section of the adrenal gland. Epinephrine, however, works in ways almost entirely opposite of flight adrenaline. It *decreases* a person's peripheral senses and actually focuses, or tunnels, the perceptions and responses.

Fight adrenaline not only triggers emergency senses, but also emergency reflexes, to aid a person whenever he or she cannot, does not, or will not avoid danger. It makes the person quicker and stronger—assets sorely needed to confront and meet danger.

In addition, fight adrenaline greatly increases a person's pain threshold anywhere from mild to superhuman, just as it does a person's strength. It also increases the dysfunctional override capacity: the ability to resist and even aggress after incurring physical damage. Fight adrenaline can allow someone to function despite a dislocated joint or broken bones, after the breath has been knocked out of him or her, or even when that person has been knocked almost unconscious. And, in extreme cases, it allows a person to function, at least temporarily, with severe brain damage.

How can the differences between flight and fight adrenaline be best described?

Here's the best analogy. Flight adrenaline is what rabbits have 99.99 percent of the time. Fight adrenaline is what grizzly bears are imbued with 99.99 percent of the time.

Rabbits are always alert and ready to run. Only the rarest of rabbits, in the rarest of instances, will fight. Even in the most extreme cases—when cornered and being eaten alive—rabbits will simply acquiesce to shock or continue their attempt to escape.

The grizzly very rarely thinks of avoiding danger, much less running from it. Grizzlies have been filmed attacking automobiles! They normally only run to catch or attack a meal. Very rarely will they run to escape. If they do, it's only because of conditioned reflexes such as to run from men with dogs and rifles. And quite often, they won't even run then.

Each human being also has a certain proportional amount of rabbit and grizzly reflexes, obviously in vastly different degrees per individual. The proportion depends completely upon a person's genetic DNA dispersal.

ACCEPTING FEAR

What can an individual do about his or her personal degree of adrenal dispersal or proportion?

Absolutely nothing! In fact, that is the exact reason for the earlier elaboration on the adrenal secretions of norepinephrine and epinephrine.

Each human being has inherited a specific amount of flight and fight adrenaline. Consequently, you must accept your normal reactions to fear, regardless of how desirable or undesirable, or how acceptable or unacceptable it may be to you.

So many people, especially fighters (and even would-be fighters) berate themselves because of their personal "fear factor." Fear factor means those feelings of fear encountered prior to, or at the initial outset of, a confrontation, match, or fight. Although it is normal to feel irritation or disappointment in yourself because of your fear, it is absurd to *blame* yourself for something you have absolutely no control over—something you were either born with or without. That is like berating yourself for not being handsome or beautiful, intelligent, muscular or shapely, tall, or dark- or light-complexioned.

People have inherited all of their physical characteristics, mental faculties, and emotional responses. From the moment the first human ancestor fell out of his tree, through generations of ancestors in everyone's family trees, down to the present population, no one has had any control whatsoever over what traits they have or what they pass on to their children.

Certainly, every parent would give his or her child every desirable asset and attribute they could possibly think of—beauty, brawn, brains, and *bravery*—if they possibly could. They can't, and you can't.

Are people then helpless to change their inherited conditions? Can a person, despite inherited degree of fear, develop more courage than he or she was born with?

What a person does to change, control, or counter any undesirable or unacceptable characteristics he or she was born with is greatly, if not entirely, up to that person. Of course, parents, teachers, and mentors can considerably help guide an individual. Nevertheless, only people themselves can deliver the goods— through desire, discipline, and determination.

If you lack intelligence, for example, you can improve your knowledge through education and determination. If you are physically weak, you can improve your physical structure and strength through hard work and determination. If you lack emotional discipline and fortitude, you can, again, improve your attitude, discipline, and self-control through sheer desire, willpower, and determination.

Determination is based upon desire, in this case the desire to strengthen any inherent weakness, whether internal or external. The degree of passion behind the desire will largely determine the outcome. How badly do you want to improve? And how willing are you to do what it takes to succeed at self-improvement?

Only you can answer those questions.

So does that mean I can learn to control my fear?

Absolutely. Human beings can learn to improve and control almost any characteristic or handicap they have—that is, if they sufficiently desire to and have, or will develop, the will and determination to do so.

OVERCOMING FEAR

As a martial artist or fighter, how can I learn to control my natural fear?

First, you need to understand what you are up against. That, again, is why technical information was provided to initiate this chapter. It's essential for you to understand the problem before you can effect a remedy.

Second, you need to find a solution to the problem. There *is* a solution, and it must be worked at in stages. So third, you must learn the stages that a fighter will normally need to improve his or her level of bravery, and you must then, systematically, follow them.

There are three stages to the process of overcoming natural fear and increasing your courage. But every stage of this solution will be a very difficult challenge for anyone who has not traveled this path before. Of course,

what worthwhile goal in this world isn't difficult?

Where do I start the process of learning to overcome fear?

Stage one starts in the gym, dojo, or studio. The training there should be rugged and demanding, sometimes even brutal and intimidating. And it often *is*, especially so in the case of boxing gyms, judo dojo, and wrestling and sambo halls. In fact, if the training isn't tough and hard, you may as well forget about becoming a real fighter.

Instead, you will simply be and remain a wannabe, with only dreams and wishes. Because in any lesser or weaker atmosphere—found in the run-of-the-mill or average karate, aikido, kung-fu, and taekwondo schools—you will develop a considerably lesser amount of actual fighting ability and warriorlike attitude. Worse, you may develop false confidence. False confidence will always betray you when you need the real warrior's attitude, which is gained only from *true* confidence.

It's very simple. If you want to swim, you will have to get wet. To be a champion swimmer, you will also get tired, cold, and half-drowned—regularly. And if you are forced to swim with sharks, you better be

The first stage in overcoming fear takes place in the martial arts school, where the training should be rugged and demanding. Such training, coupled with other factors, can make the difference between how Denver, Colorado's Karen Eden reacts to an ambush at her vehicle and how St. Petersburg, Florida's Sarah Cunningham reacts.

Photos courtesy, respectively, of Karen Eden and the John Graden Archives.

trained for it as if your very life depends on it—because usually it does!

What would be required of me in that kind of tough training environment?

In the tough gym or dojo, you must attend classes, practice sessions, and workouts regularly and consistently. Don't permit yourself excuses for missing practice, unless your reasons are honest and legitimate (injury, illness).

Preferably, you must train daily, or at least every other day. You must work hard and train hard. You must work through fatigue, discomfort, and all obstacles except potentially disabling injuries and mental stress. Further, you should never slack off.

You must be willing to shed sweat, blood, and even tears.

You should organize a schedule and curriculum that is more demanding than you think you can endure, and stick to it. Then *increase* it. You must *train* yourself to be tough before you can *be* tough. The tougher and rougher you train, the rougher and tougher you will become.

Tough and consistent training is the first step in overcoming fear. Learn to overcome the fear of work, regimentation, discomfort, pain, and frustration. Take any setbacks in stride and overcome them as quickly as possible.

To put it in brutally frank terms, strive to reach the point where you simply cannot, will not, and do not accept failure!

Three stages are cited in this process of overcoming fear. Wouldn't stage one—rugged training—accomplish this alone?

No. Now you must put your training skills to the test. Robin Webb, a former British heavyweight boxing champion and a former sparring partner of Muhammad Ali, once said, "No coward steps into the ring twice." To successfully build courage, you will have to step into the ring for perhaps the first time in your life, and no matter what happens, step into it again and again.

Stage two involves competition on the mat, in the ring, and in the arena. Having the determination to prepare as well as possible, and the fortitude to show up and do the job as well as you can, is the mind-set necessary to overcome your natural, inherited adrenal dispersal—no matter how it is proportioned. It is a matter of mind over fear. Courage!

So after you have prepared (stage one), you must systematically test yourself sometime against a worthy opponent in a competitive environment. That takes courage. Then you must continue to select or challenge more and more worthy opponents. Each time you choose a worthy opponent, it will require more courage of you. But be careful: there's an old saying, "Don't bite off more than you can chew, but don't spit it out if you do!"

What is the third and final stage in this process?

Stage three involves the street or combat zone. Tournaments and ring fights are always planned in advance; you know the date and even the approximate time that you will fight. Consequently, you have plenty of time to think and to worry about the possibility of losing.

Street fights, however, are spontaneous eruptions and consequently you have little if any time to anticipate them and little time for the flight adrenaline to activate. In most self-defense situations, you know only that there is impending danger. If a law-enforcement officer, you usually realize when a combat situation might develop—but not always. In military combat, and certainly with a SAD team, you know that combat is definitely impending; it's just a matter of when.

In police situations and military combat, you also know that there's a very likely chance you will be wounded, crippled, or killed. In the sport ring, of course, the chance of injury, and especially death, is much more remote.

Therefore, two different types of fear are involved in these two different environments. The fear of humiliation and possible injury in the sport context versus the fear of serious injury and possible death in the others. ·

In competition, ring fights to the knockout are more decisive, but they still are conducted with restricting rules and by a referee who can stop the fight. In combat, it's a fight for life or death, with no rules and no referee, only your brains, skill, experience, conditioning, determination, and luck. Without rules, the man with the best ability to improvise, and who will take the greater risk, is usually the winner—providing that Lady Luck doesn't interfere. But even then, you can sometimes outsmart her, or better yet, win her favor with courage and boldness.

You are renowned as a fearless warrior. What do you fear more than anything else?

Although I was touted as being totally fearless by most of my peers, I readily admit being scared before every match, gunfight, firefight, or battle I have engaged in. For some stupid reason, though, I feared losing in competition more than I did dying. I feared the humiliation and self-recrimination of losing a match more than I feared the potential for pain, injury, or even death.

Dying, of course, would have been the ultimate humiliation. But if I had died, I'd have never known that I had lost, would I have? Perhaps I never accepted that I would be the one dying, even though others, including friends or police and military teammates, were dying all around me. I fully realized the possibility, even the probability, of being crippled or killed. Still, I somehow always thought that I would be the killer, not the dead person.

I guess I felt the same way in the ring. I simply was not going to lose, although it was often difficult to totally convince myself of that beforehand. My sheer determination and

Overcoming fear is a matter of courage. Not being afraid is stupid. But to stand and advance into the jaws of fear simply is to conquer first yourself, then your opponent. And conquering your opponent may be easier.

Photo courtesy of John Graden Archives.

fortitude wouldn't allow me to do anything less than my best. Fortunately, my best was always better than my adversary's.

Before matches, I would distress myself over common and even remote possibilities (some stroke of bad luck) that might cause me to lose. But from previous experience, I knew that the instant the match began my anxiety would evaporate. In fact, the prefight demons were often more of a threat than many of my opponents. Not to have overcome these demons, however, would have been more humiliating to me than ever losing.

To me, losing a physical fight could somehow have been accepted; dishonor could not have been!

Where is the turning point in overcoming fear?

In whatever game you play that involves risk, it is essential that you prepare yourself both mentally and physically. However, you must normally push yourself just to enter the game, and that is the critical turning point. You must actually, and perhaps often, force yourself to step on the mat or into the ring, climb out on the wing of a plane, paddle into the rapids, and so on. Basically, you need to take that step from which you simply cannot retreat.

The rest is easy. Because there you are: in the match, in the air, in the canyon, or in the fight. Then you simply do your best to not only survive, but to excel and to win. It just takes that first difficult step, jump, or leap.

Once you take that crucial step you more often than not will find the experience exhilarating. So go for it. Even when you lose or fail, you will feel better for having tried. You will then say to yourself, "I'll do better next time." With that attitude, "next time" will surely come.

Overcoming fear is a matter of courage. Not being afraid is stupid. But to stand and advance into the jaws of fear is to conquer first yourself, then your opponent. And conquering your opponent may be easier.

In the final analysis, fear and courage represent a two-edged sword. One edge compels you to become aware and alert and to prepare. The other edge allows you to succeed against formidable adversaries—especially yourself.

How can I develop an attitude of unadulterated confidence in the ring or in combat?

I don't know that everyone can. I can only relate my experience of how I did it, and how many of my students and the fighters I've coached have also done it. But I do know that unless you try, you will never know if you are one of those people who can or not. You begin by having enough initial confidence in yourself to believe that you are one of those people who can develop unswerving confidence, and you give it your best shot for as long as you can handle it and then longer.

First you begin by initiating the steps set forth earlier. Work out in a tough training hall including a tough instructor or coach, and tough teammates and sparring partners. Compete in sport contests, formal bouts, and matches. Finally, if this is your desire, test your skills, conditioning, attitude, and fortitude on the street in self-defense or in combat.

Like I said before, to learn to swim you're going to have to get wet.

Suppose I'm a relative beginner who trains in the martial arts for fitness and health. Does that mean my skills may never work in a real self-defense situation—because I may or may not freeze out of fear? How can I know?

You can't. The student skydiver who climbs into the airplane, the rookie fighter pilot who takes off on his first sortie, and the beginner boxer climbing into the ring for the first time never knew if they could perform effectively, if at all, that first time. However, most do, and few completely freeze.

In the first place, you won't have any choice in a street confrontation. If you cringe and cower when attacked, you may very well be killed. Therefore, your only chance will be to go for it.

Second, understand that you will not normally perform in a real fight as well as you did in practice. Fear causes you to be emotionally uptight and consequently hinders or restricts your ability to think quickly and accurately. Fear also tightens you up physically and makes your moves—in this case, punches and kicks—stiffer and slower than normal.

There are a rare few, natural fighters who actually "turn on" in real and serious fights or in battle. But even these rare types also draw on their previous practice and experience.

For most people, fear-driven stiffness is totally unavoidable. Only experience will allow you to loosen up. Often, however, as a real fight progresses you will find that you will loosen up, too. Further, the sum total of your training sessions and ring experience will promote self-confidence, which leads to a more relaxed attitude in combat. The less you think about what can happen to you, the more you can focus on what you have to do to defend yourself.

Finally, when another person picks the fight with you or assaults you, that person is the one in the wrong. You are right, and being right, especially feeling right, will empower you immensely. So, in any attack situation, give yourself a big dose of "righteous indignation" and go for it. Don't lose your temper. Keep cool, calm, and collected. And explode into action!

Of course, I can't go out looking for street fights to prove that my martial arts skills are effective. That would be contrary to the self-defensive nature and philosophy of peace practiced throughout the martial arts. So how will I know if my skills will work in real life?

This is a very difficult question to answer—especially today, in this age of convoluted and ambiguous values, rules, and laws. Fortunately, I was raised at the end of an era in which it was considered honorable to—and dishonorable *not* to—challenge any insult or attack, whether it was verbal or physical. Fighting to protect your honor, or someone else's, was as important as fighting to protect yourself physically.

Today, people are rarely allowed to even protect themselves physically because of decisions made by those who control the rules, laws, and courts. Everyone must "turn the other cheek" even if it would be fatal. The law will deal with the perpetrator of the crime—if, of course, they somehow happen to catch *and* convict the culprit. Further, because of the senseless violence, misuse of weapons, and the cowardly "gang mentality" prevalent in today's society, it is extremely dangerous to defend yourself.

I can only speak for myself, and not for anyone reading this. If I'm confronted with a serious threat, I invariably take appropriate and aggressive measures to protect myself—regardless of whatever potential legal or other consequences may result. I can worry about that later, because if I don't win that encounter, I may not have to worry about anything since I could be crippled or dead! I subscribe to the old adage, "I'd rather be judged by twelve than carried by six!"

I suggest avoiding most confrontations. There are simply too many inherent dangers—physical, legal, and civil—to justify fighting nowadays. If, however, you are attacked, you are not only justified to fight back but are forced to. If you wish to live and avoid injury, you have no choice.

When that happens, you can rely only on your martial arts training and ring experience to carry you through and help you survive an attack. If that training has been tough, practical, and realistic, you will, more often than not, prevail. Remember, however, your attitude is more important than your skill.

President Theodore Roosevelt once stated so poignantly, "It's not the size of the boy in the fight. It's the size of the fight in the boy." Truer words were never spoken—and they apply to warriors of all ages and both genders.

America's Bill "Superfoot" Wallace (left) knocks out Germany's Bernd Grothe with a crushing hook kick. Wallace was the first "TV fighter" in professional kickboxing competition.

MARTIAL SPORTS

The great advantage of martial sports is that they offer something for participants of every level from white belt to black belt—in myriad arts and styles. Martial sports can appeal to all age groups and genders. In some of the more popular martial sports, there are divisions for young children all the way up to senior competitors, as well as separate divisions for women. Participants can compete in both amateur and, once sufficiently advanced in skill, professional events.

The wide spectrum of martial sports includes competitions for percussive arts like karate, karate-do, taekwondo, wushu, and kickboxing; for grappling arts like judo, jujutsu, and sambo; for weapons arts like kendo; and for the increasingly popular mixed-discipline combat sports such as shootfighting, shootboxing, valetudo, and no-holds-barred or ultimate fighting.

Furthermore, a number of these events include forms competition to satisfy the tastes of those who prefer aesthetic performance over fighting.

Martial sports date back to the beginning of time when many warring countries created indigenous forms of wrestling. Pankration (a.k.a. pancration), a pre-Christian mix of Greek wrestling, throwing, and kicking, was a popular sport in the ancient Olympic Games. Over the centuries, more and more martial arts were spawned specifically for combative applications. When their use in combat eventually waned, almost all of them were given an innovative competitive dimension by which to safely practice some semblance of the real art.

To martial artists today, these various competitions test their abilities and effectiveness against practitioners of the same style or against those of other styles. To audiences, martial sports, both live and televised, are a form of entertainment that demonstrates exhilarating technique, power, and individual will. To promoters, martial sports—like the no-holds-barred contests, formerly a pay-per-view ratings bonanza—have proved to be very lucrative.

But martial sports haven't always enjoyed commercial success. The United States, for one, had already adopted boxing as its combat sport of choice by the late 1800s. Originally devised in England under the Marquis of Queensbury rules, boxing was considered the top fighting form in the Western world. But after World War II, small groups of Americans started to become familiar with judo, karate, and other martial arts, possibly because they had encountered these styles on the battlefield or where they were stationed in the Orient. That initial interest has led to a virtual explosion of martial arts competitions today. Indeed, for karate competition alone, it is estimated that there are over a thousand tournaments held every year just in the United States.

Most martial sports have a definitive set of rules to ensure that the art aspect remains intact. Even with rules, however, these contests have remained a point of dispute and controversy among different factions of martial artists. Purists feel promoting the sporting aspect of the martial arts obscures the philosophy and true spirit of martial arts training. Legendary karate master Gichin Funakoshi, the acknowledged father of modern karate, once stated that the degradation of the martial arts would be tournament competition.

Some styles refuse to compete against other styles. Others want to find out if their training actually works under pressure. This latter attitude has created a nonstop evolution in modern martial sports, an evolution that has been a hard pill to swallow for rigid traditionalists.

Despite any conflicts, however, it is very clear that martial sports are here to stay, and just as certain that they will continue evolving and offering something for everyone.

Why do boxers and professional wrestlers consistently earn more money fighting than martial artists do?

When the first kickboxing shows were broadcast in the United States on ESPN and network TV, starting in 1974, promoters and fighters were optimistic that the audiences would embrace them as they had boxing. But they didn't. The commercial success of martial sports in the United States seemed elusive.

Although boxing was invented in England, the U.S. has adopted it as its own. It's not considered foreign. Also, boxing's publicity campaigns lead the public to believe that the fights are legitimate. But very rarely do two top fighters in the same weight class compete against each other. Therefore, the outcome to most boxing matches is fairly predictable.

When the outcome of a contest can be controlled, it can be easier for a promoter to build a fighter's record and lengthen a fighter's career. Through careful orchestration, a boxing promoter can suddenly have a fighter who is undefeated and who the public has been indoctrinated to believe is the best, yet hasn't fought tough competition.

The theory is that by controlling the press and marketing this now-popular new top contender against a current "world" champion, the promoter makes more money because the public will subscribe to a pay-per-view program that features familiar participants.

But professional wrestling is different, isn't it? Aren't these matches genuine?

Professional wrestling doesn't pretend to be legitimate. The outcome of the bouts is predetermined, and the ring "combat" is blatantly choreographed for entertainment purposes. Children love pro wrestling's flamboyant personalities and histrionic moves. So do many adults. That's why it pulls enormous ratings and has been called the most profitable overall combat sport.

Then what hinders martial sports champions from earning just as much as pro boxers and wrestlers?

Since the worldwide success of Bruce Lee and other martial art film stars, the public has been trained to believe that martial arts competition should match the fantasy of TV and movies. They have been invariably disappointed. Many times in a televised kickboxing or muay Thai contest, the fighters will fight defensively and strategically. This can be frustrating for a home-viewing audience weaned on the high-flying theatrics of martial art films, the gymnastics of pro wrestling, and the hype of boxing.

ULTIMATE FIGHTING

What is ultimate fighting?

Hatched in the United States in 1993, ultimate fighting is aptly named after the successful pay-per-view event The Ultimate Fighting Championship (UFC). The UFC is very similar to the valetudo competitions held in Brazil. *Valetudo*, when translated from Portuguese to English, means "anything goes."

UFC contests are conducted elimination-style, like karate tournaments, in a fenced-off area called the Octagon. Martial artists of any style are invited to enter these competitions. There are no weight divisions.

The no-holds-barred contests became an instant hit with pay-per-view TV audiences in the 1990s, but also drew stiff criticism of and opposition to the brutality of its matches. Here Ultimate Fighting Championship V winner Dan Severn displays the spirit of an intrepid warrior.
Photo courtesy of Carol Klenfner, SEG Sports.

In recent years, these types of events have come to be known as no-holds-barred competitions.

What are the ways to win in the UFC?

There are five ways: knockout, your corner throws in the towel, the referee stops the fight, disqualification, or submission.

How can a contestant be disqualified in ultimate fighting?

There are three rules of disqualification in the Octagon. No biting, no eye gouging, and no "fish hooking" (tearing the mouth and lips open or apart with the fingers). An infraction of these rules is cause for a warning and then disqualification. Entrance and prize money is also subject to being withheld from a fighter who is disqualified.

What is "tapping out"?

Inside the UFC's Octagon, tapping out is a way to submit or give up when a contestant gets into a position where he feels his match is unwinnable. A fighter who submits is generally regarded with as much respect as the fighter who causes him to tap out. Just stepping into the Octagon is considered a sizable act of courage.

What techniques are most effective in the Octagon?

The plethora of martial arts techniques is showcased in the Octagon. Chokes executed with the arms, legs, or even clothing (such as a gi lapel); hair-pulling; armlocks; leg locks; foot locks; groin shots; head butts; knees; elbows; punches; and kicks have all been legitimately used.

At the first UFC events, grappling generally dominated over stand-up fighting. Most notably, Brazilian jujutsu stylist Royce Gracie won three of the first four events. All of his matches ended via a chokehold or armlock.

But in recent UFC competitions, stand-up fighting and striking has had a huge influence with fighters. UFC VIII champion Don Frye, for example, won all his fights by knockouts!

Do martial artists universally embrace ultimate fighting?

No. Where there is success, there will be opposition. Many traditional martial artists adamantly oppose the UFC. So does a large faction of the boxing community.

Because of the success of ground-fighting in the Octagon, most martial art systems have had to reevaluate their techniques. Many martial artists have openly embraced the inclusion of grappling into their styles. Some, though, have stubbornly resisted. They possibly feel threatened that exposing a weakness in their training might result in an exodus of students to a style that includes some ground-fighting.

How realistic are these mixed-discipline freestyle contests?

These contests seem to divide martial artists into two distinct camps. One says the barbaric nature of these fights is exactly opposite of what the martial arts stand for, namely self-control and respect for others. On the other side are those who claim that the martial arts are about fighting, pure and simple, and that these contests show who is the most effective fighter.

Indeed, these fights have proved that many techniques formerly thought to be the most devastating actually have little effect on a charging opponent. Thus, these events have had at least some positive influence on the technical evolution of martial arts.

Who is John McCain?

Arizona Senator John McCain spearheaded boxing's opposition to ultimate fighting competitions. McCain is a former boxer himself. On NBC's *Dateline* McCain said, "I'm a strong supporter of boxing. I believe that Damon Runyon was correct when he called it 'the sweet science.'"

McCain acknowledges there have been more than three hundred deaths in boxing since 1940. Yet he has spent years mounting an outright ban on no-holds-barred events, even though there have been no deaths in ultimate fighting competitions.

Is ultimate fighting the most extreme martial sport?

No. Hard-core martial artists have always wondered what would happen if there were *no* rules at all. Enter so-called freestyle full contact. Conducted underground, freestyle full contact is similar to ultimate fighting, with one major difference: there are no rules whatsoever.

Biting and eye-gouging are both legal. Because of this, fighters don't usually want to go to the ground and grapple. Many fights end after a single eye poke while both participants are standing.

These competitions usually attract military types like those in Special Forces and mercenaries. There are no weight divisions or drug testing and fighters wear whatever they want, including combat boots. The participants are paid cash.

Full-contact competitions sound like nothing more than street fights. Are they?

Quite simply, these *are* street fights and are usually held by crime bosses for entertainment purposes. Most of these events are illegal, although in the Thai cities of Ubon Ratchathani and Motoban, the local military sanctions freestyle full contact fights for gambling purposes. Many of these contests also occur in Laos and Okinawa.

Not unlike a cockfight, many times a loser will not survive after the contest is over. A similar, albeit fringe, underground circuit seems to be growing in the United States.

What makes the UFC so unique?

Until the inception of the UFC, no martial arts event could rival boxing or wrestling in television ratings or financial profits. Defying all logic, the UFC debuted on pay-per-view television in 1993 without the benefit of a single household-name competitor. Nevertheless, it captured the public's imagination through its rugged format—a no-holds-barred, mixed-style form of combat in an elimination format, the winner of which would earn $50,000.

Over three hundred thousand U.S. households have consistently paid to view the UFC events. And although the purses for UFC winners, so far, pale in comparison to boxing, public interest in these types of no-holds-barred events continues to grow.

SEMI-CONTACT KARATE

What is semi-contact karate competition?

More commonly referred to as "point karate," the main objective in this type of fighting is to encourage safe, fun, and exciting competition for both adults and children. Clearly, the goal is not to hurt the opponent, but to strike him or her with a controlled blow that could have caused damage if it was meant to do so.

What are the rules for semi-contact karate competition?

In semi-contact fighting, the rules are simple. Both competitors must report to the ring in the appropriate uniforms and equipment when their names are called. The matches are run by a referee and two to four corner judges. The referee has the power to issue warnings and penalty points without the consent of the other judges.

Semi-contact matches consist of two minutes of actual running time. The first competitor to reach five points, or the one with the most points at the end of regulation time, wins.

A point is defined as any legal technique that strikes the body (not the back), face, or head with control and focus. Legal techniques include all hand strikes using a part of the hand covered by approved safety equipment, and all kicking techniques. No takedowns are allowed, but a person may grab an opponent's leg or arm for one second to offset his or her balance or to deliver a blow or kick.

After a technique strikes a legal target area, the referee stops the action and calls for a point. Then a majority vote from the judges determines if a point is awarded. In most tournaments, adults are awarded two points for a kick and one point for a legal hand technique. The level of contact is light to the head and medium to the body. However, in the under–black belt childrens' divisions, all successful techniques are awarded one point and no face contact is allowed, just light contact to the headgear.

What divisions are available in semi-contact karate?

Nationally rated events, such as those promoted by the North American Sport Karate Association (NASKA), are required to have at least 129 divisions. These include divisions

Forms competition is similar to a mix of Olympic gymnastic floor exercises and prearranged shadowboxing. Nine-year-old Ashley Lane exhibits the drama and intensity of forms competition en route to winning the junior weapons title at the Texas Challenge National Karate Championships in Houston, Texas.

Photo by Ray Galicia; courtesy of Al Garza.

for forms, sparring, and weapons, and cover every possible age group and rank from six-year-old beginners to forty-five-year-old black belts. This kind of variety is offered in order to provide the fairest possible competition for all participants involved.

What is forms competition?

A form is a choreographed set of martial arts moves performed without a partner, and it is the aesthetic aspect of karate and wushu competitions. Forms competition is similar to a mix of Olympic gymnastic floor exercises and prearranged shadowboxing. The moves are usually performed to music and scored by a panel of judges on a ten-point system. Forms competition also has separate weapons divisions.

Frequently, forms champions make a smoother transition into the movie business than do fighters, because their precision and control is tailor-made for film and TV fight choreography.

Is there a single national American karate championship?

While there are some very large open tournaments (anything over five hundred competitors is considered a very large American competition), no individual event has universal recognition as the single ultimate national championship. The United States has many different martial arts organizations, some big and some small. They often conduct tournaments with names like National and World attached to their titles, but these tournaments are sometimes held in an elementary-school gym somewhere in small-town America.

The deciding factor is not the name of the event, but the number of nationally recognized black belt competitors who show up. This is a good gauge of the tournament's prestige.

Who decides the nationally recognized competitors and champions?

There are many so-called rating systems for American karate tournaments. The two oldest that have the recognition of most competitors themselves are NASKA and the National Blackbelt League (NBL).

This doesn't mean that all other rating systems are inferior or unprofessional; but they are more likely to be regional than national in scope.

What is an open karate tournament versus a closed competition?

Open tournaments are exactly that. They are open to anyone of any art or style who wants to enter: karate, taekwondo, kung-fu, it doesn't matter. Whoever can afford the entry fee can compete.

Closed tournaments are held exclusively for the members of a particular school, style, or organization. Many groups do not choose to compete openly with other schools. Critics say it is because they do not want to risk defeat or a perception of having inferior techniques. While that sometimes might be the case, most teachers who advocate closed tournaments do not like the frequent bickering and lack of courtesy and sportsmanship found in too many open tournaments.

Closed tournaments permit tighter control, which provides a disciplined environment and fosters attitudes of camaraderie and sportsmanship over winning and losing.

Should the average student competitor care if the tournament is open or closed, rated or not?

No. Unless you are a black belt trying to gain rating points for an achievement award from a particular sanctioning group, your goal in a competition should be to test your abilities against others of your same level of training. Tournaments should be an enjoyable way to learn and practice your martial arts skills among your peers.

Are there many injuries to participants in semi-contact karate tournaments?

Considering the nature of karate—kicking and punching at each other's vital spots—there are surprisingly few injuries in a typical well-run point-karate competition. Protective sparring pads for the hands and feet have greatly reduced the possibility of injury, and the rules generally prohibit any kind of face contact for children and beginning students.

When was the first karate tournament held in America?

Although there were earlier tournaments, most historians cite the 1st World Karate Tournament in Chicago in 1963 as the first important and national-caliber event, because it drew a number of high-quality black-belt competitors from around the country.

Other important events soon followed. In 1964, Jhoon Rhee held his first tournament in Washington, D.C., the U.S. Nationals, and that same year, Ed Parker promoted his first competition, the International Karate Championships, in Long Beach, California.

Today, karate tournaments are held throughout the country almost every weekend. One estimate, combining both major and minor events, placed the average number of annual U.S. karate tournaments at over a thousand.

Why aren't karate tournaments broadcast on network television?

Back in the 1960s, ABC-TV's *Wide World of Sports* taped a couple of karate tournaments, but some of the matches during this Blood-'n'-Guts Era were deemed too violent and bloody for the network to broadcast, so they suspended their coverage of the sport. Although competitors soon cleaned up their acts through the institution of safer rules, network executives didn't think the public would take to karate competition. The nature of sport karate's "pulled blows" often confuses spectators and leaves unanswered the question of whether or not a point was clearly scored. It is therefore difficult for a viewer to determine who is winning a match.

That reasoning turned out to be somewhat prophetic because, even today, most of the spectators attending a typical live American karate tournament are composed of the competitors' families and friends. Karate might never become a true spectator sport.

Why aren't karate tournaments more popular?

That question has been debated for decades as promoters have tried to come up with various hooks for gathering interest in American karate. Point-karate competition, while exciting for the competitors, has often left spectators bewildered, wondering who scored what, as mentioned earlier.

For many, the answer was full-contact karate (a.k.a. kickboxing), which was launched as a televised sport in 1974. Here, the fighters were allowed to go for the knockout, something the public was familiar with from years of televised boxing matches.

What is karate-do competition?

Karate-do competition is similar to semicontact karate competition, except the participants are primarily athletes from traditional Japanese and Okinawan styles. Karate-do contests feature both forms (kata) and fighting (*kumite* or free-sparring) competitions.

What are the rules for karate-do competition?

Karate-do competition is different from other forms of sport karate, for instance, semicontact, because its rules and decorum are based on traditional Japanese and Okinawan karate. A traditional karate gi must be worn, and a large emphasis is placed on good sportsmanship and manners. Most matches take place on an unenclosed mat.

In kumite, the bare-knuckled competitors are permitted to deliver full-contact punches or kicks to the body and controlled punches to the head. Full-contact kicks are

Karate-do competition is populated by athletes from primarily traditional Japanese and Okinawan styles. In this photo from the fifth World Shoto Cup Karate Championships in Philadelphia, Belgium's Jeannot Mulolo fires a beautifully executed hook kick that's blocked by South Africa's Pavlo Protopapa.
Photo courtesy of the fifth World Shoto Cup Karate Championships.

also allowed to the head since this dramatically increases the degree of difficulty for the fighters. Sweeps, takedowns, and leg kicks are usually permitted as well, and some tournaments even allow kicking to the groin.

The reverse punch, front kick, and backfist are frequently used techniques in karate-do contests. Although these are three of the most basic techniques and appear simple to defend against, karate-do fighters deliver them with a pile-driver force that can be extremely difficult to block or deflect.

In a typical karate-do match, the referee will halt the action and award a point when a clean, focused strike is achieved. Karate-do contestants develop *kime* (focus) and usually try to strike one target at a time. Unless a knockout occurs, the match is won by the first participant achieving three points.

In Thailand, Muay Thai is the equivalent of pro football or pro baseball in the United States. It is the national sport of Thailand. One of the most rugged ring sports in the world, fighters are permitted to kick, knee, punch, and elbow anywhere on the body except the groin.

Photo courtesy of Master Toddy.

KICKBOXING

What is muay Thai?

Muay Thai, also known as Thai kickboxing, is revered as one of the most brutal martial sports because it allows contestants to kick, knee, punch, and elbow anywhere on the body except the groin.

Its origins date back over a thousand years, but the first Muay Thai matches fought in a ring, with boxing gloves and under the ten-point-must scoring system, were held in 1935. The length of all Muay Thai fights is five rounds of three minutes each, and a referee is present. Traditional Thai music is played during the bout.

Muay Thai seems like a very tough sport. Is it popular?

In Thailand, Muay Thai is the equivalent of pro football or pro baseball in the United States. It is the national sport of Thailand. Muay Thai champions adorn major billboards and are sought after to endorse major products. Since it's deeply embedded in the culture, Muay Thai can be seen almost every night on Thai television.

Gambling is a large part of this sport. At Lumpini or Rajadamnern stadiums, the two meccas of Muay Thai, the audience is free to stand and place cash bets among themselves before each fight and even before each round. This takes on a look not unlike the New York Stock Exchange during heavy trading.

What are some frequently used techniques in Muay Thai?

Front push kicks, roundhouse kicks, low kicks (leg kicks), and knee and elbow strikes are all permitted. Techniques are usually delivered at full power, occasionally sacrificing grace for brute force. The Thai roundhouse kick usually is thrown to go *through* the target.

Even though the techniques are few in number, their effectiveness is legendary. The training is the difference: repetition and drills of single moves are prioritized over multiple, flashy techniques.

What is the difference between full-contact karate and kickboxing?

They are basically the same thing. Some promoters liked the name kickboxing better because it tied into the popularity of the sport of boxing. Also, Muay Thai had already been called kickboxing by the time full-contact karate was created in 1974.

Traditional karate instructors accepted the name full-contact karate because, back when the bouts were often sloppy and technically unrefined, it didn't give the "art" of karate a bad name.

By the 1990s, kickboxing became the standard name of the sport. Today, many kickboxing events are held, not only in the United States, but also throughout the world.

What is "clinch fighting?"

In Muay Thai, fighters are allowed to continue fighting after they have grabbed hold of each other and are into a clinch. A fighter's objective in clinch fighting is to gain control of the upper torso or neck of the opponent. Also referred to as neck wrestling, this allows a fighter to manipulate the foe off balance and deliver knee strikes to the body and head.

What is the wy kru?

The *wy kru*, or *ram muay*, is the ceremonial dance that all Muay Thai competitors perform before a bout. Traditional Thai music is played during the dance as well as during the fight itself. The wy kru is stylized to pay tribute to the instructor and gym the fighter represents.

Who is known to have the strongest kicks in Muay Thai?

Perhaps surprisingly, it's not a champion competitor, but one of its most famous coaches, Master Toddy of Las Vegas, Nevada.

According to John Corcoran, this book's coauthor, "During a magazine photo session, I watched Master Toddy kick a large muscular student holding a banana bag completely *off his feet* about six feet backward! He proceeded to do this several times, and each time he used only a waist-level roundhouse kick! Bruce Lee used to do the same thing, but he used a side kick, which is easier."

Master Toddy has trained thirty-six world kickboxing champions from fifteen countries. This accomplishment is even more remarkable because most of these fighters won world championships within one year of starting their training and in less than ten fights.

Who is Samart?

Samart Payakarun is widely regarded to be the Muay Thai equivalent of Muhammad Ali. He not only was dominant in Muay Thai, but also held a world title in Western boxing, in the World Boxing Council. Whereas most Thai fighters stand directly in front of their opponents and duke it out, Samart was one of the few champions who extensively used ring movement.

Do foreigners compete successfully in Muay Thai?

Yes and no. Generally, bouts held in Thailand are won by Thais. They have been involved in this form of competition from an early age—sometimes as young as six years old—so this stands to reason. Lumpini Stadium champions are considered to be among the most dangerous stand-up fighters in the world.

Occasionally, a former Thai champion will be defeated when fighting abroad. This usually happens when his career is over in his homeland, and he gets offers to fight in other countries. The government controls Muay Thai fights in Thailand and frowns on current champions, in their peak, fighting outside of Thailand. So if a person wants to fight the best Muay Thai fighters, that person has to do it in the sport's native country, Thailand.

There is a tremendous amount of pressure on the Thai fighter when a *farang* (foreigner) challenges him on his home soil. The Thai is expected to win. Losing is just short of dishonor.

Have foreigners defeated Muay Thai champions in Thailand?

Yes. On a few rare occasions there have been documented cases when foreign fighters, such as America's Don "the Dragon" Wilson (who's also a martial arts film star), were subjected to a last-minute weight-class change, having to lose as much as eight pounds on the same day of their fight in Thailand. This type of handicapping slants the outcome toward the local competitors. Wilson, an intrepid warrior, nevertheless won.

Other fighters, like internationally respected Ramon Dekker of the Netherlands, have found it nearly impossible to win a decision by points in Thailand, even without weight tampering. If a foreigner wants to win in Thailand, he usually has to do it by a knockout.

In which other countries is Muay Thai popular?

Japan and a number of European countries—especially Holland, which has produced several legendary champions like Rob Kaman, Ernesto Hoost, Peter Aerts, as well as top Muay Thai gyms like Chakuriki, Vos, and Miero.

What is the world's foremost amateur kickboxing organization?

The World Association of Kickboxing Organizations (WAKO), founded in 1973, today has eighty-four member countries and has sanctioned hundreds of both amateur and professional kickboxing events.

Headquartered in Milan, Italy, WAKO offers more variety of competitions than any other martial-arts sanctioning body in the world. Its sanctioned events offer semi-contact fighting, semi-contact continuous fighting, musical forms (forms done to musical accompaniment), conventional kickboxing, and kickboxing with permissible leg kicks. All but the leg-kick competitions are offered for both male and female athletes.

WAKO's pro division has individual world champions by weight class in both male and female divisions.

KUNG-FU AND WUSHU

Are there exclusive kung-fu competitions?

Yes. In North America, several exclusively kung-fu tournaments are conducted every year, and some large-scale competitions are held every other year. Most of these are very well-organized and attended, since for years kung-fu athletes had to compete as the minority in open martial arts events. Every year, the numbers at the all-Chinese-style events grow.

Is Chinese kung-fu an Olympic sport?

Kung-fu is not an organized sport internationally. Two major organizations, the International Wushu Federation (IWF) in Beijing and the International Chinese Kuoshu Federation in Taiwan, are in the process of developing an international body of countries to create world-class competition.

The IWF has made substantial progress. Its congress contains over fifty-five countries and regions as members, and it has a working relationship with the International Olympic Committee. Most Chinese-style practitioners have high hopes that one day wushu will be included in the Olympic Games.

Are there world kung-fu championships?

Any tournament can use the titles World, International, or even Intergalactic. Inflated titles are common in martial sports. Competitions that truly represent the international level of kung-fu have been held in China, Taiwan, Malaysia, and the United States. Since the early 1980s, the standard of these events has risen substantially.

Has wushu been included as a demonstration or competitive event at any international sports festival or competition?

Yes. The Asian Games have listed wushu as a competitive event numerous times, and wushu was demonstrated for the first time in the Western Hemisphere at the 1936 Berlin Olympics. The Pan American Wushu Federation is planning a campaign to have wushu included in the Pan Am Games in the near future.

What are the events contested in a wushu tournament?

There are three distinct categories of events:

The first category is competition *taolu* (routines), which include *changquan* (long fist), *nanquan* (southern fist), *taijiquan* (tai-chi fist), *daoshu* (broadsword play), *jianshu* (swordplay), *gunshu* (staff play), and *qiang-shu* (spear play). There are both compulsory and optional routines in various tournaments. Sometimes added are *nandao* (southern sabre), *nangun* (southern staff), and *taijijian* (tai-chi swordplay). Competition routines have been created for four major styles of tai-chi boxing as well, including *chen*, *yang*, *wu*, and *sun* styles.

The second category, exhibition taolu, includes routines of other types, such as two- or three-person sparring routines, group routines, traditional boxing styles, and traditional weapons routines. Some tournaments open separate divisions for each of these. For example, they have a flexible weapons division for three-sectional staff, nine-section whip, rope dart, and so on.

Third, *sanshou*, also called *sanda*, is full-contact free-sparring according to various rules. The bout takes place on a padded platform, and contestants win points for throws, strikes, and kicks, and knocking the opponent either off the platform or unconscious.

What countries have been successful in international wushu competitions?

The Chinese, of course, have dominated international tournaments since their inception. However, in recent years several other countries have begun to develop world-class athletes. Some of these include Japan, Hong Kong, Chinese Taipei, Malaysia, Macao, the Philippines, Singapore, Korea, Vietnam, Britain, Canada, and the United States.

Are the rules for wushu competition the same at every event?

A very detailed set of rules and requirements for competition has been drafted by the IWF in Beijing, and an even more comprehensive set of rules is used in Chinese national wushu tournaments. The former is the template for most events outside China, although these rules vary depending on the level of the event. So a grassroots-level competition might not enforce the requirement for length and weight of weapons, whereas in the Chinese national tournaments, such details can make or break an athlete's chances.

The International Chinese Kuoshu Federation in Taiwan has a list of rules for competitions. These rules, however, are not very detailed, with the exception of the rules for *leitai*, the Kuoshu equivalent of sanshou—full-contact fighting on a platform.

How is scoring for taolu conducted?

Five judges observe the athlete's performance of a routine and assign scores based on the number of deductions, which are determined by the standard set of rules for that particular event—long fist, for example. The high and low scores are dropped, and the three remaining scores are averaged. This average score is then adjusted by the chief judge, who deducts points for unconformity in opening and closing forms, over or under the time specifications, and re-performance for whatever reason.

MISCELLANEOUS COMPETITIONS

What is judo?

Judo is an Olympic sport and a martial art that was founded by Dr. Jigoro Kano in 1882. Principally a throwing and grappling art, judo competition allows no striking.

Judo competitions are conducted on mats, and the contests are officiated by one referee and two judges. Matches, on an international level, are four minutes in duration for women and five minutes for men.

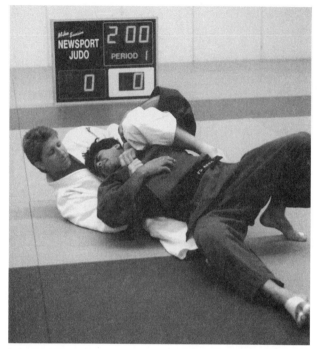

Judo is an Olympic sport and a martial art that is principally a throwing and grappling art. In judo competition, no striking is allowed. Here Mike Swain of Campbell, California, performs a judo pinning technique.

Photo courtesy of Mike Swain.

The object in a judo match is to score an *ippon* (one point), the equivalent of a pin in wrestling or a knockout in kickboxing. An ippon is awarded for either throwing an opponent onto his or her back for thirty seconds or by using a submission hold to cause surrender. An ippon scores one full point and constitutes an automatic victory. If an ippon is not achieved, cumulative points decide the match.

How are judo matches scored?

The scoring system in judo also awards a half point for a *wazaari*, which is the term used to describe a successful throw with lesser impetus than an ippon. A competitor can also receive a quarter point for a *yuko* and an eighth point for a *koka*, depending on the level of technical quality demonstrated. In addition to an ippon, a combination of two wazaaris constitutes an automatic victory.

Should a match end with no score or in a tie, the winner is determined by a majority vote as decided by the referee and judges, based upon the athletes' performances. This type of decision is similar to an award made at the conclusion of a boxing match when there is no knockout, with the more aggressive and dominant athlete being awarded the win.

What is kendo?

Kendo means the "way of the sword" in Japanese. Founded by the samurai of ancient Japan, kendo is the art of Japanese fencing. It develops the mental and physical skills necessary for sword-fighting while using a *shinai* (bamboo sword) instead of a live blade.

Kendo practitioners require a variety of protective equipment when they compete. Their armor consists of four different parts. *Men* is the helmet that protects the face, throat, and top and sides of the head. *Do* is similar to a breastplate and covers the chest and stomach. *Tare* is the waist protector. Finally, *kote* resemble gauntlets that protect the hands and wrists.

What are the rules for kendo competition?

In kendo, there are four general areas that practitioners try to strike on both the left and right sides of the body. Each of these vital targets is worth one point when struck and include the head, wrist, torso, and throat. In order to be considered successful, the attack is to be a coordination of spirit, proper sword usage, and correct body movement.

An official kendo match is a three-point bout with a five-minute time limit. Typically, kendo tournaments are held in direct-elimination form. Three referees judge whether or not a point is scored, and the first player who scores two points wins the contest. If neither player scores two points before the end of regulation time, then the one who is in the lead at the end of the match is declared the winner. If the score is tied after five minutes, an infinite sudden-death overtime is held until a winner emerges.

What is sumo?

Sumo is the traditional national sport of Japan. Each year six Grand Sumo tournaments held, in each odd-numbered month. Three are held in the capital, Tokyo, and one is held in each of the cities of Osaka, Nagoya, and Fukuoka.

The sport is noted for the gargantuan size of its participants, who sometimes weigh over five hundred pounds. The sport is professional in nature, and champions earn a substantial living.

What are the rules for sumo competition?

In the sport of sumo, there are only a few things to know. Each match consists of two wrestlers, standardly of gargantuan size and weight, wearing thick silk belts around their waists. Meeting in a ring that is 4.55 meters across, their objectives are to force the opponent out of the ring, or to make any part of the opponent's body (except the soles of the feet) touch the playing surface. The competitors are permitted to push, slap, trip, and throw. They are not allowed to pull hair, gouge eyes, or strike with a closed fist.

The matches are overseen by a referee and several judges who ultimately decide the winner. Normally, these bouts are very brief, averaging only a few seconds in length. However, some matches actually go on for two or three minutes.

At the end of a bout, the competitors stand on their sides of the ring and lower their heads to each other. Customarily, the loser exits the ring first. The winner stays behind to express his gratitude to the three gods of creation. He does so by swiftly swinging his hand in the four cardinal points while crouching on his heels before the referee's paddle. He then receives a white envelope containing a predetermined monetary reward.

What is the sumo lifestyle like?

Sumo is very much a way of life as well as a sport. The practitioners lead a very regimented existence and most daily activities occur in order of rank. They live communally in a lifestyle that is completely dedicated to the sport. In the life of a sumo wrestler, there is little time off.

They begin their day in the early morning with a practice session, and then start their assigned duties, which include cooking and cleaning the commune. Throughout the day, they train, eat, and nap. In the evening, they are permitted to enjoy some personal freedom outside of the barracks up until the time of their curfew.

They wear distinctive clothing, eat certain meals, and must be role models for their country all year round.

What is sport sombo?

Sport *sombo* (a.k.a. sambo), otherwise known as jacket wrestling, is a type of wrestling that was officially created in the USSR (Union of Soviet Socialist Republics) on November 16, 1938. The first national championship was held the following year.

Sport sombo actually started some years earlier as an intermilitary sporting event, and then it underwent a transition into a safer, more competitive activity—similar to the way jujutsu evolved into judo in Japan.

A sombo competitor's uniform (*kurtka*) consists of a red jacket, red shorts, a red belt, and a pair of soft-soled wrestling shoes. This same combination can also be worn in blue. The jacket is made of a heavy canvaslike material, and the sleeves must extend down to the wrists. On each shoulder is a cuff for gripping. The jacket must be tight-fitting and can't extend more than eight inches below the belt.

The belt must pass through at least one of two loops sewn onto the jacket to keep it in place during the match. The trunks must also be tight-fitting and cover at least one-third of the hip.

Sport sombo is a type of wrestling that was officially created in the USSR. It is a grappling sport with many possibilities for joint-locks, throws, and a variety of submission holds, as demonstrated here by Milwaukee, Wisconsin's Adrian Serrano (foreground).

Photo courtesy of Adrian Serrano.

What are the rules in sport sombo?

In sport sombo no striking is allowed. This defaults to a grappling fight with many possibilities for joint-locks, throws, and a variety of submission holds. The matches are six min-utes in length for adults and less for children. If the match time expires without a submission, the contestant with the most points wins.

What is a total victory in sombo?

In sombo, *total victory* is the term used when one of the wrestlers executes a maneuver that is worthy of an instant win. For example, when one of the players executes a perfect throw causing the opponent to land flat on his or her back, that player automatically wins the match. This also occurs when one of the wrestlers successfully applies a submission hold to the elbow, knee, or ankle. However, in sombo competition, no choke holds are allowed.

Finally, if one of the competitors gains twelve technical points in excess of his opponent's total, or when one of the wrestlers becomes injured, forfeits, or gets disqualified, a total victory is awarded.

How are points scored in sombo?

At the beginning of the match, both contestants start on their feet. Points can be scored through throws and hold-downs. If the aggressor remains standing, a throw to the buttocks, shoulders, or chest scores two points. A throw to the side yields four points.

If the aggressor falls during the throw, one to four points will be awarded, depending on the positioning of the landing. If the opponent is lifted off the mat and thrown while the aggressor remains standing, then two points are awarded. If the aggressor falls during this type of throw, only one point is given.

During a sombo match, a competitor can only score points from a hold-down once. If the opponent is held down on his or her back (torso-to-torso) for ten seconds, two points are awarded. A twenty second hold-down in this manner yields four points. During a hold, if the opponent slides off the mat, two points are awarded to the aggressor.

What is sport savate?

Savate ("boot" or "shoe" in French) is a French martial art and sport that has many elements in common with certain Asian martial art systems and even American boxing. Sport savate promotes three categories of competition that are analogous to American sport karate tournaments: light-, medium-, and full-contact matchups.

Light-contact savate is akin to point tournaments. Medium-contact savate resembles semi-contact continuous fighting competition. Fighters wear protective gear and decisions are based on a cumulative point total; knockouts are prohibited.

The final stage is full-contact savate and this resembles Americanized kickboxing, even insofar as the exclusion of knees, elbows, and head butts—techniques still present in the nonsport version of savate.

What types of kicks are used in savate contests?

As befits a fighting method based upon kicking, savate exhibits a tremendous variety of kicks and kick deliveries. Since shoes are worn, the tip of the shoe is a common striking point, yet the heel, edge, and instep are also used.

Front-leg kicks are snapped out and used as jabbing and probing blows. The side kick is also a favorite weapon for this feeling-out process. Low kicks are much more frequent than high head kicks, which are used primarily as a feint to gauge an opponent's reaction.

Occasionally, savateurs will initiate their attacks with a high kick, only to target the legs with the downward trajectory of the missed kick.

What is shootboxing?

Popular predominantly in Japan, shootboxing is a combination of kickboxing and judo. Points are awarded for punching, kicking, and throwing. Knee blows are also legal. The length of a bout is five five-minute rounds. Fighters wear tights, shin and knee protectors, and boxing gloves.

What is shootfighting?

Also known as shootwrestling and pankration, shootfighting is a mixture of kickboxing, judo, and professional wrestling. Contests are held in a traditional boxing ring with a referee present. A bout's length varies, depending on the organization and importance of the fight. There is no punching or elbowing to the head. Open-handed strikes are allowed, as are kicks to the legs, body, and head.

Actors Ralph Macchio (left) and Noriyuki "Pat" Morita in a scene from the 1984 box-office blockbuster *The Karate Kid.* This gem of a picture, written by real-life black belt Robert Kamen, was a major breakthrough in the depiction of the philosophic and human-development aspects of the martial arts. Morita won an Oscar nomination for his role, and the picture caused a massive influx of kids into martial arts schools that has continued up to the time of this writing.

MARTIAL ARTS IN ENTERTAINMENT

Since the film and TV mediums portray a wide variety of subject matter and historical time periods, it was only a matter of time before the martial arts made an appearance. And since the martial arts originated in Asian culture, it would only follow that they were showcased first in Eastern cinema as far back as the 1920s.

Martial arts sequences, typically as unrefined rough-and-tumble fights, occasionally found their way into early Western films and TV shows, but it was not until Bruce Lee exploded onto American television in *The Green Hornet* in 1966 that U.S. audiences really sat up and took serious notice of the martial arts. With the high-quality production of the TV series *Kung Fu* and the profitable releases of *Five Fingers of Death* and *Fists of Fury* in the early 1970s, a new genre had been born in the United States: the martial arts movie.

Martial arts films spread like wildfire, and the new genre found great success in the early and mid-1970s before its popularity waned. Karate champion Chuck Norris then stepped into the martial arts movie spotlight and drove the genre strongly into the 1980s. Since then, stars such as Steven Seagal, Jean-Claude Van Damme, Jackie Chan, Don "the Dragon" Wilson, and Cynthia Rothrock, among others, have kept martial arts movies alive and kicking.

The martial arts movie genre today boasts a long and successful track record. From 1971, when *Billy Jack* became a surprise runaway hit, martial arts films—combined with action films starring martial artists—have grossed an estimated $2 billion at the worldwide box office.

A few—like *The Karate Kid I, Karate Kid II, Under Siege, Rush Hour,* and *Mortal Kombat,* among others—became blockbusters, grossing over $100 million each by the time they completed their global theatrical run. And that figure does not take into account all the various ancillary revenues that multiply each picture's profits, stemming from lucrative markets such as pay-per-view, video rentals, cable-TV broadcast, and so on.

Today, audiences are more sophisticated and demanding about fight action. So it is only inevitable that the Asian martial arts have replaced the old-fashioned Western brawls and unrefined fisticuffs of earlier eras. When it comes to films and television, the martial arts are definitely here to stay.

What is a martial arts movie?

There are two schools of thought on what exactly a martial arts movie is. One definition is that it is a film that deals with the art and philosophy of war and fighting. By this strict definition, films like *Rocky* or *Sands of Iwo Jima* can be considered martial arts films.

Another more popular definition is that a martial arts film deals with the arts and philosophies of the Asian fighting disciplines. For the purposes of clarity and brevity, the questions and answers in this chapter will adhere to this latter definition.

In which film were the martial arts seen for the first time?

The martial arts were first featured in *Jiu-Jitsu, the Japanese Art of Self Defense.* This American-produced silent film, by American Mutoscope and Biograph, was made in 1901 by director F. S. Armitage (who also directed a number of documentaries and short subjects) and starred J. J. O'Brien.

Which other silent films featured the martial arts?

Some other silent films that featured martial arts sequences are *Japanese Warriors in Ancient Battle Scenes* (1904, made by Thomas Edison's Edison Company), *Lady Athlete, or The Jiu Jitsu Owns the Footpads* (1907, Great Britain), *Lessons in Jiu Jitsu* (1918, France), *A Dangerous Affair* (1919, starring Herbert Rawlinson), *Peggy Does Her Darndest* (1919, starring May Allison), *Outside Woman* (1921), and Hong Kong silent films such as *Thief in the Car, The Burning of the Red Lotus Temple* (1929), and *How Wu Song Killed His Sister-in-Law* (1927).

What was the first film to feature an actual fight?

Thomas Edison made the first actual fight film in the United States in 1894. The film featured a boxing match between "Gentleman" Jim Corbett and Peter Courtney.

Which famous literary sleuth was a martial arts practitioner?

Sherlock Holmes was an expert in the fictional art of *baritsu* (a style very much like jujutsu, according to Holmesian historians). Holmes uses this art in several of his adventures, starting with *The Final Problem* in 1903. Holmes also got to display baritsu in the 1965 film *A Study in Terror* (starring John Neville).

Which famous Asian sleuth routinely used the martial arts in his 1930s film adventures?

Peter Lorre played the Japanese sleuth Mr. Moto in a number of 1930s film adventures. Moto was a jujutsu expert who displayed his skills in *Thank You, Mr. Moto* (1937), *Think Fast, Mr. Moto* (1937), *Mr. Moto's Gamble* (1938), *Mr. Moto Takes a Chance* (1938), *Mysterious Mr. Moto* (1938), *Mr. Moto's Last Warning* (1939), *Mr. Moto in Danger Island* (1939), and *Mr. Moto Takes a Vacation* (1939).

Which early American movie star held a legitimate black belt in judo?

Oscar-winning actor James Cagney was a certified black belt in the Japanese art of judo

and used it in a number of his films, including *Blood on the Sun* (1945), *13 Rue Madeleine* (1946), *White Heat* (1949), and *Never Steal Anything Small* (1959).

What was the first film on the Western screen to feature the ninja?

The ninja was first featured on the Western screen in the 1967 James Bond adventure *You Only Live Twice*. Bond (Sean Connery) is trained in the art of *ninjutsu*, the art of feudal assassination, and he and a group of modern "ninja commandos" lay siege to the evil villain Blofeld's secret volcano hideout.

Connery studied karate with the late legendary master Mas Oyama for his work on this film and was awarded an honorary black belt by Oyama for his promotion of karate through film. Also of interest to martial arts buffs, it was the late celebrated author and martial arts master Donn F. Draeger who doubled for Connery in some of the action scenes.

Which James Bond films showcased the martial arts?

The character James Bond, Agent 007, is a trained martial artist who applies his skills in each film. However, the martial arts were showcased to a larger degree in *From Russia*

With Love (1963), Goldfinger (1964), You Only Live Twice (1967), The Man With the Golden Gun (1974), and Moonraker (1979).

Which James Bond actor made several martial arts films in Hong Kong?

George Lazenby, who played James Bond in On Her Majesty's Secret Service (1968), later traveled to Hong Kong to make the martial arts films Stoner (1974, with Angela Mao Ying) and The Man From Hong Kong (1977, with Jimmy Wang Yu).

The first martial arts movie boom in the United States can be traced to the 1973 Warner Brothers release of Five Fingers of Death.

Photo courtesy of Warner Bros. Studios.

When did the first martial arts movie boom occur in the United States?

Although the martial arts had been popular for a number of years on American TV (largely due to Bruce Lee and The Green Hornet TV series), the first martial arts movie boom in the United States can be traced to the 1973 Warner Brothers release of Five Fingers of Death (a.k.a. King Boxer, starring Lo Lieh).

The sudden and unexpected major success of this film in the United States, coupled with the release of Bruce Lee's Fists of Fury soon after, led to a new fascination with the martial arts. The TV series Kung Fu was also very popular in the early 1970s, once hitting number one overall in the TV ratings.

This success prompted many production companies to produce martial arts films and import such genre films to the United States from Hong Kong and Japan.

Who were some of the stars of the first martial arts movie boom?

Some of these early 1970s martial arts movie stars included Lo Lieh (Five Fingers of Death, Executioners from Shaolin), Bruce Lee (The Chinese Connection, Way of the Dragon, Enter the Dragon), Sonny Chiba (The Street Fighter, Return of the Street Fighter), Jimmy

Wang Yu (*The One Armed Swordsman*, *The Chinese Professionals*), Angela Mao Ying (*Enter the Dragon*, *Deadly China Doll*), Ron Van Clief (*The Black Dragon*), Jim Kelly (*Enter the Dragon*, *Black Belt Jones*), Tamara Dobson (*Cleopatra Jones*, *Cleopatra Jones and the Casino of Gold*), and Tom Laughlin (*Billy Jack*, *The Trial of Billy Jack*).

Who is considered the first female martial arts superstar?

This title goes to Angela Mao Ying (a.k.a. Angela Mao). Angela was born on September 20, 1950, in Taiwan and studied many Chinese martial arts as a child at Taiwan's Fu Shing Academy. She also studied Korean hapkido and became famous for her graceful, yet powerful, kicking techniques.

She started her film career with *Angry River* in 1970 and went on to appear in *The Invincible Eight* (1970), *The Thunderbolt* (1970), *Lady Whirlwind* (a.k.a. *Deep Thrust*, 1971), *Lady Kung Fu* (a.k.a. *Hapkido*, 1972), *Deadly China Doll* (1973), *Fate of Lee Khan* (1973), *When Taekwondo Strikes* (a.k.a. *Sting of the Dragon Masters*, 1973), *Enter the Dragon* (1973, as Bruce Lee's sister), *The Himalayans* (1974), *Naughty, Naughty* (1974), *Stoner* (1974), and *Return of the Tiger* (1976).

Angela retired from movies in the late 1970s to raise a family and concentrate on a singing career.

Who was the first African-American martial arts movie star?

The first African-American martial arts movie star was Jim Kelly. Kelly was born in Paris, Kentucky, and began studying karate with Parker Shelton and later, Okinawa te with Gordon Doversola.

After a successful tournament career, Kelly broke into the movies in 1972 with *Melinda*. He followed up with roles in *Enter the Dragon* (1973), *Black Belt Jones* (1974), *Golden Needles* (1974), *Three the Hard Way* (1974), *Black Samurai* (1975), *Take a Hard Ride* (1975), *Hot Potato* (1976), *Death Dimension* (1977), *Tattoo Connection* (1980), and *One Down, Two to Go* (1981).

Kelly's role as the cocky karate fighter Williams in *Enter the Dragon* remains his most famous.

Which vintage mainstream movies contained martial arts sequences?

Martial arts sequences in mainstream (non–martial arts) movies extend back to the silent-movie era. Some of these pre–martial arts movie-boom films include the Pink

Panther film series, *Daughter of the Dragon* (1931), *G Men* (1935), *Across the Pacific* (1942), *Behind the Rising Sun* (1943), *Blood on the Sun* (1945), *Halls of Montezuma* (1950), *Go for Broke!* (1951), *Forbidden* (1953), *Bad Day at Black Rock* (1955), *Five Against the House* (1955), *The Sad Sack* (1957), *The Barbarian and the Geisha* (1958), *The Crimson Kimono* (1959), *Hell to Eternity* (1960), *The Manchurian Candidate* (1962), *55 Days at Peking* (1963), *A Study in Terror* (1965), *Murderers' Row* (1966), *Our Man Flint* (1966), *The Silencers* (1966), *The Sand Pebbles* (1966), *Born Losers* (1967), *The Dirty Dozen* (1967), *Good Times* (1967), *In Like Flint* (1967), *The President's Analyst* (1967), *The Ambushers* (1968), *The Devil's Brigade* (1968), *The Green Berets* (1968), *Marlowe* (1969), *The Wrecking Crew* (1969), *Billy Jack* (1971), and the James Bond film series.

Which classic samurai film was remade as a western in 1960?

Director Akira Kurosawa's classic film *The Seven Samurai* was remade in the United States as the classic western *The Magnificent Seven* (1960). Kurosawa's other classic samurai film, *Yojimbo* (1961), was remade as *A Fistful of Dollars* (1964), starring Clint Eastwood, and also served as the basis for the Australian film *The Road Warrior* (1981), which brought its star, Mel Gibson, to the attention of Hollywood filmmakers.

Who is Akira Kurosawa?

Akira Kurosawa is one of the world's most respected and admired film directors. He is renowned as one of the premier directors of

Starting in the early 1950s, the late Toshiro Mifune starred in over a dozen samurai films directed by Akira Kurosawa. The Japanese samurai genre, which featured striking cinematography and awesome swordfights, drew a huge international cult following.
Courtesy of the John Corcoran Archives.

the "samurai film." He was born in Tokyo, Japan, in 1910, and started his career as an illustrator and painter. He began working as a screenwriter and assistant director in the 1930s and directed his first film, *Sanshiro Sugata* (a.k.a. *Judo Saga*), in 1943.

Some of Kurosawa's most well-known films include *Rashomon* (1950), *The Seven Samurai* (1954), *Throne of Blood* (1957), *The Hidden Fortress* (1958), *Yojimbo* (1961), *Sanjuro* (1962), *High and Low* (1963), *Kagemusha* (1980), and *Ran* (1985).

In 1990, Hollywood filmmakers saluted Kurosawa with an ultimate honor: the Academy Award for Lifetime Achievement.

What is Chanbara?

Chanbara is a Japanese word meaning "swinging sword" and is also the term for the film genre known as the samurai film. Chanbara has been a very popular art form in Japan ever since the Japanese film industry originated in the 1920s. Many have described Chanbara as the Japanese equivalent of the American western.

Which Japanese film is said to be one of the main influences for Star Wars?

Star Wars creator George Lucas has acknowledged that one of his main inspirations for his epic science-fiction classic was director Akira Kurosawa's 1958 comedy-action masterpiece, *The Hidden Fortress*. The film stars Toshiro Mifune as a loyal general who must guard a princess and her treasure as they make a perilous journey to their homeland. One of Kurosawa's personal favorites, this film won the Best Director Award and the International Critics Prize at the 1959 Berlin Film Festival.

Who is Japan's most famous martial arts star?

Japan's most famous martial arts star was also one of the world's most revered actors, the late Toshiro Mifune, who died in 1997.

Mifune was born in Tsingtao, China, in 1920. After serving in the Japanese army and studying photography, Mifune joined Toho Films in 1946 and made his acting debut in *These Foolish Times*.

Mifune studied a number of martial arts disciplines, including kendo. He won praise from critics the world over for his acting abilities and has equally won many martial arts fans over with his immaculate on-screen sword-fighting skill. His gruff, scowling samurai persona and lightning-fast swordplay have left a permanent impression on millions of moviegoers.

Some of Mifune's more memorable film roles are *Rashomon* (1950), *The Seven Samurai* (1954), *Throne of Blood* (1957), *The Hidden Fortress* (1958), *Yojimbo* (1961), *Sanjuro* (1962), *Red Sun* (1972), *Shogun* (1980), and *The Challenge* (1982).

Who are some of Japan's most famous martial arts movie characters?

At the top of this list is Japan's legendary swordsman Miyamoto Musashi (1584–1645). Widely regarded as Japan's greatest swordsman, he was also a calligrapher, sculptor, poet, *sumie* painter, and writer (*A Book of Five Rings*).

Musashi has been played by a number of different actors, in dozens of film and TV adaptations of his life. Toshiro Mifune played Musashi in the classic *Samurai Trilogy* (*Samurai I* won the Academy Award for Best Foreign Film in 1954). Some other actors who have played Musashi are Kinnosuke Nakamura in the *Musashi* film series (1960–1965), Hideki Takahashi in *Sword of Fury* (1973), and Rentaro Mikuni in *Miyamoto Musashi* (1965).

Other popular Japanese film characters include Toshiro Mifune's Yojimbo, Shintaro Katsu's Zatoichi (the Blind Swordsman), Tomisaburo Wakayama's Itto Ogami, and Raizo Ichikawa's Kyoshiro Nemuri.

Who is the Blind Swordsman?

Zatoichi is one of the most popular characters in Japanese movie history. The character is a wandering blind swordsman, gambler, masseur, trickster, and con man. He was played by Japanese star Shintaro Katsu in twenty-five films and a TV series.

Zatoichi made his first appearance in the 1962 film *The Life and Opinion of Masseur Ichi*. Some of the best films in the series include *Return of Masseur Ichi* (1962), *Zatoichi, Fugitive* (1963), *Zatoichi's Pilgrimage* (1966), *Zatoichi Meets Yojimbo* (1970), *Zatoichi's Fire Festival* (1970), *Zatoichi Meets His Equal* (1971), and *Zatoichi* (1989).

Zatoichi was the basis for the American martial arts film *Blind Fury* (1990), starring Rutger Hauer and Sho Kosugi.

What is the Baby Cart from Hell series?

The *Baby Cart from Hell* series (a.k.a. *Lone Wolf and Cub* series) was a popular string of movies chronicling the life of Itto Ogami. Ogami (played coolly and efficiently by Tomisaburo Wakayama) is the shogun's executioner, who is betrayed and becomes a wandering assassin for hire. After his wife is killed by ninjas, Ogami and his son, Daigoro, roam feudal Japan and bounce from one bloody adventure to another. Ogami wheels his son around in a specially made wooden baby cart that secretly houses a wide variety of lethal weapons.

There were six films in this series as well as a TV series starring Kinnosuke Yorozuya as Ogami. Several of these films were edited together and released in the United States as *Lightning Swords of Death* (1974) and *Shogun Assassin* (1980).

What is the Samurai Trilogy?

The *Samurai Trilogy* (a.k.a. *Samurai I, Samurai II*, and *Samurai III*,) is a series of films that tell the life story of Japan's greatest swordsman, Miyamoto Musashi. The films were produced by Toho Studios in 1954 and 1955, directed by Hiroshi Inagaki, and starred Toshiro Mifune as the legendary Musashi.

The full names of the films in the series were *Samurai Part I: Miyamoto Musashi, Samurai Part II: Duel at Ichijoji Temple*, and *Samurai Part III: Duel at Ganryu Island*.

Inagaki had made *Miyamoto Musashi: Duel at Ichijoji Temple* in 1942, but the film was thought to have been burned by post–World War II U.S. occupational forces, due to its violent content. Inagaki remade it in 1954 as the *Samurai Trilogy*.

Who is Sonny Chiba?

Shinichi "Sonny" Chiba is one of Japan's most popular and enduring action stars. He was born in 1939 and studied at the Japanese University of Physical Education. Chiba won Toei Studio's "New Faces" contest in 1961 and entered the movie industry.

He studied the art of *kyokushinkai* karate under Grandmaster Mas Oyama and brought his martial and gymnastics skills to the role of Karate Kiba in the 1970 film *The Bodyguard*. Chiba gained worldwide fame when he played the scowling Terry Tsurugi, a mercenary who would do anything if the price were right. He played Tsurugi in *The Street Fighter* (1975), the first film to receive a Motion Picture Association of America X-rating for extreme violence; *Return of the Street Fighter* (1976); and *The Street Fighter's Last Revenge* (1977).

Chiba portrayed Mas Oyama in *Champion of Death* (1976), and also appeared in such films as *The Executioner* (1974), *Kowloon Assignment* (1977), *Sister Street Fighter* (1978), *The Bushido Blade* (1979), *Message from Space* (1978), and the U.S. films *Aces: Iron Eagle III* (1992) and *Immortal Combat* (1993).

What is the Japan Action Club?

The Japan Action Club (JAC) was founded by Sonny Chiba as a martial arts school and stunt association. Students were put through a rigorous training course, and as a result, many dropped out. Those who did graduate found work as actors, stunt people, and directors in many Japanese action films and TV series.

Two of the more famous JAC graduates were Etsuko "Sue" Shiomi (*Sister Street Fighter*, *The Kowloon Assignment*, and *The Street Fighter's Last Revenge*) and Henry "Duke" Sanada (*Roaring Fire*, 1982, and *Ninja in the Dragon's Den*).

What is Yakuza-eiga?

Yakuza-eiga (pronounced *ya'koo-za eye'ga*) is a Japanese term that describes a Japanese film genre about the Yakuza, crime, or gambling. Yakuza are Japanese gangsters. Two popular examples of Yakuza films are the American productions *The Yakuza* (1975), starring Robert Mitchum and Ken Takakura, and *Black Rain* (1989), starring Michael Douglas and the same Ken Takakura. Takakura is one of Japan's top movie stars and a popular figure in the Yakuza-eiga.

What was the earliest appearance of the martial arts on television?

Although the very first TV appearance of the martial arts is not specifically known, karate practitioners Ed Parker and Bruce Tegner brought the martial arts to television shows as early as the late 1950s. Ed Parker made appearances on *I Love Lucy* and taught actor

Rick Jason for the show *Case of the Dangerous Robin* (1960–61). Bruce Tegner made appearances on episodes of *The Adventures of Ozzie and Harriet* and *The Detectives* (1959–61).

On which other films and TV shows did American kenpo pioneer Ed Parker work?

Some of Ed Parker's numerous credits include the TV shows *Mike Hammer, Detective* (1958–59, starring Darren McGavin), *The Kraft Mystery Theatre* (1961–63), *I Spy* (1965–68), and the films *The Wrecking Crew* (1969), *Revenge of the Pink Panther* (1978), *Kill the Golden Goose* (1979), *Seven* (1979), and *Buckstone County Jail*.

What other early TV shows featured the martial arts?

Martial arts could be seen regularly on such early TV shows as *Have Gun Will Travel* (1957–63), *Peter Gunn* (1958–61), *Mr. Lucky* (1959–60), *The Avengers* (1961–69), *Dangerman* (1961), *The Saint* (1963–66), *The Man from U.N.C.L.E* (1964–68), *Honey West* (1965–66), *I Spy* (1965–68), *Secret Agent* (1965–66), *The Wild, Wild West* (1965–69), *The Green Hornet* (1966–67), *Mission Impossible* (1966–73), *Star Trek* (1966–69), *T.H.E. Cat* (1966–67), *The Time Tunnel* (1966–67), *Mannix* (1967–75),

Longstreet (1971–72), and *The Phantom Agents.*

Who played the Green Hornet and Kato before Van Williams and Bruce Lee?

Although Van Williams and Bruce Lee are best remembered for playing the masked crime fighters on the TV show *The Green Hornet,* the characters also appeared in two 1940 thirteen-chapter, movie-serial adventures produced by Universal Pictures. Gordon Jones (best known for playing Mike the cop on the *Abbott and Costello* TV show) played Britt Reid (a.k.a. the Green Hornet) in *The Green Hornet,* and Warren Hull played the role in *The Green Hornet Strikes Again.* Keye Luke (later, *Kung Fu's* Master Po) played Kato in both serials.

The Green Hornet started as a radio show, which ran from 1936 to 1954, and the character Britt Reid was the grandnephew of John Reid (*The Lone Ranger*).

What was the significance of the TV series Kung Fu?

The series was significant for several reasons. *Kung Fu* (1972–75) was the first bona fide American martial arts TV show. It built on the excitement that Bruce Lee had generated earlier on *The Green Hornet* and *Longstreet* series and was a major contributing force behind the martial arts boom of the early 1970s.

The groundbreaking series introduced audiences to Eastern philosophy, history, and the fighting arts of the Shaolin Temple. In that capacity, *Kung Fu* lived up to television's highest ideal: it educated and entertained. It was also the first series to feature an Asian character in the lead (although main actor David Carradine was not Asian), and the show made frequent use of inventive filmmaking techniques, as illustrated by its now-famous flashback sequences.

The series made a star of Carradine and generated a large and loyal following of viewers. Furthermore, two of its shows won Emmy Awards, and at one point the series reached number one in the Neilsen ratings, outperforming every show on American television.

Kung Fu has been shown in reruns since it left the air in 1975 and has led to the TV-movie *Kung Fu, The Movie* (1986) and the series *Kung Fu, The Legend Continues* (1992–98), again starring Carradine. This continuation is a testament to the show's enduring appeal and popularity.

Who choreographed the martial arts scenes for the original TV series Kung Fu?

The technical advisers and fight choreographers for *Kung Fu* were veteran martial artists

David Chow and Kam Yuen. Yuen also doubled for David Carradine in some of the show's fight sequences.

Besides Kung Fu*, were there any other martial arts TV series?*

There were a number of martial arts TV series, including *The Master* (1984), *Sidekicks* (1986–87), *Street Justice* (1991–93), *Highlander* (1992–currently), *Kung Fu, The Legend Continues* (1992–98), *Raven* (1992–93), *Renegade* (1992), *Mighty Morphin' Power Rangers* (1993–currently), *Vanishing Son* (1994–95), *Walker, Texas Ranger* (1994–currently), *The Masked Rider* (1995–96), and *WMAC Masters* (1996–97).

What was the most ambitious martial arts movie ever produced for TV?

The most ambitious and most expensive movie with a martial arts theme ever made for TV was *Shogun* in 1980. The ten-hour, five-part, Emmy-winning miniseries was based on James Clavell's epic novel and centered on a shipwrecked English sailor in feudal Japan. The series starred Richard Chamberlain, Toshiro Mifune, and Yoko Shimada, and remains one of the most popular and highly rated miniseries in television history.

Shogun was also produced as a Broadway musical in the mid-1980s. The series' depiction of the ninja, in fact, helped fuel the ninja movie craze of the 1980s.

Were there any other made-for-TV martial arts movies?

There have been only a few made-for-TV martial arts movies, including *Kung Fu* (1971),

Teenage film and TV star and martial arts sensation T. J. Roberts poses with the high-tech vehicles he used in his 1995–96 television show, *The Masked Rider*.

Photo courtesy of Bob Gilroy.

Men of the Dragon (1974), *Samurai* (1979), *The Last Ninja* (1983), *Blade in Hong Kong* (1985), *Kung Fu, The Movie* (1986), *Kung Fu, The Legend Continues* (1992), and *Year of the Gentle Tiger*.

What was the ninja movie craze of the 1980s?

Although ninja had appeared in a number of films over the years, their popularity reached a new high in the 1980s. As a result of the mysterious, deadly, and effective ways the ninja were portrayed in the miniseries *Shogun*, more martial arts films were produced with ninja characters as main heroes and villains.

The 1980s saw a sharp increase in ninja projects such as the films *The Octagon* (1980), *Enter the Ninja* (1981), *The Last Ninja* (1983), *Revenge of the Ninja* (1983), TV shows such as *The Master* (1984), *Ninja III: The Domination* (1984), *Nine Deaths of the Ninja* (1985), *Pray for Death* (1985), *Teenage Mutant Ninja Turtles* (1990), the *American Ninja* film series, and dozens of other projects.

The word *ninja* was often deceptively attached to a film title to try and ensure a successful release, even if the film had nothing to do with ninja characters.

Who were some of the more notable martial arts actors who portrayed ninja?

Tadashi Yamashita played Chuck Norris's evil ninja brother, Sakura, in the 1980 film *The Octagon*, and Sonny Chiba played ninja characters in such films as *The Executioner* (1974), *Shogun's Ninja* (1982), and *Ninja Wars* (1982).

Perhaps the screen's most well-known ninja is Sho Kosugi. Kosugi, born in Japan in 1949, dominated the ninja subgenre throughout the 1980s by appearing in a string of such films as *Enter the Ninja* (1981), *Revenge of the Ninja* (1983), *Ninja III: The Domination* (1984), *Nine Deaths of the Ninja* (1985), *Pray for Death* (1985), *Wings of the Dragon* (1986), *Rage of Honor* (1987), *Aloha Summer* (1988), *Black Eagle* (1988), and *Blind Fury* (1990).

Kosugi studied ninjutsu and holds a black belt in Shito-ryu karate. He was also the first Asian action star to receive a star on Hollywood's Walk of Fame.

Which popular martial arts movie star choreographed action scenes for the film The Challenge?

While living in Japan, Steven Seagal choreographed martial arts action for the 1982 film *The Challenge*. The film starred Scott Glenn,

Toshiro Mifune, and Donna Kei Benz, and centered on the feud between two brothers and their obsession to possess a pair of valuable samurai swords. It was directed by John Frankenheimer (*The Manchurian Candidate*, 1962, *The Birdman of Alcatraz*, 1962) and is considered to be one of the finest American-produced martial arts films.

How did Steven Seagal win his first starring role?

After spending years in Japan studying martial arts and operating his own aikido school,

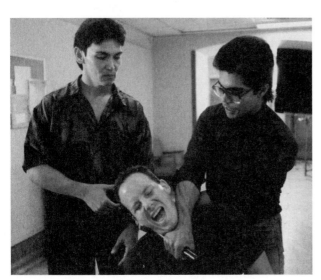

Art Camacho (right), one of Hollywood's best martial arts choreographers (and today a director), works with film star Don "the Dragon" Wilson (left) on the 1993 film *Red Sun Rising*.

Photo by Byron J. Cohen; courtesy of Maslak/Friedenn Productions.

Steven Seagal returned to the United States and set up aikido schools in Los Angeles and Taos, New Mexico. In Los Angeles, Seagal began giving private lessons to superagent Michael Ovitz, recognized as the most powerful person in the entertainment business.

Ovitz believed that Seagal had what it took to become a new action-film hero and arranged for Seagal to demonstrate his skills for Warner Bros. executives in an audition. He wowed them with a high-impact presentation of "combat aikido," a martial art unlike anything they had ever seen.

After an impressive screen test, Warner Bros. signed Seagal to a three-picture deal. His first film was *Above the Law* (1988), an action picture containing a number of memorable martial arts fights characterized by Seagal's brutally realistic skills. The movie was profitable and launched Seagal's rise to major stardom.

What was Chuck Norris's film debut?

Chuck Norris made his screen debut as a henchman in a fight sequence for the 1968 Matt Helm spy adventure *The Wrecking Crew* (starring Dean Martin). He had no lines. The film also featured martial arts legends Ed Parker and Joe Lewis in similar roles, and Mike Stone, who doubled for Dean Martin. Bruce Lee choreographed the film's fights.

Norris then went to Hong Kong to appear with Bruce Lee in *Return of the Dragon* and, back in the United States, costarred in the awful *The Yellow Faced Tiger* (a.k.a. *Slaughter in San Francisco*, 1981), made on a shoestring budget by a Hong Kong production company. Norris's first leading role was in *Breaker! Breaker!* (1977). The success of *Good Guys Wear Black* (1978) and *A Force of One* (1979) paved the way for the action star's successful career.

Is it true that Chuck Norris's sons are also involved in the film business?

Chuck's son Mike Norris is an actor who has appeared in numerous films including *The Octagon*, *A Force of One*, *Young Warriors* (1983), *Born American* (1986), and *Delta Force 3* (1991).

Chuck's other son, Eric Norris, is an experienced Hollywood stuntman and stunt coordinator who works on the TV series *Walker, Texas Ranger*, as well as on feature films.

Who is considered the top U.S. martial arts movie director?

Although the quality of some of his work can be strenuously debated, Robert Clouse can certainly be considered one of the most experienced and prolific U.S. martial arts movie directors. His credits include *Enter the Dragon*, *Black Belt Jones* (1974), *Golden Needles*, *The Ultimate Warrior* (1975), *The Big Brawl* (1980), *Force: Five* (1981), *Gymkata* (1985), *China O'Brien* (1988), and *China O'Brien II* (1989).

How was Robert Clouse chosen to direct Enter the Dragon?

Warner Bros. producers Paul Heller and Fred Weintraub, and Hong Kong's Golden Harvest producer, Raymond Chow, were looking for a director for their new film, *Blood and Steel* (later changed to *Enter the Dragon*). Bruce Lee had seen a film that Clouse had directed called *Darker Than Amber*, a 1970 action-mystery starring Rod Taylor as private detective Travis McGee.

Bruce liked Clouse's directing style, especially the way he directed the film's climactic fight sequence between actors Taylor and Bill Smith. Bruce suggested to the producers that Robert Clouse direct his new project, and Clouse was hired.

Which Hollywood directors also practice the martial arts?

Perhaps the most prominent practitioner is veteran director William Friedkin (*The Exorcist*). Others include film stars Jean-Claude Van Damme (*The Quest*), Steven Seagal (*On Deadly Ground*), and Phillip Rhee

(*Best of the Best III* and *IV*); karate black belts Art Camacho (*The Power Within*), Rick Avery (*The Expert, Deadly Outbreak*), and Paul Maslak (*Sworn to Justice*); tang soo do black belt Aaron Norris, Chuck Norris's brother (Braddock: *Missing in Action III, Delta Force 2: Operation Stranglehold*); and Emmy-winning television director Eric Laneuville, a former kickboxer.

Former directors who are also black-belt caliber include the late, great Bruce Lee (*Return of the Dragon*) and Tom Laughlin (*Billy Jack*).

Which epic U.S. film depicted the Chinese Boxer Rebellion?

Samuel L. Bronston's 1963 epic, *55 Days at Peking*, depicted the historical Boxer Rebellion of 1900. The action-packed picture starred Charlton Heston, Ava Gardner, David Niven, Flora Robson, and John Ireland.

Which film was billed as the first martial arts movie musical?

This honor goes to 1985's *The Last Dragon*, produced by Motown music mogul Berry Gordy. The film featured a campy script, a solid cast, good martial arts action, and hip musical performances. It starred Taimak, Vanity, Julius Carry III, Michael Schultz, and Ernie Reyes, Jr.

Who is Tom Laughlin?

Tom Laughlin (born in 1938) is an actor, writer, producer, and director. His major claim to fame was the successful *Billy Jack* film series of the 1970s. He wrote, directed (under the name T. C. Frank), produced, and starred in *Billy Jack* (1971). The film cost $800,000 to make and brought in over $18 million at the box office.

This success led to the sequels *The Trial of Billy Jack* (1974) and *Billy Jack Goes to Washington* (1977). Laughlin hired hapkido master Bong Soo Han to double him and choreograph the films' martial arts action. Han also played Laughlin's sidekick in *The Trial of Billy Jack*.

Laughlin also starred in the films *The Born Losers* (1968, the first screen appearance of the Billy Jack character) and *The Master Gunfighter* (1975, a remake of the Japanese samurai film *Goyokin*).

Through his films, Laughlin brought hapkido and Master Bong Soo Han into prominence.

Did Elvis Presley use the martial arts in any of his films?

Elvis Presley was a longtime karate enthusiast and practitioner. He began his studies with Jurgen Seydel in 1958 while stationed in Germany with the U.S. Army.

Elvis also studied briefly with Bill "Superfoot" Wallace and, chiefly, Ed Parker, who promoted Elvis to eighth-degree black belt in kenpo karate. Elvis used his martial arts skills, sparingly, in the films *Follow That Dream* (1962) and *Harum Scarum* (1965).

What is special about Shaw Brothers Studios and Golden Harvest Productions?

Both Hong Kong–based production companies are famous for the huge number of martial arts films and stars they have produced. Shaw Brothers is the oldest Hong Kong film studio. Sir Run Run Shaw produced Hong Kong's first sound film. He was also knighted by the queen of England.

Some famous martial arts stars to get their starts at this studio were Bruce Lee, Jackie Chan, Sammo Hung, Yuen Biao, David Chang, Alexander Fu Sheng, Gordon Liu, Lo Lieh, Ti Lung, and Jimmy Wang Yu. Shaw Brothers Studios was most active in the 1960s and 1970s and produced hundreds of martial arts movies. They were renowned for their lavish period pieces and costume dramas.

Golden Harvest came into prominence in the 1970s and, under Raymond Chow, produced a good number of martial arts films. After hiring Bruce Lee, whose films broke all Asian box-office records, Chow and Lee became partners and together with Warner Bros. coproduced *Enter the Dragon*. This was the first coproduction between Hollywood and Hong Kong filmmakers.

Chow's company acquired Jackie Chan in 1979 and has been behind most of his biggest hits, including *The Young Master*, *Project A*, *Armour of God*, *Drunken Master II*, *City Hunter*, and *Rumble in the Bronx*.

Golden Harvest also coproduced the American productions *The Big Brawl*, *The Cannonball Run*, *Cannonball Run II*, and *The Protector*.

Who are some of Hong Kong's best-known martial arts–action film directors?

Some of Hong Kong's best-known martial arts–action film directors include John Woo (*A Better Tomorrow*, *Hard Boiled*, *The Killer*), Lo Wei (*Fists of Fury*, *The Chinese Connection*), Chang Cheh (*Chinatown Kid*, *Ten Tigers of Kwangtun*, *Five Deadly Venoms*), Tsui Hark (*Twin Dragons*, *Once Upon a Time in China*, *Zu: Warriors from the Magic Mountain*), Jackie Chan (*Project A*, *Armour of God*, *Police Story*), Sammo Hung (*Eastern Condors*, *Wheels on Meals*, *Dragons Forever*), Stanley Tong (*Police Story III: Supercop*, *Rumble in the Bronx*), Liu Chia Liang (*Master Killer*, *Legendary Weapons of China*, *Challenge of the Masters*), and Yuen

Woo Ping (*Drunken Master, Snake in the Eagle's Shadow, Tiger Cage*).

Which Hong Kong director has launched the most successful career in the United States?

Acclaimed Hong Kong director John Woo turned his sights to the United States in the early 1990s and has directed Jean-Claude Van Damme in *Hard Target* (1993); the 1996 box-office hit *Broken Arrow*, starring John Travolta and Christian Slater; and two more recent blockbusters, *Face/Off* with Travolta and Nicholas Cage, and *Mission: Impossible 2*, starring Tom Cruise.

Who are the most prominent martial arts fight choreographers in Hollywood?

Some of the most prominent martial arts fight choreographers are Rick Avery, a major stunt coordinator with over 250 film and TV credits who is now a director too; Art Camacho, who has choreographed over twenty-five films and is now a director; Jeff Imada (*Rapid Fire*, among many others); Pat Johnson (*The Karate Kid* films, among many others); Eric Lee, who works prolifically in this capacity; James Lew (*Big Trouble in Little China, Undercover Blues*); Jeff Pruitt (*Mighty Morphin' Power Rangers: The Movie*); Simon Rhee, brother of martial arts star Phillip Rhee,

who coordinates fights and stunts (*Best of the Best* film series, among others); and Benny Urquidez (*Street Fighter, Road House*).

Which film can be called the first horror–kung-fu film?

Legend of the Seven Golden Vampires (a.k.a. *The 7 Brothers Meet Dracula*) from 1973 is the first horror–kung-fu film. The movie was a coproduction between England's Hammer Films and Shaw Brothers Studios.

The story involves Dracula, who assumes the identity of a Taoist priest and raises an army of zombies. Dr. Van Helsing, with the help of a group of kung-fu experts, sets out to put an end to the evil count and his army. The film starred Peter Cushing and David Chang and was directed by Roy Ward Baker.

Who is the most popular character in Chinese cinema?

The most popular character in Chinese cinema would have to be legendary folk hero Wong Fei Hung (a.k.a. Huang Fei Hong, 1847–1924). Hong was a kung-fu master, a practitioner of medicine, and an expert in the Lion Dance. He was also a son of one of the famous Ten Tigers of Kwangtung.

Countless films have been made chronicling Hong's life, including *The Story of*

Huang Fei Hong (1949), *Drunken Master* (1978), *The Magnificent Butcher* (1979), *Dreadnaught* (1981), and the *Once Upon a Time in China* film series.

Another popular character is One-Armed Swordsman, played in a number of films by Jimmy Wang Yu.

Who is the most famous of the many Bruce Lee imitators?

After Bruce Lee's sudden death in 1973, many Hong Kong producers scrambled to make Lee biographies and capitalize on the late star's name and box-office popularity. One odd phenomenon was the hiring of martial arts actors to act as Bruce Lee clones in Hong Kong action films. While dozens of actors made their careers as Bruce Lee imitators, the most famous and successful of them was Bruce Li (a.k.a. Ho Tsung Tao).

Li (pronounced Lee) had good kung-fu and gymnastic abilities and somewhat resembled Bruce Lee, so he was given starring roles in such films as *Bruce Lee: the Man, the Myth* (1976), *Fists of Fury II* (1976), *Bruce Lee, Superdragon* (1974), *Goodbye Bruce Lee, His Last Game of Death* (1975), *Exit the Dragon, Enter the Tiger* (1976), *Bruce Lee the Invincible* (1977), *Bruce Lee's Secret* (1977), *The Three Avengers* (1979), and *Dynamo* (1980).

Chuck Norris (left) and David Carradine (right), seen here with costar Barbara Carrera on the set of the 1983 film *Lone Wolf McQuade*, had a huge collective impact on the growth of the martial arts genre in the 1970s. Courtesy of the John Corcoran Archives.

Other Bruce Lee imitators included Bruce Le, Dragon Lee, Bruce Liang, Bruce Lei, Bruce Rhe, and Bruce Leong, and so on.

Which rising Hong Kong martial arts star died in a tragic car accident?

Alexander Fu Sheng, who was one of Shaw Brothers Studios' brightest young stars, died in a car wreck on July 7, 1983. Fu Sheng was born in 1954 and was one of the first graduates of the Shaw Brothers Studio training system. He was an expert acrobat and martial artist who often played the young, hotheaded hero. Among his most popular films are *Chinatown Kid*, *Ten Tigers of Kwangtung*, *Legendary Weapons of China*, *8 Diagram Pole Fighter*, and *Disciples of Death*.

Who is Jet Li?

Jet Li (a.k.a. Li Lian Jie and Lei Lin Git) is a remarkable wushu performer who hails from the People's Republic of China (PRC). In China, Li is a real-life hero and five-time wushu champion, and starred in the PRC's classic martial arts film *Shaolin Temple* (1982).

Li moved to Hong Kong and quickly became one of the top stars in Asia. He is best known for playing Wong Fei Hung in the three-part film series *Once Upon a Time in China*. He has also appeared in *Shaolin Temple II* (1983), *Martial Arts of Shaolin* (1986), *Fong Sai Yuk* (1993), *The Last Hero in China* (1993), *The Tai Chi Master* (1993), *The Bodyguard from Beijing* (1994), *Fist of Legend* (1994), *The New Legend of Shaolin* (1994), and *My Father Is a Hero* (1995).

Li relocated to the United States in the mid-1990s and made a scorching screen debut as the ice-cold Chinese killer in *Lethal Weapon 4* and made his American starring debut in the box-office hit *Romeo Must Die* in the spring of 2000.

Which kung-fu practitioner made a film about his adventures in China?

Kung-fu stylist and author Mark Salzman starred in the critically acclaimed 1990 film *Iron and Silk*. The film followed Salzman's true-life adventures in mainland China as he taught English and furthered his kung-fu studies under the legendary master Pan Qingfu.

What are the all-time best martial arts movies?

Any list of this type would be only based on opinion. However, a number of martial arts films have received excellent critical reviews and would probably make most martial arts movie connoisseurs' lists of all-time favorites. These films include *The Forty-Seven Ronin* (1942), *Judo Saga* (1943–63), The *Samurai* Trilogy (1954), *The Seven Samurai* (1954), *The Hidden Fortress* (1958), *Yojimbo* (1961), *Hari Kiri* (1962), *Sanjuro* (1962), *Goyokin*

Two martial artists who used their impressive skills to launch big movie careers are (left) Jean-Claude Van Damme and (right, at left, fighting Tommy Lee Jones in *Under Siege*) Steven Seagal.

Jean-Claude Van Damme photo courtesy of the John Corcoran Archives. Steven Seagal photo courtesy of Warner Bros. Studios.

(1969), *Machibuse* (1970), *Zatoichi Meets Yojimbo* (1970), *The Chinese Connection* (1973), *Enter The Dragon* (1973), *Return of the Dragon* (1974), *Lightning Swords of Death* (1974), *Drunken Master* (1978), *Master Killer* (a.k.a. *36th Chamber of Shaolin*, 1978), *Fearless Hyena* (1979), *Shogun* (1980), *The Young Master* (1980), *The Challenge* (1982), *Legendary Weapons of China* (1982), *Shaolin Temple* (1982), *Project A* (1983), *Yes, Madam* (1983), *The Karate Kid* (1984), *Police Story* (1985), *Armour of God* (1986), *Eastern Condors* (1988), *Once Upon a Time in China I* and *II* (1991–92), *The Yakuza* (1995), *Blade* (1998), and many of the films in both the *Zatoichi, the Blind Swordsman* and *The Baby Cart from Hell* series.

Which noted martial artists have used their fighting skills to launch film and TV careers?

This long list includes Billy Blanks, Art Camacho, David Chow, Randall "Tex" Cobb,

Keith (Hirabayashi) Cooke, Mark Dacascos, Gary Daniels, Master Fumio Demura, Dan Inosanto, Pat Johnson, Jim Kelly, Master Tak Kubota, Gene LeBell, Eric Lee, Al Leong, James Lew, Joe Lewis, Jet Li, Kathy Long, Dolph Lundgren, Chuck Norris, Richard Norton, Ed Parker, Ernie Reyes, Jr., Phillip Rhee, Cynthia Rothrock, Harold "Odd Job" Sakata, Steven Seagal, Karen Sheperd, Mike Stone, Jerry Trimble, Benny "the Jet" Urquidez, Keith Vitali, Bob Wall, Bill "Superfoot" Wallace, Cheryl Wheeler, Donnie Williams, Don "the Dragon" Wilson, and Michael Worth.

Most of these artists were national or world champions in some form of martial sports before they launched their entertainment careers.

Which film and TV stars have studied the martial arts?

Among the film and TV stars who have legitimately studied the martial arts are Kareem Abdul-Jabbar, Bob Barker, John Belushi, Honor Blackman, Danny Bonaduce, James Caan, James Cagney, David Carradine, Jim Carrey, James Coburn, Sean Connery, Robert Conrad, Robert Culp, Tamara Dobson, James Franciscus, James Garner, Richard Gere, Louis Gossett, Jr., Pam Grier, Robert Ito, Steve James, Lorenzo Lamas, Tom Laughlin, George Lazenby, Brandon Lee, Jason Scott Lee, Mako, Dean Martin, Steve McQueen, Toshiro Mifune, Audie Murphy, Hugh O'Brian, Donny Osmond, Chris Penn, Elvis Presley, Diana Rigg, Eric Roberts, John Saxon, Arnold Schwarzenegger, William Shatner, Sinbad, Wesley Snipes, Patrick Swayze, Sharon Tate, Irene Tsu, Robert Wagner, Damon Wayans, and Fred Williamson.

What is considered to be the best martial arts movie fight of all time?

The general consensus is that the fight between Bruce Lee and Chuck Norris in the Roman Coliseum at the end of *Return of the Dragon* (1974) is the greatest martial arts movie fight of all time. The frenzied battle between Jackie Chan and Benny "the Jet" Urquidez in the 1983 film *Wheels on Meals* could also rate as the best screen fight of all time.

Which popular video games have been turned into martial arts movies?

Double Dragon (1995), *Street Fighter* (1995), and *Mortal Kombat* (1995) were all popular video games that had movies derived from them. Jackie Chan's *City Hunter* (1993) included a sequence derived from the *Street Fighter II* video game.

Which martial arts superheroes are also known as the Heroes on the Half Shell?

The Heroes on the Half Shell are otherwise known as The Teenage Mutant Ninja Turtles. The crime-fighting foursome started out as a bloody, tongue-in-cheek, underground comic. The comic's popularity led to a hit TV animated series, a successful toy line, and the films *Teenage Mutant Ninja Turtles, The Movie* (1990), *Teenage Mutant Ninja Turtles II: The Secret of the Ooze* (1991), and *Teenage Mutant Ninja Turtles III* (1993).

Who was the first martial arts superhero?

One of the first—if not the first—martial arts superheroes was Japan's Starman. Starman (a.k.a. Supergiant) was a Japanese version of Superman. From 1956 through 1959, he appeared in a series of *Supergiant* films that were released in the United States as *Atomic Rulers of the World*, *Attack from Space*, *Evil Brain from Outer Space*, and *Invaders from Space*.

In the series, Starman battled alien invaders that threatened Earth, by using a unique blend of gymnastics and martial arts. The popular Japanese superhero was played by Ken Utsui.

Starman is the forerunner of Japanese superheroes such as Ultraman, Kamen Rider, Kaku Ranger, Zone Fighters, VR Troopers, Gavan, and Zyu Rangers (known in the United States as the Mighty Morphin' Power Rangers).

In which films did the late Brandon Lee appear?

Brandon Lee (1965–1993), son of the late, great Bruce Lee, made his first appearance in the 1986 TV pilot *Kung-Fu, The Next Generation* (where he played Caine's son). From there, Brandon went on to appear in *Legacy of Rage* (1988), *Laser Mission* (1990), *Showdown in Little Tokyo* (1991), *Rapid Fire* (1992), and *The Crow* (1993). He was accidentally killed in a freak shooting accident while filming a scene for *The Crow*.

Who are considered to be the top martial arts movie stars of all time?

Using the start of the martial arts movie boom of 1973 as a starting point, there have been a number of international martial arts actors who have found success at the box office. These include Yuen Biao, David Chaing, Jackie Chan, Maggie Cheung, Sonny Chiba, Billy Chong, Joyce Godenzi, Sammo Hung, Jim Kelly, Cynthia Khan, Sho Kosugi, Lorenzo Lamas, Bruce Lee, Jet Li, Lo Lieh, Gordon Liu, Ti Lung, Chuck Norris, Yukari Oshima, Cynthia Rothrock, Steven Seagal, Alexander

Fu Sheng, Sue Shiomi, Yang Sze (a.k.a. Bolo Yeung), Jean-Claude Van Damme, Don "the Dragon" Wilson, Donnie Yen, Michelle (Khan) Yeoh, Angela Mao Ying, and Jimmy Wang Yu.

Who are the top U.S. current martial arts stars?

Some of the top current U.S. martial arts movie stars include David Bradley, Mark Dacascos, Gary Daniels, Thomas Ian Griffith, Olivier Gruner, Lorenzo Lamas, Dolph Lundgren, Jalal Merhi, Chuck Norris, Richard Norton, Ernie Reyes, Jr., Phillip Rhee, Cynthia Rothrock, Steven Seagal, Wesley Snipes, Jeff Speakman, Jean-Claude Van Damme, Don "the Dragon" Wilson, Jeff Wincott, and Michelle (Khan) Yeoh.

Who is the top U.S. female martial arts movie star?

Since the mid-1980s, the top U.S. female martial arts movie star has been Cynthia Rothrock. Rothrock began studying the martial arts as a teen and went on to become one of the foremost tournament forms champions in the country.

The five-time U.S. forms and weapons champion has starred in a large number of films in both Hong Kong and the United States. Some of her best work includes

Inspectors Wear Skirts (1985), *Yes, Madam!* (a.k.a. *In the Line of Duty: The Super Cops*, 1985), *Righting Wrongs* (a.k.a. *Above the Law*, 1986), *The Blonde Fury* (1988), *China O'Brien*, Parts I and II (1988–89), *No Retreat, No Surrender II* (1989), *Martial Law* (1990), *Honor and Glory* (1991), *Rage and Honor* (1991), *Tiger Claws* (1991), *Angel of Fury* (1992), and, perhaps her best film to date, *Sworn to Justice* (1996).

What is Jean-Claude Van Damme's real name?

The martial arts movie star was born Jean-Claude Van Varenberg in Berchem–Sainte Agathe, Belgium, on October 18, 1961.

In which film did Jean-Claude Van Damme get his start?

After winning the European Professional Karate Association's middleweight championship, Jean-Claude Van Damme came to the United States in 1981 in search of a film career. He worked as a chauffeur, carpet layer, pizza delivery person, and bouncer before he found work in Hollywood.

Van Damme got his first martial arts role in *No Retreat, No Surrender* (1985) as a Russian kickboxer. Then he played another Russian villain opposite Sho Kosugi in *Black*

Eagle (1988). His first starring role was in the 1988 film *Bloodsport*, a box-office winner that paved the way for Van Damme's worldwide success.

He has also had starring roles in the hit films *Kickboxer* (1989), *Cyborg* (1989), *Lionheart* (1990), *Double Impact* (1991), *Universal Soldier* (1992), *Hard Target* (1993), *Timecop* (1994), *Street Fighter* (1995), *Sudden Death* (1995), *Maximum Risk* (1996), *The Quest* (1996), *Double Team* (1997), *Knock Off* (1998), *Legionnaire* (1998), and *Universal Soldier: The Return* (1999).

Which top female kickboxing champion served as Michelle Pfeiffer's stunt double in Batman Returns?

Michelle Pfeiffer, who played Catwoman in the 1992 box-office smash *Batman Returns*, was doubled in many of her fight scenes by world kickboxing champion Kathy Long. Long, one of the all-time great champions of her sport, has launched an acting career with starring roles in *Knights* (1994) and *The Stranger* (1995).

Who is the most recognizable martial arts movie villain?

One of the most famous and recognizable martial arts movie villains is Yang Sze (a.k.a.

Bolo Yeung), a Chinese bodybuilder and martial arts expert who has appeared in more than 250 martial arts films. He first came to the attention of American fans by playing Han's mute, bone-breaking henchman in *Enter the Dragon*, where he fought John Saxon.

Among his Hong Kong film credits are *Five Fingers of Death*, *The Tattoo Connection*, and *The Young Dragon* (a.k.a. *Bruce's Deadly Fingers*). His U.S. film credits include *Tiger Claws*, *Shootfighter*, and the Jean-Claude Van Damme films *Bloodsport* and *Double Impact*.

Another recognizable martial arts movie villain is Bob Wall, a veteran karate black belt and former tournament fighter who played the memorable scarred villain O'Hara, who fought Bruce Lee in *Enter the Dragon*. Wall also played heavies in *Return of the Dragon*, *Game of Death*, *Black Belt Jones*, and Chuck Norris's 1988 film *Hero and the Terror*.

Who is the most popular martial arts movie star of all time?

Although Jackie Chan is the most popular martial arts–action star in the world, many still consider Bruce Lee to be the all-time greatest martial arts movie star.

Thanks to motion pictures, the ninja and his arsenal of exotic espionage weapons became a pop-culture phenomenon.

EXOTIC MARTIAL ARTS
AND WEAPONS

America has proven to be fertile ground for the Asian martial arts. Five decades ago, American servicemen returning from stints in Japan and Okinawa planted the seeds of karate. Later, various Korean and Chinese systems made their way into the American consciousness. However, lesser-known, yet just as highly evolved, martial arts remain undiscovered—or misunderstood by the martial arts community and the general public.

Many of these arts previously flourished only in isolated regions of the Far East and Pacific Rim. Yet no matter their country of origin, the fact that these martial arts are practiced much as they have been for hundreds of years is a testament to both their effectiveness and the tenacity of the cultures that sustained them.

Both mainstream combative disciplines and their more exotic counterparts reinforce their unarmed techniques with a formidable array of indigenous weaponry. The term *martial arts* itself refers to military arts. It is foolish to separate weaponry from unarmed combat; the two complement each other. To pretend that martial arts techniques are confined to unarmed applications is unrealistic. In most situations, from battlefield clashes to personal duels, hand-to-hand fighting is a last resort, and skill in unarmed combat is a backup to weapon skill.

Moreover, the basic concepts, techniques, and strategies undergirding armed and unarmed confrontation remain consistent within a given art. Obviously, wielding a katana calls upon a different set of skills than delivering kicks and punches. That said, principles of body movement and balance, focus, spatial awareness, and timing are equally valid in either context. One can look to weapons training not as an add-on or substitution for empty-hand skills, but a requirement for warriors in any culture in any era.

Unarmed techniques are not rendered irrelevant by the presence of a weapon. To the contrary, unarmed techniques clarify the skills of the armed warrior. Long and short range, edged, impact and flexible, these weapons reflected the character of the people, who developed them in response to the challenges of the particular environment. Practitioners used these weapons not only against occupying forces but also just as often against their countrymen in bloody internecine warfare.

These weapons are seen today for one reason: in the most unforgiving arena of human endeavor, these fighting systems helped their proponents survive.

While martial arts weapons may appear archaic, they are anything but. Weapons serve as a link to the culture and traditions of the past as well as a reminder of what ingenuity can accomplish with modest means and materials.

Both subtle and significant variations of bladed weapons exist all over the world. Los Angeles, California's Master Eric Lee (left) displays the Chinese broadsword, which distinctly differs from (right) Japan's katana popularly used by the samurai.

Photos courtesy of, respectively, Master Eric Lee and the John Corcoran Archives.

It is true that many martial arts weapons have become little more than movie props, with techniques modified and stylized to the extent that traditional applications are no longer recognized. Fortunately, some of the lesser-known martial arts have largely avoided such commercialization and can still provide the interested practitioner with a wealth of history, as well as a valuable perspective toward his or her own art.

Why did the sword play such a central role in a samurai's life?

The sword held a place of almost inestimable importance for the samurai, not only as a weapon but also as a cultural and spiritual centerpiece. In fact, writers have called the katana (long sword) the "soul of the samurai" for good reason.

Samurai displayed reverence for the blade, which was an omnipresent indicator of their samurai station. Indeed, samurai life was punctuated with rules of etiquette involving the sword, and any breach of these rules—no matter how slight or accidental—bespoke an insult that had to be avenged.

Even the placement of one's katana while visiting another's home was an occasion for care, since it was considered an insult to place the sword down with the handle facing toward the host. Such placement signified a lack of respect for the host's skill. Also, touching a sword without the owner's permission, or even inadvertently brushing against its scabbard, was grounds for a duel.

Such bloodletting not only occurred between members of the bushi (warrior) class, but also included any hapless commoner unlucky enough to draw the ire of a samurai. As members of Japan's privileged class, samurai could and did slaughter commoners with impunity for such perceived insults as bumping into a sheathed sword. (The much vaunted code of Bushido did not apply to commoners.)

Beyond the many opportunities to draw blood with it, higher-level samurai viewed the sword and mastery of it as a means to self-enlightenment. The training and preparation of the samurai was closely intertwined with Zen Buddhism, developing within the mature warrior stoicism, self-denial, and single-minded devotion to duty. All of these aspects secured for the bushi an esteemed station in Japanese society.

How was the samurai sword made, and how did its quality match up against the edged weapons of other countries?

Quite simply, the samurai sword had no peer. While it is true the earlier straight-bladed versions copied from the Koreans and Chinese were of inferior quality, the later curved-blade swords were of superlative design and quality. The curved-blade version originally was used by the cavalry and proved so effective that all samurai eventually adopted it.

Although the size of the sword varied to individual tastes, generally the katana was about three feet in length, with a blade of about two feet. The *wakizashi* (short sword) was about a foot shorter with a comparable blade-to-handle ratio as the katana.

Blades were about a quarter-inch thick, and due to the unique tempering process they were amazingly resilient. During the tempering process, the blade—with the exception of the edge—would be covered with a clay mixture so that when the heated blade was immersed in water, the edge would harden, but the clay-covered portion would remain softer.

This made the samurai sword less brittle than its European counterparts yet provided it with an incredibly keen edge that has, with some heirloom swords, lasted for centuries. This tempering method reinforced the basic composition of the blade.

The forging process itself required weeks, as bars of iron and steel were hammered into the desired shape and repeatedly folded back on top of each other. This process sandwiched exquisitely thin layers of the softer iron between equally thin layers of steel, thereby giving the untempered blade the hardness of steel without the characteristic brittleness.

What was the samurai's purpose for carrying two swords?

The right to carry two swords was exclusive to the samurai class and thus immediately denoted their status. The katana was the primary weapon for battle; however, the shorter wakizashi was used as a backup weapon, or in some ryu both swords were wielded simultaneously. The short sword was also occasionally used to sever the head of a defeated enemy.

How was the sharpness of the samurai blade tested?

Tamashi-giri is the art of test-cutting with the Japanese sword. Translated as "spirit cut," tamashi-giri tests not only the sharpness of the blade but the perfection of the cut, and by extension, the spirit of the sword-wielder.

Three major cuts are used on a suspended object: *kesa-giri* (downward diagonal), *yoko-giri* (horizontal), and *kesa-age* (rising diagonal). In contemporary times, the preferred test-cutting material is either live bamboo (to simulate bones) or bamboo wrapped in wet tatami matting. In feudal

Japan, samurai tested their blades on the corpses of criminals. A good sword could slice through a stack of five corpses—at the hip—without a hitch!

Experts explain that true tamashi-giri skill requires a different approach than most other weapons. Usually a practitioner is advised to treat a weapon as an extension of the hand. However, that equation is reversed with the katana; the wielder instead strives to use the body as an extension of the weapon.

In other words, at a transcendent level, the sword has a life of its own; the swordsman no longer thinks about technique, but frees himself to let the sword deliver the cut.

What modern martial arts sustain the tradition and techniques of the Japanese sword arts?

Kendo and iaido are the present-day legacy of kenjutsu and *iaijutsu*. Kenjutsu dealt with the postures, techniques, and strategies associated with the bare blade. Later, kenjutsu stylists moved toward training and even dueling with the *bokken*, a hardwood replica of the regular katana.

Though made of wood, in capable hands the bokken could easily inflict lethal injuries during spirited practice. However, as peace became a greater reality in Japan, the hard bokken was replaced in training by a more flexible bamboo training sword called a *shinai*. Along with the shinai, protective head and body armor (also made largely of bamboo) made mock matches possible as the *jutsu* (combat) aspects were deliberately de-emphasized by Japanese authorities and transformed into a *do* (way of enlightenment) discipline.

With standardized protective gear and judging criteria, kendo is currently practiced along the lines of a sport. Points are awarded for focused strikes to three areas of the head, the wrists, and two areas of the torso, and for a direct thrust to the throat. Kendo also requires extensive solo training, including the practice of thousands of repetitions of the basic strikes or cuts. That, along with the grueling mock duels in full kendo armor, makes the art one of the most physically demanding martial traditions currently in practice.

Iaido, like kendo, is a do form that evolved from the earlier combative discipline of iaijutsu. Iaijutsu was essentially the quick-draw art of the samurai. Techniques focused on drawing the katana, cutting down an enemy, and wiping the blood from the blade all in one smooth motion. Many of the techniques were designed to enable a warrior to clear his sword and either block or attack directly from a sitting or kneeling position.

With the waning of the samurai, the combative applications of iaijutsu gave way to Iaido. Iaido retains many of the traditional techniques of its predecessor. However, the art now concerns itself much more with the development of character and spiritual discipline than the idea of cutting down an opposing swordsman.

What Filipino weapon was used as a holder for round-bottomed earthenware pots?

Made of bamboo or rattan, the *dikin* is a hollow circular ring about two inches thick and twelve to fourteen inches in diameter. (The size varies, of course, according to the pots placed on top.) Taught in the *pananandata* system, the dikin is used for both strikes and for capturing an opponent's arm or neck.

For striking, the dikin may be used in a slapping motion, much like a giant palm. For captures, the dikin works very much like a stiff, ready-made noose. Typically, a practitioner will use the dikin in a sweeping motion to block an opponent's weapon, deliver a one- or two-hand strike while closing the distance, and then loop the weapon around the neck or arm.

Unlike a rope, where slack has to be taken up, the dikin's rigidity means that a quick twist against a captured arm can break it at the elbow. The neck is even more vulner-

able, as an opponent may easily be pulled to the ground with a sharp yank on the dikin.

What is a pingga, and what was its original function in everyday life?

The *pingga* is one of the many versions of the Filipino staff. Originally designed as a shoulder pole to carry heavy loads, the first pinggas were made of flat bamboo, which tapered to the ends to ensure distribution of the load over a wider area of the shoulders. Pinggas designed for fighting were made of rattan and measured between forty-four and sixty inches long.

The pingga is wielded with two hands and, although its ends are blunted, it is used much like the Filipino spear. The pingga lends itself more to strikes than thrusts—although thrusts and stabbing techniques are still an important aspect of its use. Common targets are the head, shoulders, sides of the body, fists, forearms, and legs.

The pingga is usually held with one hand near the tip and the other about eight inches away. However, a sliding grip may also be used for close-quarter fighting. The grips and strikes more closely resemble that of the fifty-inch *jo* stick used in aikido than more-familiar long-staff weapons such as the bo.

Though obsolete in terms of their original purposes, the dikin and the pingga vividly illustrate the proclivity of the Filipino martial arts to turn common implements into formidable weapons.

What is Filipino pananandata? Who teaches it in the United States?

Pananandata is a comprehensive system of armed and unarmed combat originating in the Tagalog-speaking region of Pambuan, Nueva Ecija. Pananandata comprises many subsystems, including the single and double *yantok* (thirty-one-inch stick), yantok and knife, short rope, staff, *balisong*, and the horsewhip, as well as many other weapons.

Master Amante P. Marinas, Sr., is the only person known to teach pananandata in the United States today. Pananandata is, in fact, the hereditary art of the Marinas family. Master Marinas, the possessor of a master's ranking in arnis and the author of many books and articles about the Filipino martial arts, has practiced and taught pananandata for over four decades.

Who introduced ninjutsu in the United States?

Though author Andrew Adams could be credited with introducing ninjutsu to the Western world through his book *Ninja: The Invisible Assassins*, it was Stephen K. Hayes who popularized the art in America. Hayes, already a third-degree black belt in karate at the time, was inspired by Adams's book. So in 1975, he journeyed to Japan to seek instruction from Dr. Masaaki Hatsumi, the thirty-fourth-generation grandmaster of the Togakure-ryu tradition.

Hayes became the first American live-in student of Dr. Hatsumi and earned a license to teach ninjutsu. He eventually opened the first Bujinkan training hall in the United States.

Intelligent, charismatic, and a natural promoter, Hayes authored numerous magazine articles as well as several books, including *Ninjutsu: The Art of the Invisible Warrior* and *The Mystic Arts of the Ninja*. Through his writings and demonstrations, Hayes can be credited with presenting ninjutsu as more than a collection of arcane combat techniques.

The Togakure system encompasses a deep, esoteric, and spiritual tradition that supports the physical training. For those martial artists who were searching for more depth in their training, Stephen Hayes tapped into the void by offering a martial art that went beyond punching and kicking.

How did the sword carried by ninja differ from the katana used by samurai warriors?

The *ninja ken*, or *shinobikatana*, was considered as much a tool as a weapon. Longer than a tanto (knife) but shorter than the samurai long sword, the ninja ken not only was effective in close-quarter combat, but also was easily transported while moving through narrow corridors and crawl spaces—not an unlikely scenario for the types of missions the ninja were charged with.

Moreover, the *tsuba* (hand guard) was wider than its samurai counterpart and was even used as a stepladder when propped alongside a building. The squarish tsuba was also useful as a prying device; samurai would never deign to use their fine blades for such utilitarian purposes.

Since a ninja sword did not possess the incredible edge of a fine katana, the ninja could not rely upon precise cuts, so he compensated with powerful slashes powered by the weight of his body behind each cut.

What two weapons are closely associated with ninjutsu in the public's mind?

The *shuko* (spiked hand band) and the *shuriken* (throwing blade). Shuko were invented by the Togakure ninja and were used to first block an opponent's sword and then rip it out of his hands. Naturally, strikes also became exponentially more damaging with the steel shuko. These spiked hand bands were complemented by *ashiko* (spiked foot bands) with which ninja could scale walls, cliffs, and trees.

Shuriken ("throwing stars") are perhaps the quintessential ninja weapon. Two basic types, *hira* and *bo* shuriken, yielded a multitude of designs. Hira shuriken were flat plates with anywhere from three to eight points. Bo shuriken were straight blades with one or two points. Depending upon their design, shuriken were thrown in a variety of ways, the two most common being the horizontal inside-to-outside throw (Frisbee style) and the overhead throw.

In either case, shuriken were not thrown by the arm alone but with the entire body behind it. At close range, shuriken were occasionally held in the hands and used as cutting weapons. However, with the faddish popularity of the ninja, shuriken became more than a historical footnote. Shuriken were frequently cited in incidents of misuse; consequently, many states passed legislation banning their sale and distribution.

Why is ninjutsu referred to variously as the art of invisibility, the art of stealth, or the assassin's art?

Ninjutsu earned these unsavory designations partially because of how it was marketed and partially because of the dearth of authoritative voices to set the record straight. However, the translation of *ninjutsu*, also known as *ninpo taijutsu*, gives some clues as to the historical and present reality of the Togakure-ryu.

In the Japanese language, *nin* is the process of enduring or persevering, *po* stands for life, and *taijutsu* is a term for body skills. Thus, *ninpo taijutsu* denotes the ability to endure hardship and persevere through life's difficulties—hardly the exclusive province of assassins.

As a matter of history, the Japanese ninja of centuries ago did engage in guerrilla and espionage activities, but it must be remembered that this occurred in the context of almost continual feudal warfare. In those trying times, ninja techniques were used to inflict deadly injury; yet the crafts and skills of ninjutsu should not be regarded as the martial art of criminals.

The surviving legacy is an art that focuses on efficient self-defense and realizing an individual's physical, mental, and spiritual potential. Hence, the concept of learning to endure and take control of one's life is a more profound and more accurate representation of ninjutsu than the overdone idea of invisible assassins.

Likewise, the whole tradition of making themselves invisible to their enemies may have sprung from the ninja's obvious need to remain inconspicuous. The true garb of the ninja was merely the ordinary clothing of the day. Obviously, night operations demanded dark, nonreflective clothing, but the highly stylized ninja uniform is more a product of modern marketing and movie imagery than historical fact.

What role do the natural elements of earth, water, fire, and wind play in Togakure-ryu ninjutsu?

An integral component of ninjutsu is an appreciation of the five universal elements. While the fifth element is the all-encompassing void and does not translate into a distinct mode of expression, the remaining four elements earth, water, fire, and wind have identifiable postures and physical manifestations in combat. These elements are such an intrinsic part of ninjutsu that every technique, movement, and reaction takes place within their framework.

Each element is characterized by its own posture and footwork—postures in the sense of instinctual movement, not of stances. The earth posture bespeaks stability and a patient, steady mind-set. Its movement is to block without a backward step. The water posture is reactive, allowing one to move away from an attack. The fire posture encompasses an energetic, expansive attitude wherein one is ready to explode forward and overwhelm an opponent. The wind element is benevolent; adopting this strategy is useful for defusing a potential threat without causing injury.

What is combat sombo?

Although the exact date of its origin is unknown, combat sombo (a.k.a. sambo) was an effort by first the Russian military and later by the Soviet military to develop the best hand-to-hand combat system possible. They sent their best instructors all over the former USSR to systematize various techniques from judo, karate, jujutsu, free-style, and Greco-Roman wrestling.

They then merged the best techniques from all these disciplines into a very hard-core system of self-defense, which they called sombo. *Sombo* means "unarmed self-defense."

Clearly, sombo bases itself on many traditional systems of combat and wrestling. It teaches basic strikes, submission holds, throws, joint-locks, and some of the most practical moves against weapons. Hence, combat sombo has become a specialty of military and police work.

How do ninjutsu kicks differ from karate kicks?

Ninjutsu tends to devote more energy to low, battering kicks than their karate counterparts. The objective behind a kick or sweep is not so much to outright disable an opponent as much as it is to upset his balance and weaken his fight momentum. Togakure-ryu ninjutsu uses a thrusting, body-commitment kick delivery rather than snapping the leg out independently.

Frequent targets are the lower abdomen and hips since full-power kicks to these areas can easily fold an antagonist or disrupt his or her alignment and subsequent ability to continue an attack. In addition to the lower torso, the insides of the shin and knee are often attacked with heel kicks.

Ninjutsu doesn't employ the side and roundhouse kicks—at least not in their familiar forms. According to Stephen Hayes, an American Togakure-ryu master, the side kick was never a part of the historical battlefield repertoire of the Japanese. The kick was an innovation for competition; as such, the body positioning required does not fluidly support ninjutsu's striking and grappling techniques.

Ninjutsu stylists do practice their own, pre-competition version of the side kick in which the kicker's hip does not turn over and the toes remain vertical. The heel makes contact with the opponent, who is positioned sideways to the kicker.

Likewise, the classical roundhouse is not a part of the formal ninjutsu curriculum, because its targets, even low targets such as the side of the knee, thigh, or ribs, would have been protected by armor. However, some instructors do teach a follow-through version where the striking point is the bottom of the shin.

What is a hanbo?

Meaning "half-staff," the hanbo is a three-foot hardwood stick used in many jujutsu systems. Though relatively unimposing, the hanbo is one of the most practical martial arts weapons. The ends are used for striking nerves, soft tissue, and the body's vital points. The shaft can also be used to catch and control an opponent's limbs, hence its popularity with jujutsu systems.

Like a bo staff the hanbo can be manipulated with both hands; it may also be used with one hand for snapping strikes, especially to the hand, wrist, or elbow of an opponent's attacking arm. It is long enough to be a perimeter weapon, yet it doesn't become unwieldy at close range. For example, the hanbo can be slipped under an opponent's arm and used as a fulcrum to facilitate armbars.

Its rigidity and the leverage it provides make it useful for chokes as well. Moreover, the principles that undergird the hanbo can easily apply to any medium-length extension tool.

What common mobility aid is used as a multipurpose weapon in several Korean martial arts?

Korean hapkido, Hwarangdo, and several other systems have developed an extensive collection of techniques that use the ordinary walking cane as a self-defense tool. Along with its obvious striking potential, in these arts the cane is employed predominantly as a leverage weapon against the arms, torso, and legs. Once a foe is locked up by the shaft of the cane, it is comparatively easy to apply pressure against the captured limb to set up a finishing throw.

The curvature of the handle makes the cane particularly effective for hooking an adversary's arm, leg, or neck.

What is a kris, and what is the significance of its oddly shaped blade?

The kris is a double-edged dagger with a wavy, undulating blade, usually measuring between twelve and sixteen inches. With its origins in India, the kris is considered to be the national weapon of Indonesia. Practitioners of the Indonesian and related combat arts attach deep religious and supernatural significance to the kris. Various legends abound among adepts about the kris possessing powers such as the ability to control fire or kill an enemy from a distance by stabbing the weapon into his footprints.

While superstitious by Western standards, the spiritual element of the kris cannot be underplayed. The belief in the supernatural more than makes up for the fact that the kris is not as functionally efficient as many other combat knives. Its power is not merely a function of the blade itself but rather of the blade's relationship to its owner, thus the importance of forging a compatible blade.

Although not all kris have undulating blades, the vast majority do. Some practitioners believe that the kris's deadliness increases with the number of waves fashioned into the blade (always an odd number).

What is the manrikigusari, and how was it used in combat?

The *manrikigusari*, also called the *kusari-fundo* by ninjutsu practitioners, is a steel chain eighteen to thirty inches long with weighted ends. This chain may be used as a centrifugal weapon, striking the opponent with the weighted ends. More sophisticated applications focus on close-range strikes, wherein the manrikigusari wielder holds the weapon in either or both hands and delivers nerve strikes with the weighted ends.

The manrikigusari is also an ensnaring weapon. The relative shortness of the chain makes it easy to take up the slack and wrap the chain around an opponent's neck or weapon arm.

According to the late Charles Gruzanski, the individual chiefly responsible for popularizing the weighted chain among the samurai was Dannoshin Toshimitsu Masaki, founder of Masaki-ryu, and at that time, the head sentry of Edo castle. In fact, Masaki coined the term *manrikigusari* or "10,000 power chain" due to its versatility and effectiveness.

While it was Masaki's duty to protect the castle's entrance from intruders, he felt it was unseemly to engage enemies in bloody sword battles before such a sacred place. As a result, he developed a system of combat using a short chain with weights attached to each end. The manrikigusari could then be used to defeat sword-wielding enemies without defiling the castle grounds.

What Chinese weapon has characteristics of both impact and flexible weapons?

A classical northern Chinese weapon, the three-section staff combines the offensive and defensive attributes of the staff and whip chain. Comprised of three pieces of hardwood, each slightly more than two feet in length and joined by short sections of chain, the three-section staff can be swung like a whip yet still impart the solid, bone-breaking impact of a staff.

The flexibility created by the joined sections makes the three-section staff an efficient sweeping weapon when it is swung low to coil around an enemy's ankles. More conventionally, the outer sections are used for strikes or jabs while the center section can be used for blocks.

Although seen frequently at tournaments in forms competition, most of the fancy twirling and acrobatic changes with the staff have little to do with its historical combative applications. Centuries ago, the three-section staff was one of the weapons favored by bodyguards who protected caravans and wealthy travelers from marauding thieves. This speaks volumes for the effectiveness of the three-section staff against such weapons as the sword, staff, or spear.

What Brazilian martial art was originally practiced by slaves who disguised the techniques as a dance?

Practiced by transplanted African slaves, *capoeira* is an athletically demanding martial art whose predominant techniques are kicks

A demonstration of the athletic Brazilian slave art of capoeira.
Photo by Steve Sandkohl; courtesy of Master Sid Campbell.

executed from the ground. Using their hands to support themselves, *capoeiristas* launch circular and straight kicks as well as sweeps from a fluid, rapidly changing handstand position. Since the hands are usually in contact with the ground, there is little or no blocking with the arms in capoeira. Instead, capoeiristas avoid kicks with evasive footwork or by dropping to the floor with an escape technique.

In order to continue the practice of capoeira under the eyes of their Portuguese masters, the slaves disguised the techniques as dance movements. Fortunately, the highly acrobatic nature of capoeira lent itself to this deception.

There is some dispute as to whether capoeira was originally a dance that evolved into a fighting method against oppressors or a fighting system forced to masquerade as a dance form. In either case, however, capoeira was outlawed by the Brazilian government until around 1930. Although it is once again recognized as a fighting art (and national sport), capoeira still contains many elements of dance.

Today's capoeira falls into two main styles: *angola* and regional. Capoeira angola is the older of the two and uses more ground-work. It is also more combat-oriented since it is essentially the same art used by the slave originators of capoeira. Capoeira regional contains more movements, including upright techniques, than the original and is considered to be the sport form of the art.

In a rough parallel with the common split in the Asian martial arts, the angola style would be the traditional classical method while the regional would be considered the modern, eclectic version of the art.

What role does music play in the practice of capoeira?

Music, especially percussive music, is vital to capoeira training. Since capoeira is as much a dance as a method of fighting, the rhythm of the music determines the timing and flow of the match. Tambourines, cowbells, and a *berimbau* (a bow with an attached gourd that produces percussive sound) are among the favored instruments for bolstering the fighting spirit of the combatants.

What are the Filipino martial arts called kali, arnis, and escrima, and what relation do they have to each other?

Although not entirely accurate, these terms are often used interchangeably by practitioners from different geographic regions. Generally speaking, all three of these arts include the use of the twenty-eight-inch rattan stick and knife, singly or in tandem. In addition most variants of kali, arnis, and

Numerous exotic weapons stem from the Philippines. Los Angeles, California's Diana Lee Inosanto (left) poses with the Filipino wavy-bladed kris, and (right) Chicago's Fred Degerberg poses with two weapons, a rattan escrima stick, which is a medium- to long-range Filipino weapon, and a high-tech, American-designed Gil Hibbon knife, used for medium- to close-range combat.

Photos courtesy of, respectively, Diana Lee Inosanto and Fred Degerberg.

escrima incorporate many more weapons such as the rope, spear, short stick, etc.

The terms *arnis* (translated as "stick" or "harness") and *escrima* (fencing) are a linguistic legacy of the Spanish who controlled most regions of the Philippines for about three hundred years until the turn of the twentieth century. Although the origins of

kali are in dispute, it is believed to have derived from India.

Kali (knife) is sometimes referred to as the parent art of arnis and escrima. The most notable proponents of kali were the Moro warriors, who used the kris and other knives to devastating effect, first against the Spanish and later against American occupiers.

Perhaps because of this history, kali often emphasized edged weapons, both long and short. Arnis and escrima tend to incorporate more single- and double-stick applications, although the knife is still an important part of the training. (There is no single arnis, escrima, or kali; the names are umbrella terms for a myriad of related styles.) However, Filipino stylists understand that one of the implied functions of the *baston* (stick) is to be a training substitute.

Though single- and double-stick techniques are deadly in their own right, a knife has usually replaced one or both sticks in life-and-death combat. The concepts remain identical, but the substitution of the rattan stick for the fearsome bolo knife, kris, or machete made practice less intimidating for the student—and when the Philippines were under foreign control, much less worrisome for the authorities.

Why do many Filipino martial arts teach students weapons first and then progress to empty-hand applications?

Although it is difficult to speak authoritatively on a generalized basis, Filipino martial artists begin their training with weapons for several reasons. The first is that it provides students with the flexibility to improvise. In an emergency, the principles that undergird the bas-ton can be applied to a tree branch, rolled-up magazine, broken broomstick, or almost any other handy object.

Weapons also sharpen an individual's reflexes. Anyone who has ever witnessed an expert arnis man or *escrimador* will testify that the speed of an attacking stick or blade makes empty-hand techniques appear slow by comparison. Accordingly, a student who develops the competence to defend against a weapon thus will find it much easier to neutralize an unarmed attack.

Weapons training can also develop distance appreciation. A student starts out with a longer stick, progresses to the shorter stick, to the knife, and finally, empty hands.

What do Filipino stylists mean when they talk about "defanging the snake"?

Defanging the snake refers to the act of disabling the attacking arm, a central concept to the Filipino fighting arts. Whether the confrontation involves sticks, blades, or empty hands, the principle remains the same: if you damage the fist or the arm holding the weapon, that weapon no longer poses a threat.

If edged weapons are involved, a cut to the attacking limb can sever arteries in the hand, arm, or leg to force an enemy into shock through pain and blood loss. Stick strikes shatter the bones in the knuckles, back of the hand, wrist, or elbow, thereby making it impossible for an opponent to continue the attack.

To counter a punching attack, a defender might check a punch with his front hand and guide the misdirected fist into his rear elbow to break the hand or wrist. He could then move up the opponent's arm with a series of paralyzing strikes to the nerves of the forearm, elbow, triceps, or shoulder.

This tactic also minimizes loss of life. This was a significant consideration, because life-and-death personal duels were not uncommon in the Philippines prior to World War II. By disabling the opponent's limb(s), a fighter could defeat an adversary without having to inflict lethal injury. If the fight truly required taking a life, this disabling process also exposed the opponent's vital points for killing blows.

What is the "alive hand" in kali, and what is its purpose?

The alive hand is the hand that does not contain a weapon. If both hands contain weapons or both are empty, the alive hand is usually the rear hand. The alive hand is used for checking, trapping, or locking up an opponent's weapon to prevent a counterattack in the midst of the kali fighter's own attack.

What historical legends are associated with the use of kali by the Moro warriors?

The Moro warriors were perhaps the most fanatical kali practitioners. For hundreds of years they resisted Spanish and then American domination. The Moros were, in fact, never completely subjugated despite facing overwhelmingly superior firepower. Moro resistance was so fierce that these fighters came to be known as *juramentados* or "bloodthirsty warriors."

Purportedly the U.S. Army's .45 caliber gun was developed in response to these determined fighters. Many juramentados were said to have absorbed numerous bullets from the standard-issue .38 yet still lived long enough to kill their enemy.

It has also been suggested that the Marine nickname "leatherneck" originated from the heavy leather and neck collars U.S. Marines wore to protect themselves from the decapitating swords of the Moro warriors.

What attributes are developed through training with kung-fu's double sabers?

The kung-fu double sabers (*cern do*) promote coordination and ambidexterity. The double sabers possess slightly curved blades ranging from between twenty-five and thirty inches in length. The hand guard on each blade is a half-circle so that when the weapons are combined, they fit flat against each other. This allows the sabers to be placed side-by-side in a single scabbard.

In trained hands, the double sabers are a spectacular weapon as a practitioner keeps alternating each blade from a cut to a block in a windmill-like figure-eight pattern. Historically, the double sabers were often used against the spear, and traditional forms still reflect this with spins, leaps, and backward steps designed to carry the saber-wielder out of the way of spear thrusts.

Why do the double sabers have a tassel attached to each handle?

Centuries ago, the tassel was actually a small cloth used both to confuse an enemy and to wipe blood, sweat, or mud from the saber's handle. Today, the decorative tassel does not detach from the saber's handle; however, when it was used in combat, the cloth was easily removed so it would not interfere with the vision of the saber-wielder.

What is the native fighting system of Indonesia?

Pentjak silat (or *pentcak silat*) is the native fighting art of Indonesia. As the world's largest archipelago, the islands comprising Indonesia have developed a variety of fighting methods and accompanying weapon systems. A fusion of Buddhism and Hinduism heavily influenced the early development of pentjak silat, providing it with religious significance as well as combative value.

The unarmed component of pentjak silat uses economical body movement and includes knees, elbow strikes, and joint locks along with kicks and punches. Edged weapons are quite prominent in pentjak silat, particularly the kris.

In addition to the kris, pentjak silat uses dozens of other fighting knives ranging in size from the *rentjong*, a knife with a pistol-grip handle and a blade of only a few inches, to the *parang*, a cleaver-like knife with a blade as long as thirty-six inches.

In which martial arts do practitioners use edged weapons with their feet?

Capoeira and pentjak silat offer two of the best examples of the barefoot use of a blade in combat, although this practice is not exclusive to these two systems. According to author David Steele, young boys in certain Sumatran villages would learn to carry the small *rentjong* knife between their toes by first practicing with a piece of wood under their curled toes.

Later, the wood would be replaced by the handle of the rentjong, as the blade would be positioned between the big toe and the one next to it. The boys became so adept at carrying the blade in this manner that they could run barefoot without dropping the knife or injuring the foot. When it came time to use the rentjong, usually against a Dutch soldier, the knife would be thrust out with a hard kick to impale the opponent in the stomach.

Instead of using a knife, capoeiristas used the straight razor. Landing any of the dervish-like kicks with a razor gripped between the toes would cause serious injury to an unsuspecting enemy. Even if the opponent was prepared, the scythelike circular kicks of a well-trained capoeirista could slash away while still keeping his or her own head and torso out of the way.

What popular Vietnamese martial art is a combination of several established arts both from within Vietnam and from outside the country?

Cuong nhu (hard and soft, respectively, in Vietnamese) was created in 1965 by Master Ngo Dong. Melding together principles and techniques from boxing, wing chun kung-fu, Shotokan karate, and vovinam, a martial art indigenous to Vietnam, Dong created a hybrid form that took root almost immediately in Vietnam and later in the United States. Its Chinese influence is readily apparent by the many techniques patterned after the characteristics of animals: namely the snake, crane, tiger, and monkey.

Each component art, however, has contributed to the evolution of cuong nhu, as Dong borrowed wing chun's concept of controlling an opponent's centerline and Shotokan karate's straightforward punches and kicks as a starting point for training. Taught at the intermediate level, vovinam is the art that contributes the animal concept to cuong nhu.

Acknowledging the smaller stature of the Vietnamese people (even in relation to Koreans and Chinese), vovinam emphasizes footwork, economy of motion, and simultaneous blocks and counters. Vovinam is part of the soft component of cuong nhu, and is thus introduced later in a student's training.

The focus of early training is on hard, karate-style blocks, kicks, and punches. Cuong nhu training is structured in such a manner because of the belief that students can only afford to be more creative with redirection and yielding movements after they have built a solid core of usable self-defense techniques.

What is bando?

Meaning "way of the disciplined," bando is the martial art of Burma. It is comprised of several animal systems including the bull, eagle, scorpion, python, monkey, cobra, and tiger.

Each system emphasizes its own techniques, footwork, and philosophy. For example, the tiger subsystem emphasizes powerful open-hand strikes that turn into raking, grasping, and ripping motions. On the other hand, a cobra stylist within the bando system will probably be of a lighter body type and prefer to use quick, precise nerve strikes to disable an opponent.

The other animal systems dictate similarly characteristic techniques since each practitioner usually chooses a specialization based on his or her own physical and mental attributes such as size, strength, mobility, aggressiveness, and the like. Generally, knees and elbows figure prominently in the bando system; and similar to kali, the elbow is often used to intercept and punish an opponent's attacking limb.

What fighting knife is closely associated with bando?

A legacy of the Greek short sword from when Alexander the Great conquered portions of Asia, the *kukri* knife with its distinctively curved blade is the Burmese version of the Filipino bolo knife. It is an ever present possession of every Gurkha soldier and a must in the training of every serious bando student.

What is bando boxing?

Bando boxing is an athletic contest far more brutal than its American counterpart. Traditionally, participants wore neither protective equipment nor gloves. In addition to kicks and punches, knee strikes, elbow strikes, head butts, and sweeps are legal. Finger techniques to the eyes, throat, and groin are among the few prohibitions. Contests were decided primarily by knockout or technical knockout (TKO).

Reportedly, these and similar matches have resulted in many deaths and serious injuries. Consequently, they have been halted in many countries. However, bando boxing is still practiced in Burma—albeit with some modifications.

Who introduced bando to the United States?

Dr. Maung Gyi introduced bando to America in 1960 and has remained the central figure in propagating the art, under the auspices of the American Bando Association.

In addition to being an accomplished academic and a philosophy professor, for over two decades Dr. Gyi successfully put his skills to the test in the full-contact ring under rules far less restrictive than those in today's kickboxing contests. Moreover, Dr. Gyi forged his hard-core approach to bando years before, as an adolescent fighting the Japanese in the jungles of Burma.

Not surprisingly, Dr. Gyi's formidable background has had a direct impact on the way the art has been taught in the United States, where it has established itself as one of the toughest and most pragmatic self-defense disciplines extant.

What is hapkido? How does it differ from taekwondo?

Hapkido is a Korean art not dissimilar to taekwondo in that it employs an extensive collection of kicks. However, hapkido is much more concerned with joint-locks, limb immobilization, and throwing techniques than taekwondo. Circular, flowing motions are much more evident in hapkido since blocks and deflections are designed to redirect an opponent's momentum and set him or her up for a counterattack.

In fact, the name hapkido reveals much of its methodology. *Hap* means coordination or harmony, *ki* is, of course, the inner life force, and *do* translates as "the way." Thus, hapkido is "the way of coordinated power" or force.

The idea of not meeting an opponent's force with one's own but rather blending with it is reminiscent of aikido for good reason. Hapkido and aikido share a common heritage since the founder of aikido, Morihei Uyeshiba, and the founder of hapkido, Yong Shul Choi, both studied daito-ryu aikijutsu in Japan, under Sokaku Takeda. Yet, while Master Uyeshiba developed aikido as a non-aggressive art with little offensive technique, Master Choi took his art in the other direction. Combining the strikes, joint-locks, and throws of daito-ryu aikijutsu with the heavily kick-oriented Korean arts of Hwarangdo and tae kyon (the forerunner of taekwondo), Master Choi developed a much more offense-directed system.

Hapkido's preference for circular, momentum-based kicks make the system less compatible for tournament competition than taekwondo. The art's powerful spinning wheel, ax, and crescent kicks (delivered with a straightened leg) cannot be effectively pulled short of contact; thus many hapkido techniques must be altered for competitive purposes. Neither does hyung (form) play a role in hapkido. Some instructors teach portions of ancient kicking forms, but these resemble combinations more than formal hyung.

Though hapkido is primarily an empty-hand system, it includes several weapons. The signature weapon of hapkido is the walking cane. Like the art itself, hapkido cane applications use sophisticated joint-locking and throwing techniques that exploit an attacker's own aggression and turn it back on him.

What was the Chinese quando's battlefield use?

The *quando* (or *kwando*) is the northern Chinese version of the European knight's halberd. Consisting of a long pole with a large, curved blade affixed to the end, the quando was a power weapon. It was used with powerful swings of momentum rather than the quick, slicing maneuvers of the Japanese *naginata*.

Its destructive capabilities were exemplified by its use by Chinese soldiers against adversaries attacking on horseback. As the horse bore down on the quando-wielder, he would cut the front legs of the horse out from under it. Obviously, the rider would then crash to the ground along with the horse, leaving him vulnerable to a finishing blow.

Conversely, the quando was also considered a commander's weapon, frequently carried by mounted generals. In fact, the quando was referred to as the "General's weapon." It was also used in one-on-one combat against other long-range weapons such as the spear.

Though there is no longer a combative use for the quando, it remains very much a part of many kung-fu systems because of its body-development attributes. The quando is a heavy, oddly balanced weapon; manipulating it requires considerable strength and balance to maintain one's equilibrium. In fact, the ability to wield an excessively heavy quando was traditionally viewed as a great test of strength and kung-fu skill.

Why did capoeira carry the unsavory connotation of being a criminal's art?

In the early 1800s, the Brazilian elite aggressively attempted to eradicate the practice of capoeira. Whether as a dance or, worse still, a fighting method, capoeira became a cultural embarrassment. Its practice became punishable by stiff prison sentences, so capoeiristas went even further underground with their art.

When the persecution against the capoeiristas increased, these men, uniformly from the lower strata of Brazilian society, retaliated by fortifying their capoeira kicks with the straight razor. Since altercations between capoeiristas and authorities became more lethal and because the art was practiced almost exclusively by black Brazilians, capoeira came to be looked down on as a predatory, barbaric activity, the province of the criminal underclass.

In this way capoeira has some parallels with savate, the French foot-fighting art that fell into disrepute due to the social standing of many of its practitioners. This reputation plagued capoeira for over a century, until

Brazil finally acknowledged it as an important part of its national heritage.

Both Hwarangdo and hapkido extensively use the cane. Do they also use a small stick?

Yes, both arts employ the short eleven-to-twelve-inch stick as an adjunct for close-in fighting. Though not much longer than a *yawara* stick, the Korean short stick or "bone-breaker" is used less for pokes and jabs than for short, snapping strikes.

Directed at the highly sensitive bony areas of the body (e.g., kneecap, elbow, wrist), the short stick is capable of transmitting bone-shattering impact. Blows are not delivered with wide swings or heavy body commitment; it's all in the wrist, since a quick snap and an equally quick retraction provide all the necessary power to disable a hand, arm, or leg.

Of course, the head is a prime target for strikes, while chokes on the neck and throat may also be performed with the short stick. In addition, a strap that can be looped around the wrist is often attached to the short stick to help retain the weapon in the midst of combat.

What is the history of traditional, nonsport savate?

While the exact origins of savate are unclear, a hardcore street-fighting version of it existed at least as early as the 1700s. Later, savate became more systematized as more advanced kicking techniques, footwork, and open-hand blows were added.

Savate was well established by that time with many French nobles receiving instruction in the art. It retained a dual nature as a fighting and self-defense system and as a sport, since both formal and informal matches were frequent. Moreover, through its association with the French upper crust, savate began to shed its image as a hooligan pastime. By the mid-1800s, savate underwent even more refinement, borrowing much from English boxing—including the use of gloves.

However, it was Joseph Charlemont, the father of modern savate, who synthesized the art into the form recognized today. Charlemont, an extraordinary innovator and visionary, blended a patchwork of fighting methods such as boxing, wrestling, and *chausson*, as well as the use of the sword and cane.

The inclusion of the sword and cane, which were the constant companions of French nobility, could infer that Charlemont wished savate to remain a high-class endeavor rather than the street-fighting method that it had once been. French savate continued to prove itself throughout the years, but its growth was stifled by both world wars. It was the interest in Asian martial arts after World War II that helped revive savate.

What is the Chinese fan?

The Chinese fan is an advanced weapon of the choy li fut system that was used as a weapon of surprise for striking or, if need be, for blocking a longer-range weapon. The choy li fut fan is about eighteen inches long and made out of iron or steel.

Usually containing between nine and twenty-four ribs, it was traditionally carried in the sleeve or tucked into the waistband. Since the fan offers relatively little room for error when blocking a longer and often edged weapon, superior footwork is needed to augment the block(s) as well as to close distance.

As a result, the first order of business for a student learning to use the fan is to develop fluid, evasive footwork. Only then is he or she ready to train for pinpoint striking ability on the wooden dummy. The dummy also accustoms the practitioner to the fan's recoil when solid contact is made.

What role does the fan play in Korean martial arts?

Presently taught in the hapkido, Hwarangdo, and kuk sool wan systems, combative fan techniques were practiced by members of the royal Korean court. More delicate than the Japanese or Chinese fighting fan, the Korean fan was between eleven and twenty inches in length with bamboo rather than metal ribs.

The fan was a utilitarian instrument actually used for its intended purpose; however, it also became a potent defensive or offensive weapon when necessary. Its lightness made it ideal for whipping, snapping strikes to the unprotected extremities of an enemy.

It was also effective as a poking weapon when thrust into the throat, armpit, or other soft-tissue area. Indeed, to increase their deadliness, some of the fans reportedly had metal strips placed on their outer edges as well as in each fold.

What weapon does wing chun kung-fu use to build forearm strength and reinforce empty-hand principles?

The wing chun pole, a staff between nine and thirteen feet in length, develops a variety of attributes. Wing chun divides the body into four zones, or quadrants, for defense. The elbow is the hinge that facilitates economical quadrant blocks. The long pole helps teach the correct use of the elbow, which, in turn, generates leverage and power.

The pole is also useful for helping a practitioner understand chi (inner power). As a practical matter, the wing chun pole is too long and unwieldy to be a true combative weapon. That same unwieldiness, however, becomes an asset in strengthening a practitioner's arms and teaching optimal body alignment.

How does Hakko-ryu jujutsu differ from other forms of jujutsu?

In comparison to most of its ancient counterparts, hakko-ryu jujutsu is a martial art of recent vintage. Founded by Master Ryuho Okuyama in 1941, hakko-ryu jujutsu was designed to subdue an antagonist with temporary pain caused by disrupting his ki (inner power), without inflicting serious injury.

Recognizing that an individual's energy radiates via internal meridians throughout the body, an accomplished hakko-ryu practitioner will push or strike certain sensitive points along these meridians to gain a foe's compliance. Hakko-ryu eschews the concussive bone- and joint-destroying strikes of some of the harder styles of jujutsu. Consequently, hakko-ryu is considered a less damaging and more benevolent form of jujutsu.

Master Okuyama fashioned the system after intensive study with a number of jujutsu and weapons masters in Japan. Among Okuyama's teachers was daito-ryu aikijutsu Master Sokaku Takeda (who also counted among his students aikido founder Morihei Uyeshiba and hapkido founder Yong Shul Choi). Okuyama also devoted himself to the study of traditional Oriental medicine. As a result, he combined his jujutsu and medical knowledge to create a system that does not rely on destructive techniques to neutralize a threat.

Even though it is itself a recent synthesis, hakko-ryu is extremely traditional in its teaching methods. To keep dangerous knowledge away from those who might misuse it, higher-level training in targeting the meridian points is reserved for advanced black belts.

Another indicator of its beneficent nature is the use of *shiatsu* to heal injuries and prevent sickness. Whereas attacking a person's meridian system is the negative manifestation of the art, shiatsu is its positive counterbalance, and a basic knowledge of this healing science is required of all hakko-ryu black belts.

What martial art was founded by Professor Henry Okazaki?

Danzan-ryu jujutsu was founded in the 1920s by Professor Henry Okazaki. Professor Okazaki's martial arts odyssey was somewhat unusual in that although he was a native-born Japanese, he began and received the bulk of his training in the Hawaiian Islands.

Professor Okazaki studied numerous styles of jujutsu and combined these techniques with Okinawan karate and Filipino knife techniques to formulate the danzan-ryu, or Hawaiian school, of jujutsu. Okazaki later incorporated techniques from the native Hawaiian art of lua, as well as boxing and wrestling. Concurrent with his jujutsu training, the professor also studied traditional Japanese restorative arts, a skill necessary to heal the damage wrought by jujutsu training.

Several characteristics distinguish danzan-ryu, the first being the comprehensive nature of the art. Both before and after World War II, the Hawaiian Islands attracted many accomplished martial artists. Moreover, the mind-set of most of these practitioners differed from Japanese thinking. The Hawaiian practitioners were, by and large, more willing to experiment and more willing to share their knowledge with those outside of their style.

Professor Okazaki tapped into this free-thinking wellspring, even to the point of promoting his own Kodokan in Hilo, away from the pervading influence of Jigoro Kano's Kodokan Institute of Judo.

Another interesting footnote about danzan-ryu is that it was one of the first Japanese systems to accept non-Japanese students. Okazaki was reviled in some quarters for this decision, but his belief in the positive powers of jujutsu was so strong that he felt that everyone should have the opportunity to study.

What is lima lama?

Lima lama (hand of wisdom) is a martial art derived from thirteen ancient Polynesian fighting arts. A strike-oriented system that nonetheless includes joint-locks, sweeps, and throws, lima lama techniques are characterized by fluid, circular movements and retaining blocks wherein the wrist curls around and captures an adversary's arm.

Power in lima lama is not as much a function of strength as it is of velocity. Consequently, practitioners strive for a relaxed, whiplike delivery when striking an opponent.

The indigenous Polynesian art of lua is perhaps the strongest influence on the lima lama system, accounting for many of the hooking, "sticky" blocks that control an opponent's arm. Once controlled, a foe can be jerked off balance or pulled into a blow for greater effect. Many lima lama wrist and arm movements are displayed in modified form in the Hawaiian dance *hula kui.*

What ancient Japanese fighting method did bodyguards of the shogun and other nobles use?

According to some sources, *koshiki koppo*, a derivative of the even more ancient Japanese fighting art of *tegoi*, was developed by Komaro Ohtomo, a bodyguard to Emperor

Shoumu in the eighth century. Early forms of koppo stressed wrestling-type submission holds and wide-trajectory arm-and-leg techniques. Later, various factions of koppo adepts branched out—some becoming mountain priests, others becoming ninja.

The art remained under wraps until Seishi Horibe began openly teaching koppo. In its present form, koppo emphasizes attacks on the joints via strikes and low kicks. Modern koppo also retains many of the earlier immobilizing and restraint techniques that made it effective for high-profile bodyguards.

Do kuk sool wan stylists spar?

Even though kuk sool wan places much more emphasis on the internal application of techniques, according to author Jane Hallander, several types of sparring have a place in kuk sool wan. One type tests the style's grappling aspect as partners practice throws, joint-locks, and controlled strikes. The exchange is not totally freestyle nor is it a two-man kata; it exhibits elements of both. The objective of this type of sparring is to teach practitioners to develop sensitivity to an opponent's intent and to learn efficient angles to break the other's balance.

To reinforce kicks, punches, and strikes, kuk sool wan stylists engage in full-contact sparring with hand, foot, and chest protection. The full-power nature of the contact accustoms participants to putting their all behind punches and kicks—without sacrificing their balance. Full-contact sparring is also an endurance-builder par excellence.

The third variation, freestyle sparring, is a combination of the other two: kicks, punches, throws, and locks are executed spontaneously, yet still under control. Strikes and kicks are delivered with light-to-medium contact with the exception of hitting the face. A winner is determined by a well-focused blow or when one party taps out after being pinned or locked up.

This final form is a true self-defense exercise, and together the three types of kuk sool wan sparring provide practitioners with tangible feedback about the efficacy of their skills.

What are kama?

Kama are modified sickles, with a heavy hardwood handle of about twenty inches or more (kama vary in size and configuration) with a slightly curved blade affixed near the base.

Accepted lore has it that the combative applications of the kama, often included as part of the Okinawan kobudo repertoire, were devised by Okinawan farmers to fight the katana-armed samurai who policed their island. Some historians disagree, however, noting that while the farmers did employ the kama as a cutting tool, the evidence for their development of a sophisticated combat system using double kama is not strong.

Kama techniques, then, could have been a contribution of the Japanese members of the bushi class living in Okinawa. As members of the civilian warrior class, these people would have been knowledgeable about weapons; hence, it is not unreasonable to theorize that they converted a simple farm implement into a pair of fearsome weapons.

In combat, kama were used with powerful slashing movements. Kama were effective against long-range attacks such as those from the staff, since the rear kama could be used to block while the front sickle slices or hooks an opponent's head or arm. Authentic kama kata are limited, but those that exist do not emphasize the whirling, spinning, acrobatic manipulation of the kama seen at martial arts tournaments. Traditional kama kata consist of focused blocking, striking, and slicing motions.

Due to the need for coordinating both weapons and the fact that many of the slicing techniques bring the blade perilously close to a practitioner's body, kama executed with live blades is considered to be one of the more dangerous types of weapon practice and performance.

What are nunchaku, and what is their origin?

Nunchaku are two round or hexagonal pieces of hardwood, usually twelve to fourteen inches in length, connected by a short length of nylon rope or chain. Of Okinawan origin, the nunchaku was originally a rice flail, but was converted by Okinawan peasants into a

Los Angeles, California's Dan Inosanto, the late, great Bruce Lee's chief protégé, wields the nunchaku.
Photo courtesy of the John Corcoran Archives.

striking weapon. Though it shares a common heritage with the other kobudo weapons (e.g., staff, *tonfa*, sai), the nunchaku has become perhaps the most recognized—and misused—kobudo weapon.

Swinging strikes are the most common nunchaku techniques seen in tournaments and demonstrations, yet the nunchaku can also be used to block, pinch, and poke. Used as a pincer, the nunchaku can trap and squeeze an opponent's hand, leg, or arm. The ends of both sticks can be doubled up and thrust into the opponent's vulnerable points. The shaft of the sticks may also be used to facilitate a choke.

Notwithstanding these offensive options, the temptation to concentrate on whip-type techniques is considerable, since even a person with minimal training can generate tremendous destructive force with flailing strikes. Nunchaku in motion can reach speeds easily in excess of 100 mph, thus it's easy to see how such a weapon could have been used to deadly effect by Okinawan farmers-turned-fighters.

Unfortunately, it's also evident how a practitioner can seriously hurt him- or herself when careless with the nunchaku. A pair of hardwood sticks whistling around one's head at over 100 miles per hour doesn't provide much margin for error, and more than a few individuals have learned this the hard way.

Why did the nunchaku become so popular in the United States?

Long a relatively obscure weapon on the American martial arts scene, the nunchaku became a familiar sight to millions through the cinematic efforts of the late martial arts actor Bruce Lee. In several of his movies, Lee's use of the nunchaku was so impressive that it literally made the weapon an overnight sensation.

However, the nunchaku Bruce Lee used in the movies was slightly different from the traditional Okinawan version. Lee's sticks were round and shorter relative to the lengthened chain. This design obviously contributed to the speed and visual impact of these scenes, although in reality it made the nunchaku less effective overall.

According to insiders' statements made after his death, for Lee the nunchaku was not an important cultural or combative weapon but merely a movie prop. Nonetheless, many practitioners who have gone on to become proficient with the nunchaku and other weapons got their inspiration from Bruce Lee.

What is the tonfa?

Originally, the *tonfa* was part of a millstone. The long end of the L-shaped implement was fitted into a hole in the millstone and used to grind grain. As with other farm tools,

Okinawan farmers employed the tonfa against samurai. The shaft or long handle of the tonfa varied between fifteen and twenty inches in length. About five inches from the top and affixed at a right angle is a smaller handle about six inches long. It is this small handle that a practitioner grasps while the long end is held alongside the forearm.

With the tonfa so positioned, a practitioner can use the handle as a swivel. A sharp twist of the wrist whips the long end of the tonfa for strikes. Alternately, the tonfa may be held by the long handle so that the shorter handle becomes a hook to choke or trip an opponent. The projecting handle is also ideal for hammer-style blows.

Tonfa are almost always used in pairs, and like the kama and sai, the addition of the second tonfa allows a practitioner to successfully engage long weapons such as the bo staff. Moreover, since the tonfa uses many blocks and thrusting techniques, a solid grounding in empty-hand techniques is a prerequisite for success against an armed adversary.

How has the tonfa contributed to the law-enforcement field?

The basic design of the tonfa has been adapted for law enforcement, and in fact has replaced the traditional baton (billy club) as the standard impact weapon for many police departments. Known as the PR-24 or side-handled baton, the police version of the tonfa is said to be more versatile than the straight baton.

To account for the longer forearms of Americans and to provide more of a reach advantage, the PR-24 has been lengthened by several inches. The handles on police-issue side-handled batons are usually knurled for greater grip retention.

Although a modern police officer is not likely to face threats similar to those of a seventeenth-century Okinawan peasant, tonfa techniques remain basically unchanged. However, due to the threat of litigation, police departments emphasize more locks and restraint maneuvers.

What is a sai, and how was it used in combat?

The sai can best be described as a pronged truncheon about twenty inches long. Made of iron, the sai is a heavy weapon that was usually used in pairs against a swordsman or a staff-wielding enemy. The tip is blunted; however, the two prongs above the handle are pointed and angle out slightly.

The sai's position and striking methods change through the manipulation of the wrists. One or both sai are held in the normal position with the tip forward, or, with a quick rotation of the wrist, the shaft of the sai lays along the side of the forearm and the weighted butt end becomes available for thrusts.

Even more than its striking and jabbing capabilities, the ingenuity behind the sai is best exemplified by its highly developed blocking and disarming techniques. The design of the sai allows a practitioner to catch the blade or shaft of an opponent's weapon between the prongs. From there, a sharp twist of the sai can snap an inferior blade in half or wrench an adversary's weapon right out of his or her hands.

What role does the bo play in the arsenal of Okinawan weapons?

The bo, or *rokushakubo* (six-foot staff), is the quintessential example of how an ordinary tool becomes an extraordinary weapon in accomplished hands. Although the Okinawan staff is the most recognized long-stick method practiced in the United States, it must be remembered that the staff is a universal weapon used throughout the martial arts.

As indicated by its name, the Okinawan (or Japanese) staff is a hardwood pole six feet long with a diameter between one and one and one-half inches. The Okinawan version is usually tapered at both ends for easier handling.

The staff is, of course, a long-range weapon used for blocking, striking, and thrusting against an opponent armed with a similar or shorter-length impact or edged weapon. Like its companion empty-hand art, Okinawa Te (the inclusive name for the different styles practiced on the Ryukyu Island chain), bo techniques tend toward sharply focused strikes and thrusts as opposed to, say, the Chinese staff, which employs more circular, centrifugal blows.

San Francisco, California's Jeff Chinn, one of the world's biggest Bruce Lee fans, poses in his Bruce Lee Room, dedicated entirely to Bruce Lee memorabilia (fish-eye lens photo). His collector's items appear in the pictures throughout this chapter.

BRUCE LEE

Why was Bruce Lee so special? Why is he still popular many years after his death in 1973? Because when Bruce began making martial arts movies in 1971 with *The Big Boss*, he brought the genre to its highest level, which has never been matched since.

Bruce became the standard by which all others are measured. Hundreds of martial arts films have flooded the market with many action stars hoping to become the next Bruce Lee. Compared to the master, they all seem to move in slow motion. People come and go, but Bruce will definitely last. It is safe to say that there will never be another like him. The more we discover about him, the more he amazes us.

One of the basic principles of Bruce's jeet kune do is to use what works. He applied jeet kune do to his moviemaking and knew how to bring the audience to a frenzy. Bruce had the uncanny ability to know when to hold back and when to fight. He then delivered much more than the audience would ever expect.

Bruce was able to deliver because he was an extremely gifted entertainer who could make whatever he wanted come across on the screen. He would take every ounce of his physical, mental, and emotional skills and combine them in uncanny harmony. Bruce's face would be as articulate as his body, and his intense battle cries delivered even more sensation to each of his already stinging blows. His grace, speed, power, and timing made him the total package that no one else could ever duplicate.

Bruce was rare in that he was an expert martial artist both in real and "reel" life. He knew that real martial arts wouldn't look good

NOTE: All of Bruce Lee's films cited in this chapter are referred to by their original titles as released in Hong Kong.

on screen and movie martial arts wouldn't work in a real fight. When people think of Bruce, they think of martial arts, and when they think of martial arts, they think of Bruce!

In his films, Bruce showed his human side through his warmth and humor. Viewers would always care about Bruce's different characters, although he was essentially playing himself. His movies would get you so involved that you would be sucked in and forget you were in a theater.

In Hong Kong, where the audience is usually quiet and reserved, Bruce's movies would cause them to erupt and cheer with delight. In Japan, which was the worst market for Chinese films, Bruce's movies broke all box-office records. In the United States, Bruce was the first Chinese actor in a leading role to gain widespread acceptance across racial lines. People all over the world could relate to Bruce, because he had a universal way of communicating.

When Bruce died, movie producers cranked out as many look-alike movies as possible, hoping to cash in on even a fraction of Bruce's success. Oddly enough, these terrible films elevated Bruce's films to an even higher level. On the PBS show *Sneak Previews*, Roger Ebert said, "Kung-fu fans have seen a hundred of these rip-offs. Why do they keep going back? I think it's because they had such a shock of delight with the life in those original Bruce Lee pictures that they keep hoping against hope that Bruce Lee will somehow come back."

Bruce's films will undoubtedly hold up through the test of time. Even people who aren't fans of martial arts movies admire his superior artistry.

Why was Bruce Lee so special? Find out by simply watching any Bruce Lee movie. Then join the club with the rest of the world.

Jeff Chinn, who helped write this chapter and supplied photographs of his personal Bruce Lee collection, has been a dedicated Bruce Lee fan and collector of memorabilia since 1972. Chinn is a contributing editor for *Inside Kung-Fu* magazine and writes a bimonthly column on Bruce Lee.

Was Bruce Lee Chinese or American?

Lee was born in San Francisco while his Chinese parents visited the United States, which made him an American citizen. His early martial arts training was in Chinese kung-fu in Hong Kong, but he came to epitomize the American eclectic approach when he began teaching in Seattle in the 1960s while attending college.

Historian Jerry Beasley says, "Lee stressed abandoning traditional methods (which he referred to as 'the classical mess') and instituted a more contemporary training method . . . [finding] eventual acceptance by thousands of American proponents."

What is the story behind Bruce Lee's several names?

When Bruce was born he was named Lee Jun Fan by his mother, Grace. The name meant "Return to San Francisco," because she felt he would return there to live. One of the nurses at the hospital gave him his English name, Bruce, but he didn't use it until he attended La Salle College in Hong Kong.

Bruce was also given a girl's name, Sai Fon, which meant "Small Phoenix." His parents had lost their firstborn son and they hoped to confuse the spirits so they wouldn't steal their precious new son. They even had one of Bruce's ears pierced.

A film director gave Bruce his most well-known Chinese nickname of Lee Siu Loong, "Little Dragon," when he became a child star. Many fans think that this name is carved into Bruce's gravestone, but his real Chinese name, Lee Jun Fan, is the one represented there.

What was Bruce Lee's first movie appearance?

Bruce was barely three months old when he appeared in a film called *Golden Gate Girl.*

The movie was filmed in San Francisco, with Bruce playing the role of a baby girl carried by his own father, actor Lee Hoi Chuen. Although both Bruce and his father made more films, this was their only film appearance together.

What was the final movie that Bruce Lee filmed?

Many people believe that *Game of Death* was Bruce's final movie because it was released last and was incomplete. Bruce actually shot three *Game of Death* fight scenes before he halted production in order to film *Enter the Dragon* instead.

Before Bruce could resume filming *Game of Death*, he suddenly died. Ironically, the very first fight scene in *Enter the Dragon* would prove to be the very last fight scene Bruce would ever film. Bruce decided to add this fight sequence at the last moment because he felt *Enter the Dragon* needed to have a stronger opening.

What was Bruce Lee's height and weight?

Bruce was five feet, seven inches tall and weighed around 140 pounds. Many people who knew him say that, pound for pound, Bruce was one of the most powerful men in the world.

Did Bruce Lee portray a fighter or martial artist in all of his movie and TV appearances?

No. In an episode of *Here Come the Brides* entitled "Marriage, Chinese Style," Bruce's character, Lin Sung, was a weakling. Although several scenes gave Bruce an opportunity to fight, he wasn't able to because his character didn't know how.

Bruce's voice was actually dubbed in several scenes because the makers of the show felt his Chinese accent was too strong!

Did Bruce Lee portray a good guy in all of his movie and TV appearances?

Bruce was cast as a good guy in all but one of his roles. In *Marlowe*, he portrayed a villain named Winslow Wong. Stirling Silliphant, one of Bruce's students, wrote the screenplay with Bruce's talent in mind. Bruce's incredible athletic ability was showcased in the best action scenes of the movie.

What was the original TV show Bruce Lee hoped to star in when he made the screen test for 20th Century Fox in 1965?

Bruce had planned to star in a show called *Number-One Son*, in which he would have been cast as Charlie Chan's number one son opposite Ross Martin (*Wild Wild West*) as

Kato and *The Green Hornet* memorabilia (mostly from 1966–67).
Photo courtesy of Jeff Chinn.

Charlie Chan. Bruce was to carry on the duties of Charlie Chan after his death. Bruce would have been portrayed as a new "Chinese James Bond" who uses kung-fu.

Bruce Lee got a huge amount of fan mail for the unprecedented caliber of martial arts he performed on **The Green Hornet.** *What*

unusual things did he do to promote the show?

Bruce made personal appearances around the country dressed as Kato. He rode on processional floats, opened supermarkets, and appeared at fairs. Many of the fans who mobbed him were children, and Bruce was happy to sign his autograph for them. Underneath his signature he would write *Kato*.

Besides his hands and feet, what weapons did Kato use?

Kato had green darts (hornet-shaped) that he would throw with lightning speed and incredible accuracy. Kato also had a pair of nunchaku; the very first time Bruce ever used nunchaku on the screen was while playing Kato.

What acting roles did Bruce Lee vow never to take?

Bruce never took any roles that would portray him as a stereotypical Chinese. He felt that wearing a pigtail and bouncing around saying "ah-so" would be extremely degrading to himself and to the Chinese people. Bruce was proud to be Chinese and said that he would rather starve than accept these roles.

Turning down these roles made it very difficult for him to survive in the American TV and movie industry during the 1960s and 1970s. An example of Bruce maintaining his integrity is his guest role on the ABC show *Here Come the Brides* in 1968. All of the Chinese characters on the show wore a pigtail, except Bruce.

What were some of the lesser-known TV and movie projects that Bruce Lee appeared in or was involved with in the United States?

Before Bruce did the twenty-six episodes of *The Green Hornet* for ABC (1966–67), he did fifteen minutes of test footage in 1965. In this footage, Bruce is exchanging lines as Kato to a Green Hornet character not played by Van Williams. Both are also wearing different masks.

In an ABC special called *Seven Nights to Remember*, which promoted the network's new shows for the 1966 season, Bruce and Van are seen in a thirty-second promotional clip wearing slightly different costumes. Bruce also did a ten-second commercial promoting *The Green Hornet* wearing a suit and tie.

The Green Hornet and Kato made appearances on two other shows, three appearances on *Batman* and a guest appearance on the *Milton Berle Show* in full costume.

After *The Green Hornet*, Bruce had parts in the TV shows *Ironside* (NBC, 1967) as a martial arts instructor, *Blondie* (CBS, 1968) as a karate instructor, *Here Come the Brides* (ABC, 1968) in a nonfighting role, and *Longstreet* (ABC, 1971) as Longstreet's Jeet Kune Do instructor in four episodes.

As for movies, Bruce appeared in *Marlowe* (MGM, 1969) as a villain. He was fight coordinator for *A Walk in the Spring Rain* (Columbia Pictures, 1969) and *The Wrecking Crew* (Columbia Pictures, 1969).

After Bruce Lee became famous, what were some examples of how he was exploited?

Marlowe was rereleased by MGM with Bruce Lee's name in top billing over James Garner, the actual star. 20th Century Fox pieced together a full-length movie by combining three episodes of *The Green Hornet* TV series with fight scenes from other episodes. This movie made no sense and had Bruce's name in top billing over Van Williams.

Was Bruce Lee's film Fist of Fury shot right after The Big Boss?

No. The premiere episode of American TV's *Longstreet*, co-starring Bruce, had so many favorable reviews that Bruce flew back to Los Angeles to film three more episodes after completing *The Big Boss*. Bruce then flew back to Hong Kong to do *Fist of Fury*.

After Bruce Lee filmed The Big Boss and Fist of Fury, his two-picture contract with Golden Harvest was over. What did he do next?

After almost single-handedly saving Raymond Chow and Golden Harvest from bankruptcy, Bruce was swamped with astronomical offers from producers desperate to get him to sign a contract. But Bruce decided to form his own production company in partnership with Raymond Chow, which was called Concord. Bruce was the first Chinese actor to form his own production company.

The two films produced by Concord were *The Way of the Dragon* and *Enter the Dragon*, which was a joint production with Sequoia (producer Fred Weintraub's company) and Warner Brothers.

What was special about Bruce Lee's first movie for Concord, Way of the Dragon?

In this film, Bruce was the first Chinese to star, write, produce, and direct his own film. And, of course, he choreographed all of the spectacular fight scenes.

Since the Italian authorities in Rome did not allow filming in the Roman Coliseum, how was the classic duel between Bruce Lee and Chuck Norris shot?

Bruce and his film crew illegally shot footage outside the Coliseum. Then the battle between Bruce and Chuck was filmed in Hong Kong at a Golden Harvest Studio soundstage. A set was built to duplicate a portion of the Coliseum.

How was Bruce Lee able to film a convincing battle between himself and aging actor Shih Kien, who portrayed Han in Enter the Dragon?

Shih Kien, who was almost seventy years old, had appeared in over 800 martial arts films and was chosen to star in *Enter the Dragon* as a special guest villain, Han. His battle with Bruce symbolically pitted a villain of the past against a hero of the present.

Shih Kien had to use a stunt double during several fight scenes with Bruce. During one very intense scene, even a stunt double could not be used. In this sequence, Bruce's face suddenly becomes like a madman's as he ferociously kicks Han, who ends up sailing across the room. Bruce actually kicks a fake dummy made up to resemble Han!

Did Bruce Lee see Enter the Dragon before he died?

Bruce saw a rough unfinished version of *Enter the Dragon* at Warner Bros., while visiting Los Angeles before he returned to Hong Kong and died about one month later. This

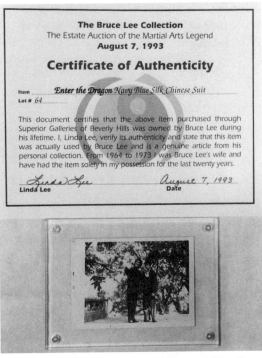

Certificate of Authenticity for the *Enter the Dragon* suit (signed by Linda Lee) and an original photograph of Bruce Lee wearing the suit in a scene from the movie.
Photo courtesy of Jeff Chinn.

version had no music, no sound or optical effects, and no fades or dissolves. It did have plenty of scratches and grease-pencil marks from the editor.

Despite this, Bruce knew a winner when he saw it. When the lights came on, Bruce reportedly had a big grin on his face and stated, "This is the one! We've got it!"

Why did Raymond Chow abandon Bruce Lee's original story concept for Game of Death?

One of the biggest reasons was that many rip-off movies with Lee look-alikes used Bruce's original story line. Raymond's fear was that audiences would confuse Bruce's *Game of Death* with the rip-off movies.

What fashion statement was Bruce Lee trying to make in Game of Death?

Bruce's opponents guarding each floor of the pagoda were dressed in traditional clothing, whereas Bruce wore a modern yellow and black tracksuit. Even his nunchaku matched his suit. Bruce's modern clothes symbolically represented jeet kune do versus each opponent who was bound by tradition.

The only opponent who didn't wear traditional dress was Kareem Abdul-Jabbar. Jabbar was guarding the very top floor and was master of the "unknown style" or "no style."

Speaking of clothing, *Game of Death* is the only martial arts film in which Bruce does not bare his chest.

What were the memorable catchphrases used to promote each of Bruce Lee's films in the United States?

The Big Boss: "Every limb of his body is a lethal weapon."

Fist of Fury: "Unstoppable! Unbelievable! Unbeatable!"

Enter the Dragon: "Their deadly mission: To crack the forbidden island of Han!"

Way of the Dragon: "Boy, can we use him now!"

Game of Death: "Bruce Lee challenges the underworld in his last and greatest motion picture adventure."

Did Bruce Lee's character die in any of his movies?

Yes, he died as Winslow Wong in *Marlowe* and as Chen Chen in *Fist of Fury*. Both movies coincidentally happened to have Bruce's character die while doing a flying kick. *Marlowe* had Winslow missing his flying kick at Philip Marlowe (James Garner) and falling off a tall building. *Fist of Fury* had Chen leap into a hail of bullets from his persecutors.

Why isn't Bruce Lee's actual voice heard on any of his original Chinese martial arts films?

Chinese movies are shot without sound and then are later dubbed with voices. Mandarin was the dialect used in the 1970s, but Bruce only spoke Cantonese, so his voice was never used.

Bruce was the first to use non-Chinese villains in these films; he had to provide all of the English-speaking voices because no one else spoke the language. Among the voices Bruce dubbed were the Russian in *Fist of Fury* and the boss, the interpreter, and the black guy in *Way of the Dragon*!

In which movies did Bruce Lee have a part in the music soundtrack?

In *Way of the Dragon*, Bruce personally sat in on one of the recording sessions and played a percussion instrument. In *Enter the Dragon*, Bruce's battle cries can be heard mixed in with Lalo Schifrin's rousing theme song.

What controversy was caused by Bruce Lee's use of the nunchaku in his movies?

Bruce introduced and popularized the nunchaku with his flamboyant use of them in most of his films. Many fans purchased or made their own pairs without realizing how deadly the nunchaku could be. Many people got hurt, which caused quite a few states, such as California, New York, and Massachusetts, to prohibit the nunchaku by law.

It is currently a felony to possess a pair of nunchaku in some states and, in fact, the punishment can be worse than being caught with a gun! In the United Kingdom, which has even stricter laws banning the weapon, all of Bruce's nunchaku scenes are edited out of his films, even in the biopic *Dragon: The Bruce Lee Story*.

Did Bruce Lee ever get hurt while filming a movie?

In *The Big Boss*, Bruce badly sprained his ankle after landing awkwardly from a jump. He also badly cut his hand after gripping a cheaply made drinking glass. The glass broke and delayed production for a whole week because Bruce needed ten stitches and time to heal. That's why his right hand was bandaged thoughout the film.

In *Enter the Dragon*, Bruce's hand was severely cut in the scene where Bob Wall uses a pair of broken bottles against him. The bottles were made of real glass, since no breakaway bottles were available in Hong Kong. Bruce's hand bled profusely and required twelve stitches, which caused him to miss a week of work.

A second accident on this film was when Bruce's hand was bitten by the cobra he was holding. Fortunately, the cobra's venom had been removed.

In *Game of Death*, Bruce attempted to get a perfect kick to Kareem Abdul-Jabbar's jaw, but due to their tremendous height difference, Bruce pulled a groin muscle. Bruce tried the kick at least three hundred times during the day; he ended up having to take it easy for a whole month before he could kick again.

Did Jackie Chan appear with Bruce Lee in any of his movies?

Jackie was the stuntman for Suzuki in *Fist of Fury* and can be seen crashing through a door screen after catching a flying kick in the throat. In *Enter the Dragon*, they fight each other in one of the cavern scenes. Bruce counters a bear hug from Jackie, locks Jackie's arm behind him, and pulls his head back until his neck snaps.

Bruce Lee statues from China.
Photo courtesy of Jeff Chinn.

What are some of the ways Bruce Lee would demonstrate his incredible strength?

One way was Bruce's use of his "one-inch punch." A volunteer would hold a punching pad against his own chest with Bruce's completely extended arm and fist one inch from the pad. After just a flick of his wrist and slight twist of his body, Bruce would send the volunteer flying backward!

Another way was for a volunteer to hold an air-filled shield while bracing himself. Bruce would kick the shield, sending the person into orbit! Bruce performs this amazing kick in *Way of the Dragon*. With no special effects whatsoever, Bruce is shown kicking an air-filled shield held by one of the restaurant workers, who crashes backward into a pile of boxes.

Just how fast was Bruce Lee in his TV and movie fight scenes?

Bruce was awesomely fast! When Bruce first filmed fight scenes as Kato for *The Green Hornet* TV series, he was told to slow his movements down. The camera could only register a dark blur when he was filmed at normal speed.

When Bruce fought Bob Wall in *Enter the Dragon*, the camera had to be sped up to thirty-two frames a second in order to see Bruce's backfist hit Bob. At normal speed, it didn't even show on film.

What was Bruce Lee's famous coin trick?

Bruce would place a dime in a person's open hand and boast that he could remove the coin before the person could close his hand. After a seemingly failed attempt, Bruce would humbly admit defeat and ask for his dime back. The person would be shocked to find that the dime was gone and in its place a nickel. This trick was one example of Bruce's amazing reflexes and physical dexterity.

All of Bruce Lee's five martial arts movies were in modern-day settings with the exception of one. Which one?

Fist of Fury was set in 1908 in Shanghai. During this time the Japanese had a strong political presence in China and their relationship with the Chinese was hostile.

What was the first documentary done on Bruce Lee?

A few months after Bruce passed away, Golden Harvest quickly put together a film entitled *Bruce Lee: The Man, the Legend*, which documented Bruce's life. The film was of particular interest to the Hong Kong audience because it showed scenes from *Enter the Dragon* and *Game of Death*, neither of which had been released yet.

Did Bruce Lee appear on any talk shows in the United States?

Bruce was to return to the United States in August 1973 to promote *Enter the Dragon* and to appear on *The Johnny Carson Show* in New York. When Bruce died, the travel tickets to New York were traded in for tickets to return his body to Seattle.

Was a TV series ever done on the life of Bruce Lee?

Yes. In 1992, Asia Television Limited (Hong Kong) produced a weekly TV series called *Spirit of the Dragon*. American-born Chinese actor David Wu played the part of Bruce, and the famous moviemaking martial artist Lau Kan Leung had the important role of Bruce's father. The hour-long series lasted thirty episodes and was loosely based on Bruce's life.

What is the basic philosophy of Bruce Lee's personal fighting method, jeet kune do?

To absorb what is useful, reject what is useless, and add what is specifically your own. To have no technique, but make your opponent's technique your technique. Jeet kune do is simply to simplify, but also to have no limitation as limitation.

In his style of jeet kune do, Bruce Lee said, "Efficiency is anything that scores." How did he exemplify this in his movies?

- In *The Big Boss*, Bruce used a flashlight, a handful of sawdust, a bag of chips, and his own jacket when weapon-wielding thugs outnumbered him.
- In *Fist of Fury*, Bruce used a bowl of rice against a samurai with a sword (Suzuki) and used his teeth to bite the Russian villain armlocking him.
- In *The Way of the Dragon*, Bruce caused a villain to knock himself out when he didn't know how to handle a pair of nunchaku.
- In *Enter the Dragon*, Bruce was able to trick an opponent (Parsons) by not fighting him, or more specifically, he used "the art of fighting without fighting."
- In *Game of Death*, Bruce was able to counterattack Kareem Abdul-Jabbar by punching holes in the paper windows and letting the sun temporarily blind his sensitive eyes.

How much did Bruce Lee charge his celebrity students?

According to Bruce's business card, he charged $275 per hour, $1,000 for a ten-session course, and instruction overseas would cost $1,000 a week plus expenses! This was during the 1960s, when nobody else charged anywhere near these kinds of fees.

What was the most ever paid for a piece of Bruce Lee memorabilia?

Twenty-nine thousand dollars (not including commission and sales tax) was the winning bid for a personal handwritten statement dated January 1969 and titled "My Definite Chief Aim." Planet Hollywood was the successful bidder, and a color copy of this unique piece has been duplicated and placed in many of its restaurants.

The statement reads

> "I, Bruce Lee, will be the first highest paid Oriental superstar in the United States. In return I will give the most exciting performances and render the best of quality in the capacity of an actor. Starting in 1970 I will achieve world fame and from then onward till the end of 1980 I will have in my possession $10,000,000. I will live the way I please and achieve inner harmony and happiness."

Why did Bruce Lee display a pair of broken eyeglasses on the wall of his office?

Bruce displayed the eyeglasses as a reminder of how poor he had been. During the difficult times of his life, Bruce couldn't even afford to have his glasses repaired. He had to use Scotch tape and paper clips to keep the glasses together.

In Dragon: The Bruce Lee Story, *Bruce Lee was challenged by a representative of the Chinese kung-fu schools in the San Francisco area. Bruce defeated him, but was severely kicked in the back and was hospitalized. He slowly worked himself back to shape. Did this really happen?*

Bruce really was challenged to stop teaching non-Chinese by a representative named Wong Jak Man. Bruce beat him, but the fight dragged on for three tiring minutes. The fighting became sloppy, and Bruce ended up having to chase after Wong.

This incident proved to be the critical turning point in Bruce's fighting and training methods, because he recognized his limitations and need for better conditioning. It was the birth of jeet kune do.

In a separate incident several years later, Bruce had a severe back injury, but he caused it on his own. Bruce often performed an exercise in which he would place a 125-pound weight on his neck and then continuously bend over at the waist. One day in 1970, Bruce performed this exercise but suddenly felt some pain in his lower back. He later found out that he had permanently injured his fourth sacral nerve. Even more shocking, Bruce was told that he would never kick again and to forget about practicing kung-fu.

Bruce ended up bedridden for three months and spent another three months of gingerly moving only very short distances around the house. According to Lee himself, this was the most depressing time of his life, but Bruce wisely used his time of physical inactivity to write notes on jeet kune do and ended up with eight two-inch volumes. These notes were later condensed by his wife, Linda, and published as the book *Tao of Jeet Kune Do* in 1975.

Bruce also refused to accept the doctor's permanent diagnosis of his back and continued to do the martial arts he loved in spite of his injury.

Was Bruce Lee born with the incredible martial arts skills he had, and did he have the perfect body?

Bruce definitely was not born with these skills, but achieved them by spending thousands of hours perfecting them. Two other important factors that contributed to Bruce's success were the strong power of his mind and will, and that he never seemed to want to relax and sit idle. As a child, Bruce's family gave him a Chinese nickname that meant "never sits still."

If Bruce didn't constantly exercise the way he did, he would not have developed his perfect body. In fact, Bruce was born with one leg shorter than the other, and was even rejected from the military draft because of his very poor eyesight, sinus condition, and high foot arches!

Would Bruce Lee have been as successful in the TV and movie business without his martial arts skills?

Probably not. Bruce's success as an international film actor was primarily due to his charisma and the way he presented martial arts on the screen. Bruce had two types of speech impediments, a stuttering problem and a funny way of speaking that sounded like Elmer Fudd, and these would generally spell doom for any actor. But Bruce's strengths as a martial arts actor far outweighed his weaknesses.

What was one of the most incredible and difficult fight sequences that Bruce Lee put on film?

In *Enter the Dragon*, Bruce filmed a spectacular scene in which he defends himself against twelve of Han's guards who were attacking from all angles. The physical strain put on Bruce was tremendous because he had to kick eleven stuntmen eleven consecutive times, nonstop, then use a backfist to strike the twelfth stuntman.

Choreographing this scene was just as difficult because each of the twelve men had to attack with split-second timing and have the right reactions when getting hit. Bruce not only had to kick with perfect accuracy, but make each move with the grace, realism, ease, and athleticism for which he is famous. Even if one of the twelve made a mistake, the entire sequence had to be reshot until it was perfect.

On top of that, not only did Bruce have to look fresh and not tired every time, but also his permanent back injury had to be cared for after each fight scene.

Where is Bruce's son, Brandon Lee, buried?

Brandon is buried right next to his father in Seattle's Lakeview Cemetery. A special bench was constructed at the base of the two grave sites with the special message, "Husband and Father, Son and Brother, You Are Always With Us—Linda and Shannon."

When and where was "Bruce Lee Day"?

"Bruce Lee Day" was officially celebrated on June 8, 1979, in Los Angeles. Mayor Tom Bradley proclaimed this special day during the U.S. premier of Bruce's last film, *Game of Death*, at the Paramount Theater in Hollywood.

Bruce Lee periodicals in various languages from around the world.

Photo courtesy of Jeff Chinn.

During the premier, a petition for Bruce's star on the Walk of Fame was displayed in the theater lobby for fans to sign when they came to see the film. Linda Lee was the first person to sign it. Bruce's star was long overdue; it took almost fourteen years to become a reality.

Where is Bruce Lee's star located on Hollywood Boulevard's Walk of Fame?

Bruce Lee's star is located on 6933 Hollywood Boulevard, which is only a few feet west of the famous Mann's Chinese Theatre. The Chinese Theatre location is the favorite spot among most Walk of Fame inductees. Bruce's star was inducted on April 28, 1993.

Did Bruce Lee ever win a Lifetime Achievement Award?

Yes. In 1994, in the 13th Hong Kong Film Awards ceremony, a special Lifetime Achievement Award was given to Bruce posthumously. After a touching montage of film clips that showcased Bruce's entire film career from 1940 to 1973, Raymond Chow presented the award to Linda and Shannon Lee. After accepting the award on behalf of Bruce, both Linda and Shannon gave very sentimental speeches completely in Cantonese to a rousing ovation from the audience.

What is the one common gesture used to charm the audience in all five of Bruce Lee's martial arts movies?

His trademark smile.

Choosing the right school is the first step to success when it comes to martial arts training. It's best to be a comparative shopper. Rob Colasanti (left), vice president of the National Association of Professional Martial Artists, says "the key is to visit a variety of schools before you make a final decision."

HOW TO CHOOSE A MARTIAL ARTS SCHOOL

The choosing of a martial arts school is in many ways described best by the old Zen parable, "A journey of a thousand miles starts with a single step." The first step toward earning your black belt is to seek out a good school and teacher to guide you on your journey.

This single decision will be one of the two major factors of your growth as a martial artist. The other is your attitude toward training and your discipline to follow through. However, keeping a good attitude and going to class is sure easier when you're in the right school.

I was so excited about the martial arts school I joined that I went to class there every day after my regular school let out. I used to spend the night at the school and train until 3 or 4 A.M. and then sleep on the floor. I'd go right back at it the next day.

Part of the reason I went to the karate school every day was because my parents wouldn't pay for the lessons. Since I had quit football a few years earlier, they thought I would quit karate too. So they refused to pay the $25-per-month tuition.

So in return for my lessons, my instructor allowed me to clean the school. I was the original "Wax on, wax off" kid. That put me in the school every day. I would vacuum the carpet, clean the mirrors, and scrub the bathroom. Afterward, I would practice. My instructors noticed my desire to excel, so they began to take me on as a training partner.

You need to realize that choosing a school is not like choosing a dry cleaner. You ought to make a good, educated decision on where to learn. Your relationship with your instructor is paramount in your success. You don't have a relationship with a building or a storefront. Relationships are between people.

Choosing the right school and the right instructor is the first step in a lifelong journey toward fulfilling your own potential and reaching your goals as a martial artist.

How do I choose a martial arts school for me or my child?

The principles of choosing a martial arts school are the same for you and your child. The following answer is addressed to parents, as there are a couple of special considerations when children are involved.

Many modern studios feature gorgeous interior layouts that are designed using the principles of Feng-Shui.

Photo courtesy of the John Graden Archives.

Step one in choosing a school is to understand clearly what you want you or your child to gain from learning the martial arts. Is it a light recreation? Then a community center program may suffice. Is it self-defense or personal development? If so, then a full-time professional school may be more suitable. Many parents view the martial arts as part of their child's educational development. With a good professional school, this is very possible.

Step two is to recognize that choosing a school really means choosing an instructor. Be sure to visit the school and watch the instructor work with other children of the same age. Every school is very different because every instructor is different. Don't get confused by claims of black-belt degrees, tournament wins, or martial art styles. The only style that matters is the teaching style of the instructor and how you or your child will respond to him or her.

Finally, trust your instincts. A professional school will have a family atmosphere, show lots of smiles, and be well kept. You'll feel comfortable with the personnel and the facility.

While this may not end up being the closest school to your house, when it comes to your safety or the safety and education of your child, an extra ten-minute drive can make a world of difference in the outcome.

Does the government license martial arts schools?

Other than business licensing, there are no regulations in the United States governing martial arts instruction or the qualifications of these who give such instruction. This is primarily due to the fact that the martial arts have always been considered an "art form."

Since instructor requirements vary from style to style and organization to organization, there is no objective way to measure an instructor's qualifications. Therefore it is very important for you to become an informed consumer when you start looking for a martial arts school.

How early should a parent start a child in the martial arts?

While martial arts study is an enjoyable and very worthwhile activity for children, it should be recognized that progress will take consistent class attendance, practice at home, and support from the family (kids can't drive themselves to class).

How early to start a child really depends on the individual child and his or her level of interest and maturity. Many professional schools have age-specific classes and curriculum programs for children as young as four, five, or six years old. These programs are very popular and can be a great way for a child to learn concentration, acquire self-control, and start to develop more coordination.

Programs for children of this age usually are less demanding than mainstream martial arts programs and bypass much of the serious self-defense training in favor of more age-appropriate and fun activities.

How many styles of martial arts are there, and how do I choose one?

There are hundreds of martial arts. Without a doubt, kung-fu has the most systems, ranging from major systems practiced worldwide to systems practiced only by one family or in one Chinese village.

When choosing a system, you should decide what you want to gain from your martial arts training. If you are solely interested in learning self-defense, a system that concentrates on sport competition would be a poor choice. And if you are small in stature and therefore interested in a system that will allow you to use your legs as weapons, you should avoid grappling systems.

The one good quality about an activity that has so many variations is that there is a style to fit everyone. By talking with instructors and watching classes, you should be able to select a style that fits your personal needs.

What kind of facility should I look for?

It's important to trust your first impressions when finding a facility. The modern martial arts school is clean, well lit, and spacious, and has a good family atmosphere. The mirrors are polished, the floor is clean, and the dressing rooms in good order. On the wall might be photographs of recent school events and outings, and there should definitely be an area for parents or family to sit and watch the classes.

Beware of any school that doesn't allow you to watch the class. Particularly if you are a parent looking for a school for your child, you should have real concerns about a school that doesn't allow you to watch them work with your child. An instructor might say that they don't want the child to be distracted by the parent, but usually the truth is that the instructor doesn't want to be accountable to the parent.

Conversely, professional instructors will try to insist that you stay and watch. They know that once you see the positive lessons they are teaching your child, you'll be even more supportive of the training. The instructor who encourages you to take the time to watch your child in class is doing you and your child a great service. In today's busy world, the tendency to drop off a child and not take the time to share his or her experience of learning a new skill is all too prevalent.

Kids whose parents are in class and are supportive seem to do much better and be more well adjusted than kids who are dropped off. Children want, more than anything else, their parents to take an interest in them and be proud. Martial arts, taught by a professional, offer a series of victories for each child ranging from a new belt or stripe on their belt to other forms of recognition for the child. That recognition is greatly enhanced when the parent is there to share in the pride.

Consider a professional martial arts instructor as part of the team whose goal is to instill a strong sense of self-pride and confidence in your child. As a parent, your pres-

Make sure that the school you select is clean and spacious, and has a viewing area for spectators.

Photo courtesy of the John Graden Archives.

ence in that classroom is critical to the success of the team.

What should I do if my child wants to quit?

There will come a time when your child says, "I'm too tired to go to class today." This is a critical point in a child's training. This is when you help teach them about follow-through and the never-quit attitude.

Don't be concerned about "pushing it on your child." Children wouldn't go to school, brush their teeth, or clean their rooms if you didn't push it on them. There's a big difference between helping a child follow through on a goal they agreed to and force-feeding martial arts to a child.

When you begin the classes, agree with your child on some short-term goals, such as earning a specific belt, with the understanding that there will be no quitting until the goal is achieved. The real goal in the training should be black belt, but until you've had a chance to really understand what it takes to earn a black belt, it's best to initially set a more reachable goal. Once you've determined that a black belt is the goal, commit to it with full enthusiasm.

However, it's unrealistic to expect a child not to, at some point, rebel against the effort. This is natural and should not lead to quitting. Quitting can quickly become a bad

This state-of-the-art martial arts school sports a fully stocked pro shop so that the students can conveniently purchase safety gear and a variety of other martial supplies.
Photo courtesy of the John Graden Archives.

habit. Facing this type of challenge is part of the training inherent in the martial arts.

How can I motivate my child to continue?

Not quitting on a goal is an integral skill a parent has to instill in a child. This is the foundation of goal-setting and achievement. Quitting is the foundation of under-performance and failure. The world is full of great starters. But you need to teach your child that it's the ability to set goals and see them through to their completion that's most important.

When you've been attending class with your child and know exactly what has been happening, you can help motivate the child to go to class by reminding him or her of how enjoyable the last class was. Also, he or she can look forward to seeing friends in class.

How much do martial arts lessons cost?

The actual cost per month will vary widely from market to market. But this question has to be approached from a slightly different perspective than money alone. In seminars around the country, I ask the black belts a simple question: "If I could give you $10,000, would you be willing to sell me back your black belt and the impact that martial arts have had on your life? Would you be willing to erase your martial arts experience from your life for $10,000? For $20,000? How about $50,000?"

I've spoken before thousands of black belts, but no one has ever offered to accept my hypothetical offer. Whether your classes are $40, $70, or $100 a month, the value of earning a black belt far exceeds the investment. What is it worth to be able to walk out to your car with a loved one late at night after a show and know that if something happens, you have the skill to deal with it? What is it worth to parents to know that their child is developing the self-pride and inner confidence to avoid negative peer pressures? What is it worth to any of us in today's violent world to empower ourselves or our children with the skills to handle a confrontation?

It's worth a lot more than it costs to gain that kind of invaluable knowledge. With the huge variation in the instructors, the facilities, and the atmospheres of one school to the next, you should never shop for the martial arts based upon price. Schools tend to charge what they think they are worth. If a school charges $30 a month, there is a reason why it's so cheap. Likewise, a school that charges $85 a month usually has a reason why it's worth a higher fee.

What's interesting is that, in most cases, the schools that charge a little more for the quality of their instruction tend to be bigger and have many more students than the bargain-basement schools that charge apologetically.

Most good schools will charge anywhere from $60 per month and up, with a small registration fee of about $149. This registration might include your membership in the National Association of Professional Martial Artists (NAPMA), your first month's dues, and possibly your uniform.

Do martial arts lessons have to be expensive?

Many excellent instructors teach at Boys and Girls Clubs, YMCAs, city recreation departments, and college clubs. These classes normally provide instruction at reduced rates since they are partly funded through taxes or donations.

Because these are public organizations that cater to children, the instructors are usually checked for legitimacy, narcotic use, and any criminal record. The disadvantage to these programs is that since they use part-time instructors and multiple-use facilities, classes are usually restricted to two or three meetings a week, normally in the evenings.

Do I have to sign a contract?

This depends on the school and your situation. Many schools do not require any contract or agreement. However, signing a contract for lessons is not always a bad idea. One advantage to signing a contract is that you lock in the cost of tuition at the current rate and thus avoid increases.

The key is to not sign for more than you're confident you can follow through on. Since earning a black belt should take three to four years, you should avoid any kind of long-term agreements over, say, four or five years. However, if you know you want to earn a black belt, it makes perfect sense to lock in the lowest tuition possible for that time period.

There are some additional items to consider when you are faced with an agreement for lessons. Check with the local merchants'

association, Better Business Bureau, and your state's consumer affairs or consumer protection agencies, to see if the school has a history of litigation or complaints.

Many schools use the agreement only as a way to clearly spell out the arrangements for the relationship between the student and the school. Such schools will not enforce any type of hard collections that may damage your credit or harass you. On the other hand, some schools will attempt to collect on the contract, and that could present a real problem for you.

Other schools go as far as selling the contracts to a third party. This third party will aggressively pursue the collections whether you are in class or not. This selling of the contract to a third party should definitely be avoided. Find out what the school plans to do with the paperwork before you sign on the dotted line.

However, it's perfectly reasonable for a school to employ a tuition billing company to process your payments. This is very different from selling them your contract. In this case, the third-party billing company simply accepts your payments, keeps a small percentage as a fee, and then sends the school the remainder. Martial artists don't always make the best bookkeepers, so it's a good idea for them to hire the processing and posting of payments out to an expert.

What if I like the school, but the school insists on having me sign a contract?

If you are uncomfortable signing a contract for yourself or your child, tell the school owner that you're uncomfortable and seek out an alternative arrangement. Most schools will work with a student in order to provide the training. However, other schools will turn away a student who is not willing to commit to training more than a month at a time.

Also, state laws can affect what types of arrangement a school can make, so find out ahead of time what to expect from a school. For state-specific advice, contact your state's consumer affairs office.

My contract mentions Electronic Funds Transfer. What is this, and should I use it to make tuition payments?

Electronic Funds Transfer (EFT) is a simple and effective method of ensuring that your tuition is paid on time each month. The exact amount of the tuition is automatically withdrawn from your designated bank account each month on the same day and transferred to the school.

While the thought of someone automatically extracting funds from your account each month may be uncomfortable for you, it is the safest and easiest method of payment available. In actuality, no one is accessing your account. It's really just two computers talking to each other. Only the exact amount can be withdrawn, not a penny more. Furthermore, no one can access that account or peek around to see how much is in there. It's all done electronically.

This is important because your relationship with the instructor, as you pursue your black belt, should be as pure as possible. Your instructor doesn't want tuition hassles interfering with your training any more than you do. EFT makes the whole process easier by guaranteeing that the student's tuition will be paid in a timely fashion each month without any problems.

The student (or parent) also remains in full control of the EFT and can cancel it at any time should there ever be any complications.

What if the instructor wants me to pay in advance for lessons?

There is a big difference between being offered the option to pay for, say, a year in advance with a discount, and being told that advance payments are required. If a school insists that you must pay for more than thirty days in advance, do not enroll. Usually this indicates a school that has a very high dropout rate and whose owner knows you may not stick around for long. The owner is going to try get as much money as possible from you before you leave.

Most schools have a standard payment plan and then a small discount of 15 to 20 percent if you pay the full amount in advance. This is simply a reasonable option. Many people prefer to pay in advance; therefore that option should be available to them.

However, if you decide to pay in advance anyway, make sure you have a written agreement that's signed by the instructor as to what is being paid for and what would constitute cause for a refund. This is an example of where signing a contract may be in your best interest. For instance, if you are in an automobile wreck or are transferred for your job, wouldn't that be cause for a refund? Your attorney would have the answer based upon the state you live in, so be sure to investigate and protect your investment before making advance payments.

Many states prohibit any advance payments of more than thirty days, so talking with an attorney is always the prudent thing to do when it comes to advance payments.

What are testing fees?

Many schools charge an additional fee when you take an exam to graduate to another belt. These testing fees can be $40–$75 or more. While it would not be fair to say that a school that charges testing fees should be held in suspicion, it can be said that, through the efforts of NAPMA, testing fees are becoming less common.

NAPMA–member schools are encouraged not to impose testing-fee charges. NAPMA's position is that a student's progress should not be tied to money.

Some schools are charged a testing fee from their parent style–association, which in turn supplies the school with certificates. These certificates, for the most part, are irrelevant to the student since they are only recognized within the association. You might ask if you can avoid testing fees by not getting your certificate. A certificate from an association for any color belt, except the black belt, rarely transfers to another school.

The only reasonable test fee is one for a black-belt test. A black-belt test is a much more involved exam and often has a number of expenses tied to it for the school. For that reason, you can expect to pay $150–$300 for a black-belt exam. This money offsets the additional preparation the school has to make in order to promote someone to black belt, and it is a fair charge.

How do I find a good instructor?

There are many sources for locating instructors. Martial arts equipment store owners, friends who are martial arts students, and even the Yellow Pages can get you started in locating a school.

Once having located a school, a prospective student should watch classes of various levels. Observe the way the instructor and students conduct themselves. Does the instructor actually instruct and physically perform techniques skillfully? Talk with the instructor and some students. Do they have the enthusiasm and attitude that you want to acquire? Is the instructor teaching what you want to learn?

To the untrained eye, a marginally skilled martial artist might look impressive and therefore can be deceiving. So never sign up with the first school you look at. Visit as many schools as it takes for you to find one that fits your needs.

Are all black belts the same?

Unfortunately, no. The requirements for a black belt vary widely, and this is true the world over, not just in the United States. In some schools, a person can earn a first-degree black belt in just a year or two. Other schools require four to six years of intense training.

If you are thinking, "Gee, I want to train in one of those schools where I can earn a black belt in a couple of years," just remember that it means your teachers won't have much experience either.

The middle road is probably the best path to take. Three to four years of continual practice under a good teacher should provide you with the knowledge and skill to call yourself a black belt.

What belt rank should my instructor be?

In most styles of martial arts, there are ten degrees of black belt, with new black belt being a first-degree. The problem is that with the lack of standardization in the martial arts, what defines a fifth-degree black belt or a seventh-degree black belt varies so drastically that the rank doesn't really convey meaning to the general public.

Joe Lewis, one of the legends of American martial arts, has a unique reply regarding black-belt rank. When asked what degree of black belt he was, Lewis would typically answer, "There are two types of black belts. Good ones and bad ones. I'm one of the good ones." Beyond earning a black belt, rank has little, if anything, to do with quality of instruction.

This is a critical point to understand. Just because someone has received a high rank within an art doesn't make that person a good teacher. Indeed, sometimes the opposite is true. Some black belts are more focused on their own achievements rather than the students'.

It's very hard to say what rank beyond black belt a professional martial artist should be. But obviously, a school owner or chief instructor should be a black belt or the equivalent, depending on the art. Also, if your goal is to earn a black belt, then you have to have an instructor who is at least a second- or third-degree black belt, so he or she can promote you to first-degree black belt. A first-degree black belt cannot promote someone else to first-degree black belt. In most systems, you have to be one or two degrees higher to promote someone. For instance, an instructor would have to be a third- or fourth-degree black belt to promote a student to second-degree black belt.

Beyond that, the rank of the instructor will mean very little to your classroom experience or the quality of your instruction. In fact, when choosing a school, you should probably avoid schools that advertise by telling you all about the instructor's ranks. What the instructor has accomplished is not as important as what he or she can do for you, so don't be misled by claims of the title "grandmaster" or a tenth-degree black belt. Those are not as important as finding an instructor who cares about the students and makes them the focus, instead of seeking all the attention him- or herself.

How do I know an instructor's credentials are legitimate?

Black-belt certificates are a lot like college degrees. Some are received after years of hard work, some are received through accelerated programs, some are from correspondence schools requiring little or no study, some are honorary, and some are just plain fraudulent.

The average time it takes to earn a first-degree black belt is three to six years. After that, most promotions normally come in two- to six-year increments. So the years of experience the instructor has invested in an art are an important factor in determining whether his or her rank is justified.

All legitimate instructors will be glad to tell you who they trained under and how to contact them or the organization they're affiliated with. If the instructor will not discuss his or her background or is evasive about certain information, it's safe to assume that the credentials might be questionable.

What kind of certification should I look for?

Instructors who have been certified through NAPMA have undergone training in classroom management and safety. This certification is signified by the ACMA (American Council on Martial Arts) designation, which is issued by the prestigious Cooper Institute for Aerobic Research in Dallas, Texas.

In the martial arts industry, the ACMA is widely recognized as the qualification that demonstrates basic, entry-level knowledge in classroom management, student safety, and working with special-needs students.

Should I find a "champion" instructor?

Looking through the phone-book ads, it's almost impossible not to find a champion. It would be harder to find an instructor who doesn't claim to be a champion of some sort. Like rank, an instructor's tournament titles mean very little, if anything, to your learning experience. Just because someone has won an event doesn't mean he or she can teach you or your child.

In fact, the hard-core competitor often has a difficult time toning down the training for novices or children. For instance, John McEnroe is a great tennis champion, but I don't know if I would want him as my child's tennis coach. That's not to say a title is a bad thing. It's just not an important aspect to look for or be concerned with.

Since just about every martial artist listed in the phone book is a champion of some sort, simply ignore the claims and focus on what they can do for you.

What is the National Black Belt Club?

The National Black Belt Club (NBBC) is a very special program within a school that is designed to aid and recognize the students who have set a goal of earning a black belt. The NBBC greatly differs from a money-oriented black-belt course.

Many schools use hard sell to get a student on a three-year black-belt course as soon as the student enrolls. This is unfair both to the student and to the school. A student should first train in the school for a while in order to fully understand the commitment necessary for earning a black belt. Only then, after a full evaluation, should a student be offered the opportunity for advanced training.

This is often an offer to join the NBBC. The NBBC best represents what a good school stands for, which is earning a black belt. Students in the NBBC are given special classes and training opportunities in order to help them reach their goal of the black belt. The NBBC works as a screening process so instructors can reserve advanced training for students who are seeking that level. This process helps the instructor in designing his or her curriculum, clinics, and lesson plans.

The NBBC is an evaluation process whereby students spend a few months in the classroom learning about the martial arts and its benefits. The instructors also spend those first few months evaluating the students to determine if they have the necessary attitude and aptitude to earn the black belt. Students who decide to make the black belt their goal can qualify for advanced training in the NBBC.

The commitment to the black belt should be very prestigious and given tremendous reverence within the school ranks. Of course everyone knows that a student should not be able to buy a black belt. However, a student should not be able to buy even the commitment on behalf of the school to train them for the black belt. It must be earned.

How does the NBBC work?

The student enrolls in a trial program to see if he or she can qualify for advanced training in the NBBC. After three months, a series of evaluations should begin with short surveys about the student's progress and goals.

Once the student joins the NBBC, he or she can qualify for additional classes and seminars, and special uniforms and patches. In addition, special social events for NBBC members are a great way to reinforce the commitment to the black belt by creating an opportunity for students to socialize and bond together.

Some schools have the attitude, "Why not get a three-year commitment when a student enrolls, then, if he or she quits, we still have the money." Again, this is unfair to the student and to the school. When instructors are measured not by how many people they sign up and how much money they take in, but by how many people they can get to share the vision of the black belt, there will be a huge difference in their performance and in the overall attitude of the school.

This process, of course, puts pressure on the instructors to do a great job. It shows tremendous confidence on behalf of the school to say to a student, "No, we won't take your money for an NBBC membership until we feel you are ready and capable of making that decision."

What are the requirements for joining the NBBC?

In most NAPMA schools, students can only enter the NBBC at the recommendation of their instructor. They cannot request acceptance into the club; they have to be recommended and have fulfilled very specific qualifications. To qualify, a student must have his or her first colored belt or above, and have his or her instructor's recommendation.

How do I get recommended?

To qualify for the NBBC, you must

1. Have set a goal of earning the black belt
2. Have regular belt-exam participation
3. Have a very positive attitude in martial arts, at school or work, and at home
4. Demonstrate the qualities of black-belt excellence in and out of the school
5. Have a high level of enthusiasm for your martial arts class

6. For students still in school, earn a good report card for your conduct and attitude from both parents and teachers
7. Support school functions
8. Have good attendance and eagerness to make up absences
9. Be current with tuition payments
10. Have full support of your family

What are the benefits of membership in the NBBC?

NAPMA schools are black-belt schools, and when a student makes the commitment to the black belt, he or she is past the trial stage. That student becomes part of the school with the following privileges:

1. Discounts on all special events
2. Special weekly seminars/workouts for NBBC members only
3. Lowest possible tuition rate through the black belt, with no yearly increases
4. Special NBBC patch
5. Special NBBC belt
6. Opportunity to wear the red uniform of the NBBC

Should I take group or private lessons?

Private lessons are beneficial because they allow you to work one-on-one with an instructor and therefore can sometimes help you advance faster. When teaching only one student, the instructor can both observe and correct mistakes quickly.

In a group class, you get to work with classmates of various skill levels. This helps you adjust to opponents who may be bigger or smaller, faster or slower, and more skilled or less skilled. It is usually hard to gauge your own progress when you work out with only one instructor and no classmates.

Another important part of the martial arts is the sense of belonging and family that a group class provides. Classmates tend to support each other while at the same time pushing each other to make progress.

The best learning situation is to attend group classes and take additional private lessons to learn the techniques you cannot grasp in the group situation.

How often should I go to class?

For the first few months, resist the urge to go more than two times a week. Most professional schools will restrict your attendance in these early stages to twice a week while they evaluate your training. Then, after you've trained for a few months, they may make more classes available for you as part of a special program, such as the NBBC.

This is a good method for both the student and the instructor. The student is prevented from overdoing it at first, and it helps the student to avoid injuries and burnout from an overenthusiastic start. Then, as the student gets in better shape and understands the training, the instructor can better determine if the student should be given the opportunity for additional training. This is often a privilege reserved for students who have made the commitment to earning a black belt.

Since new students couldn't be expected to understand what it takes to earn a black belt, the early restrictions on attendance serve to slowly indoctrinate the students in the martial arts and permit them to evaluate the potential benefits before setting a goal of gaining the black belt.

How long are classes?

The length of a class usually will depend on the age of the students. For most classes targeting four- to six-year-olds, the class should run thirty to forty-five minutes at the most. For classes targeting seven- to twelve-year-olds, forty-five minutes is usually about right, with a one-hour class for the brown- and black-belt children. Adult beginner's classes can be forty-five minutes, with an increase to an hour upon graduating to the next belt level.

Schools that still run two-hour classes tend to burn their students out very quickly. In today's world, it's very difficult for people to devote more than one hour to an activity for any length of time. Professional studies on attention spans have shown that thirty to sixty minutes is about the max for most people, depending on their age.

How many days a week should I practice?

Two to three days a week is sufficient for beginners. You will be learning new techniques all the time, and you need a few days between practices to assimilate all this information. As you become more proficient, you may wish to train almost every day. The bottom line is that you should do whatever is comfortable for your schedule and your body.

Is martial arts training dangerous?

Martial arts training is not dangerous when compared to many other contact and high-risk activities. Most karate and kung-fu schools teach students to stop their techniques just short of contact or only allow them to make light to moderate contact.

Most grappling systems conduct their training on matted floors, making their training no more dangerous than high school wrestling. Of course, accidents occasionally happen, and some systems practice full-contact sparring and kickboxing. If you are truly concerned about the possibility of injury, you should make sure to observe all areas of instruction in a school before deciding to enroll in it.

How risky is martial arts practice, in terms of injuries?

Past insurance ratings, based on data from hospitals, ranked martial arts below golf in the number of injury claims. That doesn't mean you're not going to get sore or occasionally bruised. It just means that serious injuries are not very common in the martial arts in most schools, particularly for schools belonging to a professional organization like NAPMA.

Most schools are very safe and go to extreme lengths to ensure the safety of its classes and participants. Other schools are rougher and can have a militarylike atmosphere where only the strong survive. These schools can be recognized by an almost exclusively adult-male student body and a gymlike atmosphere.

Any school you attend should have age-specific classes and use all possible safety equipment when sparring. The striking pads should be new and in good shape, and the instructors should belong to an organization like NAPMA to ensure they are receiving ongoing information in the latest methods of teaching.

While claims against martial arts schools are very rare because the training is very safe, many schools are not insured, which is a mistake. Make sure your school is insured and that the instructors are attending seminars and workshops on professional teaching methods.

What can I expect to learn?

This is an exciting question. Contrary to the media's image of a tough drill sergeant–like martial arts instructor, today's professional is well-schooled in positive motivation, modern training methods, and character development.

The schools will have special programs built into the curriculum on goal-setting, self-confidence, how to avoid violent confrontation, and other personal-development goals.

This emphasis on personal responsibility and successful attitudes was introduced into the martial arts classroom in the mid-1980s. It has come as a pleasant surprise to many students who feared that martial arts would be an only-the-strong-survive experience.

Students of all ages and athletic abilities can now train in the martial arts without the fear of injury and humiliation associated with the so-called dungeon schools of the past.

What kinds of physical training do the martial arts teach?

In terms of the physical aspects, there are two primary areas of physical training in the martial arts. First are the traditional arts and techniques of the style taught at the school. This is known as the do or the Way. These techniques and forms are not made up by the school, but are passed down from instructor to student through the years. Students honor the art by adhering to its traditional principles.

Traditional training is the most difficult to understand and to execute. However, the process of traditional training develops outstanding discipline, self-control, and coordination.

The other aspect to physical training is a more modern, practical science of self-defense. Here the focus is less on adhering to ancient arts methods than on practicing what works and discarding what may not work.

A tremendous amount of scientific data comes to us at a phenomenal rate these days, which continually improves our understanding of how the human body works. And with

Light-contact sparring helps students to apply the offensive and defensive skills they learn in class. Professionally run schools require their students to wear protective gear to ensure the highest levels of safety.
Photo courtesy of the John Graden Archives.

that understanding comes a better philosophy and better practices about how to condition the body to avoid hurting it. This is the basis of the modern method of martial arts training.

Which is better training, the modern or the traditional method?

Modern training is much more adaptable to an individual's needs, since the training can serve the student rather than the student serve a particular style. While this may sound more appealing, many of these schools are more gymlike than school-like.

With the lack of traditional ideals, there can be a lack of decorum within the school, although this certainly is not always the case. Respect, courtesy, and discipline, however, are important elements of the martial arts experience.

Most professional schools have a very effective mix of traditional arts and modern applications. The school's exams and lesson plans will be balanced between the traditional forms and basics and the more modern self-defense and fighting applications. The atmosphere is warm and family-oriented, with a strong sense of courtesy and respect throughout the student body.

So you can look forward to learning the fundamental techniques of a traditional style, the practical applications of the modern strategies, and the personal development skills of self-discipline that work as the glue that holds it all together and makes a black belt.

How long does it take to become proficient at self-defense?

It will take six months to a year, depending on your physical and mental abilities, and the number of days per week you dedicate to training. This does not mean obtaining an expert level, of course, but only acquiring the ability to defend yourself in an average self-defense situation.

How long does it take to get a black belt?

This is by far the most commonly asked question by prospective and new students. There is no cut-and-dried answer. Some organizations have promoted people to the black belt in as little as six months. Other people have had fifteen years of dedicated training before being promoted.

Most instructors believe that reaching the black-belt level of expertise, both physically and mentally, should take three to six years. These same instructors believe that a first-degree black belt is only the first step to achieving the precision possible if training is continued.

Why are the martial arts so popular?

Martial arts are so popular because no other activity can provide the same results as martial arts for each individual participant. Whether your goals are self-confidence, self-defense, personal development, fitness, flexibility, or to earn a black belt, the martial arts will take you there.

Do the children and adults train together?

This depends on the school. In most cases, it is best for adults to train separately from children. The needs of adults and children in the martial arts clearly differ. Many adults are not comfortable training with children in class.

However, some schools have family classes that are designed specifically for families to train together.

Are martial arts a good activity for children?

Parents today are recognizing that the public school system is not enough. Millions of parents are bringing the martial arts into their children's lives to supplement their education.

Carleton University, in a study reported in *Psychology Today* (January 1985), found that children in martial arts have a lower level of anxiety, an increased sense of responsibility, a decrease in willingness to take foolish risks, a higher self-esteem, a higher level of social intelligence, and a lesser likelihood of becoming radical.

Will the martial arts make my child more aggressive?

As reported in the Carleton University study just described, the martial arts often have an interesting effect on children. Some refer to it as a mediating effect. Children who are shy and withdrawn tend to become more confident and assertive with martial arts training. They learn to stand up for themselves and are more self-assured. Conversely, children who are overly aggressive tend to become more calm and centered as a result of the training.

What are the benefits of martial arts training for children?

Parents report these five important benefits for their children in martial arts:

1. The belt system improves children's self-esteem. The martial arts are not like team sports, because the emphasis is on developing the individual's self-esteem not the team's winning record. The belt system is the key. When kids earn their belts, it gives them a great sense of accomplishment that really improves the way they feel about themselves.

2. Martial arts teach children discipline. One of the things parents appreciate most about the martial arts is the improvement in their child's self-discipline. Look for a good staff of patient instructors who love to work with children, but who are also very clear about respecting limits.

3. Martial arts channel children's aggression. Many doctors actually prescribe martial arts for treatment because of the positive outlet it gives the kids for all their energy.

4. Martial arts classes enhance children's self-confidence. Confidence is one of the most important things the martial arts can give kids. Many schools have confidence-building drills included in each class.

5. Martial arts teach children essential self-defense skills. The martial arts teach practical, proven self-defense methods. A good

instructor will also be careful to teach the kids that the moves they learn in class will work, so they don't go home and try them on a sibling or neighbor.

What can an adult get out of the martial arts?

Adult students really appreciate the differences between martial arts training and standard exercise programs.

1. Martial arts workouts are a great way to get in shape. The martial arts are like an exercise program with a bonus: you learn to defend yourself while you get in shape.

2. Martial arts relieve stress. The martial arts are well-known for their stress-relieving benefits. The emphasis on mind-body training goes far beyond the benefits of standard, health-club–type exercise programs.

3. Martial arts practice sessions provide self-confidence. The confidence-building aspect of the martial arts is what students appreciate the most. Nothing can take the place of the security in knowing that you can defend yourself if you have to.

4. What the martial arts teach you could save your life. A good martial arts instructor works very hard to ensure that almost any dangerous situation you might encounter is covered in the classroom under very safe learning conditions, so you will be prepared.

5. Martial arts are a lot of fun. The reason the martial arts are so popular is because the classes are fun and exciting.

Do I need to be flexible to kick?

Most beginners are not very flexible. Like most aspects of the training, your flexibility will improve as you progress through the classes. Some styles, such as taekwondo, place an emphasis on kicking. In these systems, flexibility is a more critical factor. Other styles, such as the Okinawan systems, have less emphasis on kicking. As such, flexibility is not as critical.

What martial art is best suited for senior citizens?

Tai-chi is a gentle and graceful form of martial arts. Tai-chi also makes elderly people less likely to fall and break their brittle bones, according to research by the National Institute on Aging (NIA). It also appears to help people ages seventy and over maintain the gains from other balance and strength training exercises.

In the first study, Steven Wolf and colleagues at Atlanta's Emory University School of Medicine found in a study of two hundred participants over age seventy that a fifteen-week tai-chi program reduced their risk of falling by 47.5 percent. Many also reported that they worried less about falling, and about half the study participants voluntarily continued to keep meeting informally once the experiment was over.

In the related study, Dr. Leslie Wolfson and colleagues at the University of Connecticut in Farmington found several effective ways for the elderly to improve their strength and balance, and tai-chi helped preserve those gains for the next six months.

At what age is someone too old to start martial arts training?

A person is never too old to start training in the martial arts. One important thing about the martial arts is that there is an art or style to fit everyone.

People in their seventies may not be able to execute fancy kicks, but they can certainly execute tai-chi chuan movements. In fact, millions of elderly people in China practice tai-chi every day.

What is aerobic kickboxing?

Aerobic kickboxing is a fast-paced workout class that puts the punches and kicks of kickboxing to high-energy dance music.

Do I have to have martial arts training to do aerobic kickboxing?

No. In fact, in many schools the aerobic-kickboxing program is designed for the non–martial artist. Most of the techniques are taught in an introductory program before you actually begin the aerobic-kickboxing class.

How is aerobic kickboxing different from traditional martial arts?

In traditional martial arts, you study a specific art with a goal of progressing through the belts to achieve your black belt. The classes follow a traditional process with an emphasis on Eastern rituals such as bowing and meditating. Traditional martial arts training requires far more commitment from the student.

Aerobic kickboxing appeals to many because it does not require any long-term commitment. Also, a lot of contact is involved in a traditional martial arts class whereas aerobic kickboxing typically has none.

Is sparring an important part of martial arts training?

Some martial arts use sparring as part of their training curriculum and some do not. Sparring is beneficial, if done properly, because it allows a student to safely test his or her abilities against others of varying skills. It improves reactive speed, timing, quickness, and adds some measure of reality to a self-defense technique.

Sparring also helps develop sportsmanship and self-control. And of course, most martial artists consider it great fun.

Is forms training important in the martial arts?

As with sparring, some martial arts teach forms and some don't. In systems with forms, the forms are the component that identifies the particular system and makes it unique. Learning these forms is learning the essence and tradition of the system that has been passed down through generations of its practitioners.

In reality, forms are meant to simulate combat against multiple opponents coming from different directions. By practicing forms, a student learns many things. The ability to execute the techniques contained in the form is improved. The ability to transition from one stance or technique to another is also improved. And balance and the ability to change directions and face attackers, no matter where they come from, are improved.

Do you have to wear a gi in an aerobic-kickboxing class?

No. In fact, this is another big difference between traditional martial arts and aerobic kickboxing. Comfortable workout attire is typical in an aerobic-kickboxing class, whereas a traditional martial arts class typically requires the traditional uniform of the style being taught.

What is the difference between a drop-in and a progressive class?

Traditional martial arts are typically taught as progressive programs. This means that each class builds on what was taught in the previous class. Regular class attendance is required to progress through the program.

In a drop-in class, each class is self-contained. Drop-in classes, such as aerobic kickboxing, don't require the same commitment as does a progressive program like a traditional martial arts class.

Can I learn to defend myself in an aerobic-kickboxing class?

That's a tough question. Most black belts would answer that an aerobic-kickboxing class is too "light" to teach anything of real value. However, much of self-defense is in prevention. One of the best deterrents to an attack is self-confidence. Ask the same question to students in an aerobic-kickboxing class and they'll probably say that their training makes them feel much more confident about their ability to defend themselves. Indeed, there have been many reports of aerobic-kickboxing students actually defending themselves with techniques learned from the classes.

Is aerobic kickboxing for adults and children?

While some schools have created aerobic-kickboxing programs for children, most restrict the class to ages sixteen and over.

What are the benefits of learning forms?

Martial arts legend tells us that "forms," otherwise known in karate as kata or in tae-kwondo as *poomse*, were developed to allow martial artists to practice techniques by themselves, away from the prying eyes of government officials, who had banned the practice at certain times throughout history.

A good form can be beautiful and graceful but also exhibit power. Forms practice is one of the best full-body workouts you can get, and they are great when you don't have a partner to work with.

Forms can strengthen your stances and improve your balance and coordination. Forms can also force you to use both your left and right sides. Many forms are symmetrical; that is, both sides must perform the same movements.

Forms have also been called a "moving meditation." They require focus and concentration. Just as meditation, they distract the mind from worries and clear it of clutter and everyday stressful thoughts.

Will I have to learn a foreign language to learn traditional martial arts?

Most styles use terminology from the style's originating country. For instance, in a tae-kwondo school you would learn certain words or phrases in Korean. Typically, the forms and techniques are taught by their English names and the translations.

For the most part, the words are very easy to pick up. Since they are learned with the technique, the association is very easy.

Also, one of the benefits of traditional martial arts training is the cross-cultural dynamic it introduces the student to.

Are traditional martial arts religious?

While the roots of martial arts lie in Buddhist temples, the typical martial arts program in North America has no religious theme or underpinnings. One exception is Christian martial arts schools, and the instructor will normally inform you of that connection when you inquire about classes.

Why do I have to call my instructor Master?

Since there are no standards of rank in the martial arts, the use of the title Master is fairly arbitrary. Virtually anyone can decide to attach the title of master to themselves. Although achieving a certain rank, such as fifth-degree black belt, in some styles qualifies a person to be a master, there is no universally recognized qualification for the title.

Are martial arts a good option if I only want to learn self-defense?

Most traditional martial arts schools are devoted to teaching a specific style to their students. Typically, this involves some self-defense, but it also requires forms, one-step sparring routines, and a multitude of kicks and punches. So out of a one-hour class, ten minutes might be spent on self-defense while the rest of the class is spent learning these other techniques.

Are there martial arts programs strictly geared toward teaching self-defense?

Recognizing a demand for programs specifically on self-defense, many schools are offering special programs to meet this need. One example of a self-defense program is called EZ Defense, a highly specialized program that teaches participants to defend themselves.

EZ Defense is based on the idea that learning is best accomplished by "doing." In it, instructors create safe, yet powerful scenarios designed to help students experience the "rush" of self-defense without the danger or consequences.

All courses are taught in teams of female and male instructors trained in dealing with the physical and emotional process of an escalating confrontation.

Do I need to learn many techniques to defend myself?

For the average person, success in a self-defense scenario is more psychological than physical. Even veteran black belts with dozens of techniques under the belt have been known to freeze up when attacked.

This is why self-defense programs typically teach very few actual techniques. The theory is that, under stress, a person is far more apt to execute the most simple and effective strikes instead of more complex and flamboyant moves.

INDEX

ABOUT THE AUTHORS

John Corcoran

Recognized as one of the world's premier martial arts authors and journalists, John Corcoran has been a prime force in taking modern martial arts literature into the major-league arena. In his twenty-seven-year literary career, he has written millions of words about the subject in an acclaimed body of work encompassing books, magazines, and screenplays. Overall, he has used the power of the media to bring thousands of martial artists to public attention, and a select handful—including superstar Jean-Claude Van Damme—to stardom.

Mr. Corcoran has authored six books to date, all but one with major New York publishers, which have collectively sold over 300,000 copies worldwide. He is perhaps best known for his masterwork, *The Original* *Martial Arts Encyclopedia*, the definitive reference of the genre, which took ten years from concept to completion and has sold over 130,000 copies to date.

In addition, over the past twenty-eight years, Mr. Corcoran has served as an editor or founding editor of almost every influential martial arts magazine in the industry, starting with *Black Belt* in 1973. Corcoran was most recently editor of *Martial Arts Professional*, the industry's foremost trade publication. In 1977, he pioneered multilanguage article syndication in his field, and his stories have since appeared in six languages in over seventy countries.

Mr. Corcoran's writings on the subject have also extended into academia, motion pictures, and the mainstream media.

He was selected by the editors of both *The World Book Encyclopedia* in 1986 and

Microsoft's *Encarta (Electronic) Encyclopedia* in 1996 to write their inaugural entries for martial arts. His mainstream articles have appeared in *Parade*, the Sunday newspaper supplement, and *Daily Variety*, Hollywood's leading trade paper.

In 1993, he wrote the screenplay for *American Samurai*, the film in which Mark Dacascos (*The Crow: Stairway to Heaven* TV series) made his starring debut. He was a primary technical consultant for A&E's 1998 landmark TV documentary *The Martial Arts*, and is currently serving in that same capacity for *Modern Warriors*, produced by Oscar-nominated documentarian Peter Spirer, which was distributed in video stores by Eaton Entertainment. He has also appeared as a stunt-fighter in a dozen martial arts films.

In 1995, Mr. Corcoran launched a national public-speaking sideline, teaching martial-arts-school owners publicity-procurement techniques, for the National Association of Professional Martial Artists.

In 1998, he coedited with John Graden *The ACMA Instructor Certification Manual*. Based on the contents of the book, Dr. Kenneth Cooper, the Father of Fitness, and his world-renowned Cooper Institute for Aerobics Research, agreed to administrate the ACMA Instructor Certification Program. This endorsement provides unprecedented credibility for the martial arts with both the academic and scientific community and the health and fitness industry. Essentially, it elevates the martial arts from a fringe pastime to a mainstream fitness activity.

Mr. Corcoran's literary mentors are the late great Academy Award–winning screenwriter Stirling Silliphant (*In the Heat of the Night*), who was Bruce Lee's main Hollywood mentor, and bestselling author Joe Hyams ("Bogie"; "Zen in the Martial Arts"). Legendary Heavyweight Karate Champion Joe Lewis has been his chief martial arts mentor since 1977. A veteran black belt in karate, Corcoran began his training in 1967. He lives in Pittsburgh, Pennsylvania.

John Graden

Author, athlete, publisher, and pioneering martial arts innovator, John Graden has had a profound impact on the manner in which thousands of martial arts schools are operated worldwide since 1995.

A former member of numerous world champion U.S. kickboxing teams, Graden's two top-selling books, *Black Belt Management* and *How to Open and Operate a Successful Martial Arts School*, are considered the quintessential references for martial arts school owners.

His position as the spokesman for the martial arts instructional profession was validated with his appearance on the A&E Network in its 1998 landmark documentary *The Martial Arts*. He has been quoted in national publications such as the *Wall Street Journal*, *Playboy*, and *American Way Magazine*.

In late 1994, Graden founded the National Association of Professional Martial Artists (NAPMA), for which he serves as executive director. Dedicated specifically to strengthening the professional skills of martial arts school owners, NAPMA has mushroomed to nearly two thousand members throughout North and South America, Australia, and the United Kingdom. Graden launched two more significant support enterprises to fortify his industry leadership position.

In 1995, he capped his position as a martial arts teacher of teachers by publishing *Martial Arts Professional* magazine, the first widely accepted martial arts business journal. The slick monthly reaches over 24,000 American and Canadian school owners.

Today Mr. Graden's foremost goal—and greatest challenge—is to take the martial arts industry into the twenty-first century by revolutionizing how the arts are taught to the public, through the creation of an unprecedented instructor certification program. To accomplish this, in 1999 he created the American Council on Martial Arts (ACMA), whose board of advisers is composed of sports physiologists, psychologists, and motivational, legal, and fitness experts, all of whom also practice the martial arts. These advisers have contributed their expertise to *The ACMA Instructor Certification Manual*, which equips martial arts instructors with state-of-the-art standards for teaching, communication, and safety. He seeks to take the martial arts industry—and with it the public and corporate perception of them—to an unparalleled level of quality and credibility.

Due to the high quality of the ACMA program and manual, Graden was able to partner with the world-renowned Cooper Institute for Aerobics Research in Dallas, Texas. Founded by famed physician and fitness pioneer Dr. Kenneth Cooper, the institute is one of the world's most respected resources on fitness education.

A former successful school owner himself, Graden was a five-time member of the World Championship U.S. Karate Team (1985–91). He is married and lives in Palm Harbor, Florida.

Other books by John Corcoran

The Complete Martial Arts Catalogue

The Overlook Martial Arts Dictionary

The Martial Arts: Traditions, History, People

The Martial Arts Companion

The Original Martial Arts Encyclopedia (an updated reprint of *The Martial Arts: Traditions, History, People)*

The Martial Arts Sourcebook

How to Become a Martial Arts Star in Your Town

The ACMA (American Council on Martial Arts) Instructor Certification Manual (with John Graden)

Other books by John Graden

Black Belt Management

How to Open and Operate a Successful Martial Arts School

The ACMA (American Council on Martial Arts) Instructor Certification Manual (with John Corcoran)